THE TROPOHOLIC'S GUIDE TO BACKSTORY ROMANCE TROPES

CINDY DEES

CYNTHIA DEES PUBLISHING INC.

CONTENTS

INTRODUCTION

If you're reading this book, odds are good you've already read one of the first two volumes in this series describing universal tropes—The Tropoholic's Guide to Internal Romance Tropes or The Tropoholic's Guide to External Romance Tropes.

Because I was unsure which of those volumes writers would look at first, I included the same introductory information in each book describing what tropes are and how to use them.

As I explained in those volumes, I've identified about 140 major romantic tropes that are applicable to all types and genres of love stories, in any time period, any setting, and any format of storytelling, be it film, stage play, television rom com, video game, a novel, or something else.

I should also point out that love stories exist in many genres of fiction beyond the traditional romance novel, and the information in these books applies to all of those as well.

When I first started this trope project, I quickly realized that each entry was stretching as long as eight or ten pages. I did the math and, rather publish a single gigantic, 1400-page volume, I had to split my list of 140 tropes somehow.

I'm the first to admit that my categorization of tropes into internal, external, backstory, and hook tropes is somewhat arbitrary, and many tropes could arguably be included in one of the other categories. But this is the most sensible division I was able to come up with.

This arrangement also has the advantage of you being able to grab one trope out of each volume and layer all four into your story without the tropes overlapping excessively and interfering with each other.

Here are the four categories of universal romance tropes I came up with:

INTERNAL TROPES – These are the tropes of personal affliction: the wounds, fears, and personality traits that form obstacles to love inside the hearts and minds of your story's hero and heroine.

EXTERNAL TROPES – These are comprised of people, situations, and problems around your hero and heroine that prevent them from blissfully and naturally falling in love and finding their happily ever after.

BACKSTORY TROPES –As the name implies, these tropes are made up of the lingering problems, scars, and needs from your hero's and heroine's pasts that must be overcome before they can achieve happiness and true love.

HOOK TROPES – These tropes might more accurately be called Inciting Incident Tropes. They're the trope-based way your hero and heroine meet and come together as a couple and how that initial meeting establishes a set of problems that must be overcome before

the hero and heroine can achieve their happily ever after.

THE ETHICS OF WRITING TRAUMA

As a veteran of drafting the Internal and External Trope volumes, I felt pretty confident heading into the backstory trope volume. Wow, was I in for a shock.

It turns out backstory (for the purposes of fiction creation) is largely defined by past traumas, wounds, and scars as your characters bring their emotional baggage forward into their current lives.

Moreover, if that baggage is bad enough to interfere with the formation of healthy romantic relationships, it's probably pretty significant baggage.

Not only can it be tricky as a writer to understand how such traumas work, what causes them, and what recovery from them looks like, but humans are complicated beings and may approach dealing with trauma in completely different ways from one another.

And here's where dealing with backstory-based traumas gets *really* tricky. Many of your audience members have lived—directly themselves or indirectly through a loved one—trauma similar or identical to the one(s) you chose to write about.

These experiences not only leave scars in your fictional characters but also in your very real readers or viewers. And these scars can dramatically affect how your audience relates to your story.

The trickiest bit of all is that some of your audience members may never have dealt with the trauma you wrote about, never sought professional help, never researched it nor learned about it...and they may not even know that what they've lived *is* a traumatic experience that leaves wounds and scars until they read or view your story.

Your story may serve as the *first* and *only* information your reader or viewer, who is living with a horrendous trauma, consumes about this particular type of trauma.

You might want to reread that last paragraph and sit with it for a minute.

While I'm fairly sure everyone using my Tropoholic's Guides is creating fiction of one kind or another, it's entirely possible—probable even—that at least a few of your audience members will use your story as their main or only source of what they believe to be factual information about a very real, deeply harmful, truly devastating trauma that they or a loved one have lived or are living.

This being the case, an ethical responsibility lands upon our shoulders as fiction writers to think wherefore we portray backstory events that are the source of some of humanity's deepest suffering and pain.

Believe me, I had as little interest into diving into thorny ethical questions as I wrote these backstory tropes as you probably have when it comes to reading about them. But like it or not, our responsibility as content creators includes considering the ethical implications of how we portray trauma, its treatment, and its recovery.

I spent countless hours reading psychology articles and books, meeting with mental health care professionals, and picking the brains of therapists about many of the backstory tropes in this volume. I couldn't in good conscience skip doing the necessary research to get the information right that I'm passing on to you.

I've tried to be clear and concise and give you the bare basics of psychology that you need to know to tackle various backstories. But I strongly encourage you to do your own research and dig deeper than the superficial treatment of the subject I've been able to include in this writing how-to book.

My goal in tackling the basic ethical questions raised by certain tropes is to give you enough factual information for you to begin pondering the choices you'll make as you start working with a trope.

Let me be the first to say that we are all writing *fiction*, here. It is perfectly fine to explore fantasies, taboos, and wish fulfillment in the fiction space. There's no trope in this book that can't be written brilliantly and beautifully (even the one I suggest strongly that most people steer clear of).

It's important to understand that exploration of certain taboo or violent themes by readers or viewers is not always a direct representation of the fantasy at work in their minds.

The Virgin vs. Prostitute dilemma is a classic theory developed by psychologists to describe Western culture's relationship to sex. It holds that men and women both have abundant sexual urges but must find a way to reconcile having been taught that good people don't enjoy sex, don't pursue sex actively, and only have sex to make babies.

One way this dichotomy is expressed is in highly sexualized books, movies, and other content that include dubious consent (Dub-Con) or nonconsensual sex (Non-Con).

Although many people enjoy consuming content this kind of content, very few men or women actually fantasize about being violently assaulted.

However, numerous people do fantasize about some sort of power exchange or assuming a submissive role in a sexual relationship. In particular, they fantasize about not having to take responsibility for choosing to have sex with someone off limits, for doing something taboo, or for sullying their pure, good reputation.

After being forced into "dirty" sex, the character who was just ravished (and the reader or viewer living vicariously through them) can return to their good girl/boy identity and not be dubbed a slut.

Which is to say most Dub-Con and Non-Con aren't mainly about consent at all. They're primarily about assuaging guilt in your audience members for enjoying raunchy sex.

While it's important to understand what your audience is actually aiming to get out of your fictional story, you cannot forget that some of your audience members have actually experienced nonconsensual sex—and to them it was an act of violent assault.

It is these diametrically opposed experiences by audience members—factual trauma versus fictional fantasy—that are the source of writers' ethical dilemma in dealing with trauma.

If you'd like a fascinating and thorough discussion on the duality of sexual experience in Western culture, take a look at "ContraPoints Twilight", a scholarly YouTube video produced by former PhD candidate in philosophy and social commentator, Natalie Wynn. It's nearly three hours long, fully cited, and goes back to the early Greeks to trace the development of sexual values and beliefs all the way forward to the Twilight vampire-romance phenomenon.

That's all a very long way of saying **it's okay to write taboo subjects and wish fulfillment fantasies with the full understanding that they're not real. However, it's vital that your audience be aware your story is a fantasy explored and not a factual representation of trauma.**

It's very common—and accepted practice—for fiction writers to more or less ignore scientific information about certain events or conditions and to make up their own rules for how this particular thing works in their story.

This is perfectly fine as long as you're fully aware that you're fictionalizing the reality of that experience...and as long as your audience is fully aware of it, too.

The classic example is amnesia. If a person wakes up from a coma not remembering his or her name, or anything about his or her life, but is able to cook supper or drive a car, that is NOT how actual amnesiac memory loss works.

While there may be some sort of traumatic mental block in place to retrieving certain memories, memory of parts of a person's life cannot be erased wholesale while leaving the rest of the memories of that person's life intact.

For that matter, people don't just lie in a coma for months or years and then open their eyes one day, ask what year it is, and walk out of a hospital. Actual coma recovery is a lengthy process involving a great deal of rehabilitation and relearning of lost skills like walking, talking, and other motor functions.

KEY POINT: It's fine for you to write any trauma and trauma recovery however you'd like. It's just important for you to know when and where you're taking liberties. Somewhere in your project—in a disclaimer, author's note, or afterward—you have a responsibility to tell your audience where you took fictional liberties with factual information.

NOTE: It's common for writers to include information in their disclaimer about where to learn more about recovery or where to get help if you have a loved one experiencing the trauma you wrote about.

I'm confident that I'm going tick off some writers as I challenge the ethics of writing certain tropes in certain ways. But ironically, I have an ethical responsibility of my own to remind you that real, traumatized, suffering people are going to be in your audience and that you do have a responsibility to think about how they'll respond to your story.

Indeed, isn't that the point of writing fiction for popular consumption at all? We're all telling a story specifically to evoke responses from our audience, be they laughter, tears, fear, compassion, or a good jump-scare.

Ask yourself:

- Has any audience member possibly experienced this trauma or something similar?
- Is it possible that any audience member may be further harmed by reading or viewing this project?
- Might this project trigger or upset a reader or viewer?

If the answer to any of these questions is yes, **the simple solution is to include some sort of warning in your packaging, cover materials, or manuscript (preferably up front rather than in back matter). Disclaimers and trigger warnings exist for a very good reason. Don't be shy to use them.**

If you *want* to further traumatize an already traumatized person in your audience, that is, of course, a choice you're free to make. I just question personally whether it's an ethical choice.

By all means, I encourage you to make your own decisions as to how you plan to deal with the ethical questions raised by the trope(s) and events you've chosen to write about.

All I'm asking is that you at least think about the ethical implications of what you write, how your story may affect your audience, and how you can take steps to properly warn your audience in advance that there may be triggering or inaccurate information in your story.

BACKSTORY-WHEN AND WHAT TO INCLUDE

A common complaint editors make about openings of stories is that they start with too much backstory. Or heaven forbid, they start with some sort of prologue that's pure backstory.

The story editors have a point. Your audience wants to dive right into the action of the story and get sucked into what's happening now, to fall in love with the main character(s) now and find a good villain to hate. Readers and viewers rarely want to sit through a lengthy information dump about who all these people are, where they came from, and why they are the way they are.

This is probably a good spot to segue into a discussion of how **story openings are the place to plant as many questions as possible in your audience members' minds.**

Keep in mind that backstory explains past behaviors and answers questions about characters' pasts. **Openings are about sucking**

your audience into the story quickly and forcing them to read or watch on to find answers to the many rapid-fire questions they have after the first few pages or minutes of your story.

If you were to record the internal thought process of a reader or viewer as they absorb the opening of your story, you want it to go roughly like this: "What the heck just happened? Did that guy just walk up to a total stranger and do that? Why? What did that person mean by that response? Was that sarcasm, or is that person really that rotten? Why is this person acting this outrageously? How come nobody called the police? Why is this world set up this way? Why is that rule in place? Who made that rule? Who enforces it? Wow, that seems like an extreme reaction for that character; what's that all about? Why did that car blow up? Who planted the bomb? Was the bomber trying to kill the driver or the passenger? Why? Who on earth were they..."

You get the idea. We want our audience stacking up questions and more questions right out of the gate.

Humans are innately curious. In fact, our curiosity is one of our most powerful survival tools (along with our opposable thumbs and incredibly complex brains). We cannot stand unanswered questions. The more questions you plant in your reader's or viewer's head in the beginning of your story, the more compelled they will be to read or watch on in search of answers.

A powerful technique for creating question-packed openings is to layer multiple tropes in the same story and to introduce them all right away.

Take, for example, the movie Superman. (I'm envisioning the Christopher Reeve and Margot Kidder version, but the example holds for every version of the film or comic book.)

When Clark Kent first meets Lois Lane in the newsroom, nothing of great interest actually happens. He's gobsmacked by her, she barely notices him, and they both go about their work. (Trope #1: Right Under Your Nose)

What makes this moment interesting and memorable to the audience is we can't believe that an ugly pair of glasses is enough to make Lois oblivious to what a gorgeous hunk Clark is, nor do we understand Clark's instant attraction to this brusque reporter. (Trope #2: Oblivious to Love, Trope #3: Love At First Sight)

It's adorable to watch Clark try not to drop an armload of papers, keep his glasses on his face, and remember how to form words as he's completely taken with brash, confident Lois (Trope #4, Clumsy/Awkward/Bumbling Hero, Trope #5 Opposites Attract).

We wonder how long it's going to take for Clark to pluck up the courage to ask Lois out (Trope #6 Shy Hero), particularly if she continues to blow him off and steamroll him in the newsroom (Trope #7 Grumpy/Sunshine). How will his life be complicated by hiding his identity from her (Trope #7: Secret Identity) and will he ever let her in on the secret life he lives when they have their occasional trysts (Trope #8: Secret World)?

It's worth noting that all eight of these tropes are, in fact, carried through the Superman story to their logical middles, black moments, and endings.

In the meantime, in the external plot, Superman saves the world from a trio of bad guys who've followed him to Earth from Krypton—a trio that's rather clumsily introduced by way of a backstory sequence of Superman's father participating in a trial to sentence the criminals for crimes against Krypton.

So, how's a writer to introduce backstory into this soup of compelling questions? Which backstory should you include in your story and when should you share it with your audience?

In point of fact, every moment of your character's entire life, every experience, every thought, and every feeling is their backstory. Obviously, we can't include all of it, or even a tiny fraction of it, in any story.

Somehow, we have to find a way to sift through an entire life lived, distill down the most important bits, and figure out how to weave them into our story in a way that enhances our audience's understanding of this person without boring our audience or killing our story's pacing.

I don't know about you, but just writing that paragraph exhausted me. What a monumental and mind-numbing task that sounds like! I could spend weeks or months constructing a full life history for a single character and then sorting through it all. And I don't know about you, but I have deadlines to meet. I don't have time to do all of that.

Realistically, we must find a way to zero in—quickly—not only on the most important backstory in a character's life but also on the backstory that matters to the story we're trying to create.

Luckily, there is a way to do both.

LIFE-CHANGING EVENTS

Psychologists will tell you that most people, living average lives, will experience approximately two to three life-changing events in each decade of their lives. Obviously, you can give your character more or less of these events depending on how boring, difficult, peaceful, or traumatic a life your character has led.

Rather than construct an entire past life for a character, what if we writers focus solely on defining these life-changing events?

So...what constitutes a life-changing event?

Psychologists have a formal name for them: Significant Emotional Events. Dr. Morris Massey, a leading expert in values development defines these as **"an experience so mentally arresting that it becomes a catalyst for you to consider, examined, and possibly change your initial values or value system."**

In lay terms, these are life's biggest stressors, the moments so overwhelming, shattering, or soul shaking that they leave a mark on us and change us forever.

These events can be positive—the birth of a child/grandchild or graduating from an arduous academic program. But for the most part they tend to be traumatic or tragic—deaths, marriage, divorce, job loss, a child leaving home, being the victim or perpetrator of a crime, for example.

Psychologists typically rank life's ten most stressful events as follows:

1. Death of a Spouse
2. Divorce
3. Marital Separation
4. Incarceration
5. Death of a Close Family Member
6. Major Health Concern, Illness, or Injury
7. Marriage
8. Job Loss
9. Marital Reconciliation
10. Retirement

While these events are obviously life-changing, it's entirely possible that much more subtle events will dramatically affect your characters and leave lasting marks upon them, forever changing who they are.

For example, the moment when a little girl looks in a mirror and decides for the first time that she's ugly, or the moment when a coach or teacher tells a youth they'll never be any good at something. It could be repeated embarrassment over not having enough lunch money. Being laughed at by your colleagues for suggesting something new... the list of small but deep cuts that leave permanent scars is endless.

These may be insignificant events to the other person(s) involved with them, but to the person experiencing it, this moment will change them forever. It will shape how they approach the rest of their life, how they perceive themselves, and the choices they make going forward.

EXERCISE: LIFE-CHANGING EVENTS

1. Take the age of your main character and multiply it by 2.5. That's roughly how many life-changing events your main character should have experienced by this age. For a character around the age of thirty, you're looking at six to nine life-changing events so far. If he or she has had a rough past, you might come up with ten or twelve life-changing events this poor soul has already been through.

2. Start by writing down the life-changing events you know your main character has experienced. It's fine to start with the obvious ones—a parent died or left when they were young. Your main character is divorced, or their best friend has died, or they've recently been fired from a job or moved.

3. Now, write down a few less dramatic life-changing events. For example: the birth of a child or grandchild, crashing a car, leaving home, joining the military, getting a first job, inheriting (or losing) substantial wealth, or winning/losing at something this person has worked toward for a long time.

4. Now write down the subtle life-changing events that have shaped your main character. A good way to find these is to write down the key elements of your main character's personality—quirks, triggers, strongly held opinions, beliefs or values, hot buttons, insecurities, things he or she hates about himself or herself. Try to capture all the elements of the main character that will be important in your story or that you plan to explore in your story.

5. For each of these key elements, ask yourself what happened in the character's past to make him or her that way or that taught him or her that lesson or belief.
6. Repeat this exercise with every major character in your story, including your villains and antagonists.

LIFE-DEFINING LESSONS

While it's all well and good for big things to have happened to our characters, the interesting part of these life-changing events to us as writers is the life-defining lessons that characters take away from these major events.

How did a specific life-changing event actually change that character as a person? Did values, beliefs or morals shift? Did self-perception change? Did confidence or sense of safety diminish? I could keep going, but you get the idea.

It's not enough for characters to simply live through significant emotional events. What matters most to us as writers—and to our audiences—is how these events change our characters for better or worse.

People who experience a life-changing event, particularly the younger and less experienced they are when it happens, do not always draw the correct, proper, or healthy life-defining lesson from that event.

...which is the best fodder *ever* for us writers!

This is where characters go off the rails, develop hang ups, misconceptions, misbeliefs, and the gray or black morals, values, and ideas that make for rich, complex, fascinating, and messed-up characters.

This is especially where we have a chance to create interesting, believable, nuanced villains and antagonists for our stories.

Dr. Massey believes our core values develop during three major childhood periods:

1. The Imprint Period – 0-7 years old. We're sponges and absorb everything around us, accepting most or all of it as true, especially when it comes from our parents.
2. The Modeling Period – 8-12 years old. In these years, we copy people, often our parents, but also other people, e.g. teachers, coaches, or adult mentors.
3. The Socialization Period – 13-21 years old. During these years, we're primarily influenced by our friends, media, technology, music, and so forth, and tend to turn to people who seem most like us.

After the age of 21, we're pretty much fully formed and unlikely to change much at all in the absence of some sort of life-changing event that leads to a life-defining lesson.

SIDE NOTE: This is why, in various backstory trope descriptions, I prompt you to consider whether the events in your story are big enough, life-changing enough to force your main character to learn a life-defining lesson that makes it possible for him or her to engage in a healthy, long-term, romantic relationship.

When children and young people experience life-changing events, it's especially important for them to receive good advice, guidance, counseling, or therapy to help them arrive at a positive, healthy, non-traumatic lesson learned from their experience.

In the absence of this sort of wisdom and support from more experienced adults, the odds go up—a lot—of a child or young adult arriving at an unhealthy or even incorrect life lesson.

Conversely, as people reach their later years, the number of life defining lessons learned tends to slow down. It's not that elderly people stop experiencing stressful events. Far from it.

Rather, they tend to have experienced highly stressful events before and tend to have a framework of how to deal with big stressors such that these sorts of events don't change them as much as they once might have.

Also, with age there's a possibility of having attained wisdom that allows one to deal with difficult, challenging, or traumatic events with a certain equanimity and to draw the correct life-defining lessons from these sort of events.

EXERCISE: LIFE-DEFINING LESSONS

1. Go back to the lists of life-changing events you've developed for each of your characters and assign to each event a positive, healthy, life-defining lesson that could be learned from it.

2. Next, assign a negative, unhealthy, destructive, harmful, hurtful, or traumatic lesson to each event that could be learned from it.

3. Now for the hard part. Choose which life-defining lesson is more useful in the story you plan to tell.

4. Will a major character arc in your story start with a character experiencing one of the life-changing events on his or her list and end with him or her finally arriving at a correct life-defining lesson—potentially after passing through various incorrect lessons or unhealthy reactions to the event?

5. When and how does each of your villains or antagonists arrive at the life lesson(s) that send him or her down the wrong or "bad" path? Are these lessons the reason why he or she is so convinced of his or her rightness in pursuing various goals and courses of action?

6. Will your various characters' learned lessons be corrected or changed over the course of this story? If so, what is the misconception or incorrect value or belief they start with,

and what will be the steps along the way to correcting that belief? (And yes, you can plot your entire book just by answering this question for each character in the story.)

Having walked through both of these thought exercises, we can now answer the question of which backstory rises to the level of being important enough to belong in your story:

The only backstory that belongs in any story is the life-changing events and life-defining lessons that have shaped who your characters are *and* that are relevant to the story you're telling about them.

WHERE AND HOW TO INTRODUCE BACKSTORY

The common wisdom is to **never begin a story with backstory**. That said, I'm a big fan of no writing rule being unbreakable. If that's absolutely where and how your story needs to start, do it. Just make sure the backstory you open with is riveting and guaranteed to grab your audience by the throat and suck them into your story irresistibly.

Another rule of backstory, one I'm personally less inclined to break, is to **only include backstory at the moment it must be known for your audience to understand something that's happening right then** in your story.

If a seemingly innocuous event—say, baking a holiday dessert—inexplicably freaks out your main character, that's the moment to share that his or her mother used to bake the dessert every year, get drunk, and eventually throw it at the main character, ruining it before it could get eaten.

Your audience gets an ah-hah moment, they abruptly understand the character's previously inexplicable reaction, and then you move right back into the current-day action of your story.

Another general rule of backstory: **if you must drop in some backstory information, keep it as short as possible so you interrupt the pacing and forward momentum of your current-day story as little as possible**.

Some books are constructed using two parallel timelines. They bounce back and forth between the past and present throughout the entire project.

A book with a lot of backstory in it may end up looking constructed in this fashion even if it wasn't your original intent.

The trick in this sort of story is to make the backstory so interesting that your audience doesn't mind a large portion of the story happening in the past, even though the outcome is assured and has already happened. Beware, however. Already knowing how the story turned out is a recipe for disinterest and boredom from your audience if you're not especially careful.

Here are several tips for keeping this type of backstory-heavy story interesting:

- Write the past so the outcome is as unknown as possible and in doubt to your audience until the end of the story (other than something obvious like the present-day character exists or is still alive). This may mean rejiggering how you tell the present-day story so your audience doesn't know how the backstory turns out.
- Make sure both timelines are riveting and compelling enough to hold your audience's interest all by themselves.
- When you pause one timeline to shift to the other one, stop on a cliffhanger **every single time**. Make sure your reader has a powerful reason to race through the next section of the other timeline in order to return as soon as possible to this timeline to find out what happens next.

Here's one last writing hint for handling backstory: this one involves how to introduce backstory and flow easily from your current action into the backstory moment.

Most people who experience a highly stressful or traumatic event tend to remember tiny details of the event with vivid clarity. These are called sensory associations.

Interestingly, although humans are not particularly scent-oriented creatures, we do tend to remember smells very strongly with regard to important memories. Likewise, we may associate a sound, a voice, or a piece of music with a memory even more strongly than we associate a visual detail.

And of course, visual creatures that we are, we're likely to remember a few very vivid visual snapshots of the event that stay with us more clearly than any other aspect of the event.

We writers can use this tendency to make sensory associations to our advantage as we write backstory for our characters.

If you go through the lists you created in the previous exercise of life changing events your characters have experienced, you can go through your lists one last time and assign a distinct sensory memory to each life-changing event each character has experienced. (Or at least do this for the life-changing events you've decided to include in your story.)

You could assign a smell to that memory—the acrid scent of the main character's burned home, the formaldehyde and perfume smell of a funeral, the sight of some object the main character saw during a traumatic event, memory of the music playing when the event took place.

A real-life example: I witnessed a serious airplane crash in my military pilot training. Two people died (including my best friend) and a third was seriously injured. That evening, my then-neighbor and now-husband ordered Hawaiian pizza and brought me some of it —a kind gesture that was the start of our lifelong romance. However, to this day some forty years later, the taste or even the smell of Hawaiian pizza makes me physically ill.

So, how do we use these sensory associations attached to life-changing events to introduce backstory?

1. As your character is moving through the current-day action of your story, at the moment when you need to introduce a backstory snippet, write in the sensory stimulus associated with that backstory event into the current-day story.
2. Let it trigger a memory of the backstory event in your character.
3. Recount the backstory snippet you need to introduce as briefly as possible.
4. Jump back into the current-day action.

For example, your intrepid heroine is getting briefed-in to fly a dangerous mission that she may die executing. Into the lengthy briefing, someone delivers pizza for everyone. She smells the Hawaiian pizza the head briefer likes, drops into the memory of the fatal crash that made her terrified of a maneuver that's going to be necessary in this mission, and then you jerk the character's attention back to the present as someone asks her a question or resumes the briefing.

Boom. Backstory plausibly and realistically inserted into your story. Pacing and forward movement minimally interrupted. The audience has the information it needs—no more and no less—right then.

And because most people do the *exact* same thing and associate smells, tastes, touches, sounds, and sights with important memories, your audience will have no trouble following the character's momentary lapse into memory triggered by a sensory association.

If you're working in a medium where internal thoughts or internal monologue are difficult or impossible to convey—a stage play for example

—you will need to pick and choose which backstory moments are critical enough to your story to merit a few lines of narration or side monologue to share a memory triggered a sensory association in your story.

OTHER USES FOR BACKSTORY

Here are several more ways you can use backstory to structure your story or set up conflict:

- You can set up the main character and main antagonist or the main character and love interest to have experienced identical or similar life-changing events but to have drawn diametrically opposed life-defining lessons from them. Talk about a great source of conflict between two characters.

- You can, of course, set up the main characters in your story where one of them has perpetrated a life-changing event upon the other one. The fallout from such an interaction is likely to be epic and cause monumental conflict between these characters as they confront the aftermath and the life-defining lessons they both took away from this event.

- You take something viscerally traumatic that has left lingering emotional baggage, scars, or unhealed wounds and have someone else tell your main character that he or she is ALL WRONG in how he or she reacted to something that rocked his or her world and changed his or her life. This sort of fundamental conflict in values or deeply held beliefs is guaranteed to be a source of huge conflict between characters.

- One warning about placing romantic love interests in direct conflict over their core values and beliefs, however: **people are unlikely to change their core values and beliefs for the sake of possible (but not fully realized) love. It almost always takes a life-changing event and a life-defining lesson to accomplish that.**

While I'm not saying you always have to have some external crisis or external plot problem be the change agent in your story that prepares a character to be capable of loving another character, I am saying you should be cautious with how different at a core level you choose to have your lovers start out being in your story.

For example, a deeply, sincerely religious character is unlikely to walk away from his or her faith to fall in love with and be with an avowed atheist. These two aren't likely to get into a serious relationship at all because both will rule out the other one as a possible romantic partner the moment they encounter their fundamental disconnect of core values and beliefs.

If you do, indeed, choose to get these two people together, one of them is going to have to have a *serious* epiphany, a *major* life-changing event followed by a dramatic life-defining lesson, that leads him or her to finding faith or losing faith.

- You can structure your entire book around a single life-changing event and how it affects the lives of multiple characters in differing ways, based on their differing experiences and perspectives of that event.

- You can also craft an entire story by starting with a life-changing event for a single person and following the main character through his or her entire journey to a life-defining lesson.

- Or, of course, you can use a character's past trauma and experiences to create current-day problems in finding and sustaining deep personal relationships with other people.... which is the whole point of using backstory to form tropes in your story.

Hence, this book.

And with that, let's dive into the backstory tropes...

1

BACK FROM THE DEAD

DEFINITION

In this story, one of your main characters returns from the dead. This often happens at the very beginning of the story, which is why this trope is categorized with backstory tropes.

Something has happened in the past where this character a) had a near death experience or was said to have had one b) was presumed or declared dead, c) was not, in fact dead, d) returned home either knowing already or realizing upon return that he or she was thought to be dead.

This moment of return is typically where your story begins. (Even though, of course, it will be important backstory in your project to explain to your audience what really happened and how the misunderstanding occurred.)

From this return to life you'll proceed to show the complications of the mistaken "death" and the main character's journey to unraveling the mistake while falling in love or rekindling a love.

The love interest in this trope can be a loved one or even spouse from before the moment when the alleged death occurred. In this case, the person returning from the dead may rekindle an old relationship in need of repair or restoration, may pretend to be a stranger and try to get the old lover to fall in love with a new person (in reality a new or better version of himself or herself), or the disguised "dead" character may try to test the old lover's love for him or her.

The love interest may be someone totally new in the "dead" character's life, someone who didn't know him or her before, and who probably has no idea who he or she really is. In this case, the "dead" main character is taking advantage of the mistake to start a new life for himself or herself. But, when the truth is revealed, the old life and new life are bound to collide and need reconciliation in some way.

Of course, your main character can be declared dead in the course of your story and then make a secret or dramatic return from the dead at some later point—usually the black moment or climax of your story. In this case, you'll show your audience in real time, the story of how this person ended up declared dead and then you'll carry the story forward into the consequences of that mistake.

But because we're focusing on backstories that set up romantic tropes in this volume, let's stick to the traditional version where a main character is declared dead before your story begins.

Often, the circumstances leading up to the main character's presumed death and declared death are shown in snippets of backstory sprinkled into the current events as the dead character makes a return to his or her old life.

At its core, this is a story of correcting a terrible mistake or a terrible deception. Hence, forgiveness typically must be granted or justice served, consequences of the "death" reversed, an old life resumed, a new life launched, and the old and new lives meshed into one. This story is the mother of all do-overs at life.

ADJACENT TROPES

- Hero/Heroine in Hiding
- Coming Home
- Hero/Heroine in Disguise

- Dangerous Secret
- Mistaken Identity

WHY READERS/VIEWERS LOVE THIS TROPE

- who wouldn't love to spy on one's friends and family and find out how they would react if they thought you were dead
- we love to think we'd be terribly missed and things would fall apart without us
- giving someone you love a joyous surprise
- snatching life literally from the jaws of death
- your grief at losing a loved one is miraculously swept away with the revelation that he or she is actually alive
- reinventing both oneself and one's life

OBLIGATORY SCENES
THE BEGINNING:

The first decision you must make when constructing this story is whether the declaration of death of your main character was a mistake or not. The second decision is whether or not the main character actually came close to death or not. Based on these, there are multiple variations of how your story might begin.

In all variants, however, the story begins with the main character believed to be dead. You may show a funeral or grieving friends/loved ones, the dissolution of an estate or sale of a business—whatever would logically happen after the death of the main character as those around the deceased do the things that would happen after his or her death.

In the beginning, we often see the main character find out he or she is "dead". This person may return home and be shocked by the news or may find out about the mistaken declaration of death before returning home. Depending on how sinister the intent of someone declaring him or her dead was, the main character may or may not choose to reveal himself or herself as being alive right away.

I've seen variations on this opening where the main character is maimed, heavily bandaged, or in some way not recognizable as himself or herself upon returning home. Others don't realize who he or she is. He or she chooses for some reason not to reveal his or her identity or cannot reveal his or her identity immediately.

Another variation on this opening is the "dead" main character disguises himself or herself for part of the story to observe what others are doing with regard to his or her death. This is typical if the main character suspects foul play is at work—this foul play may have occurred when he or she nearly died before the story began, or there may be foul play afoot in the current timeframe as someone tries to steal a spouse, loved one, property, inheritance, or title.

The "dead" main character meets the love interest if they've not met before this.

The "dead" main character either introduces himself or herself to the old love interest as someone new, or the "dead" character may secretly or not secretly reveal his or her true identity right away to the old spouse or lover.

THE MIDDLE:

The middle of this story begins when the consequences of the "death" begin to unfold and cause complications for the back from the dead character. These may include financial problems, property problems, or family problems.

Depending on how long the "dead" character has been away from home and presumed dead, his or her life, family, property, business, wealth, and so forth may have been dismantled a little...or completely. This will determine the types of complications the "dead" character and the love interest have to deal with.

The love interest may be in on the secret that the "dead" character is actually alive, or the lover, too, may be taken in by the main character's deception.

If the main character reveals his or her true identity and very much not dead status early in your story (even as part of the beginning), then the complications of the middle will probably revolve around his or her struggle to regain the lost, sold, stolen, or given away elements of his or her old life.

The "dead" character may have to fight to regain the love of the former lover/spouse/fiancé(e).

The "dead" character may test the old love interest's love and/or grief. The "dead" character may try to get the old lover to fall in love with him or her disguised as someone else. The "dead" character may try to get the old love interest to admit he or she didn't really love the "dead" character or that the love interest is over the "dead" character and his or her death.

If some person, group, or force had dastardly intent in declaring the "dead" character dead, this plot must be investigated in the middle of the story, the motives for it discovered, and a plan hatched to foil the bad guy.

The complications of the middle have to get more complicated, more difficult to resolve, and the story builds toward a crisis. The romance between the "dead" character and the lover is becoming too complex, painful, fraught, based on lies, or devastating to sustain.

In some cases, the "dead" character revealing himself or herself to be, in fact, alive may be the incident that provokes the black moment.

BLACK MOMENT:

The relationship between the back from the dead character and the love interest collapses. The love interest may discover the true identity of the main character and be furious or distraught at being lied to. The love interest may refuse to choose a new love (the dead character in disguise) over the old love whom he or she is still grieving. A love interest, who had already moved on with his or her life and is now being asked to choose the old lover returned from the dead over a new love, chooses the new love instead of the back from the dead love.

If there was a plan to steal some aspect of the "dead" character's life, that plan succeeds, and the "dead" character loses everything. All his or her efforts to reverse the damage of having been declared dead have failed.

In some cases, the black moment may be when the back from the dead character reveals his or her true identity to the world at large and to the bad guy(s).

THE END:

The climax of this story usually involves a confrontation between the back from the dead character, whom everyone now knows to be alive, and the forces that have tried to take his or her old life away.

The climax also revolves around a confrontation between the back from the dead character and the love interest, in which they fight out and resolve their personal issues. The back from the dead character apologizes for any deception he or she pulled on the love interest. The dead character may apologize for his or her insecurity, mistrust, or complete lack of trust in the love interest when first returning home early in the story.

The "dead" character may have to forgive the love interest for having moved on after he or she "died". This moving on might even have included falling in love again.

If the love interest in this story is a new lover who didn't know the "dead" character before his or her return from the dead, the love interest must be integrated into the old life that the back from the dead character resumes at the end of the story.

The lovers may choose to return to the back from the dead character's old life, or they may choose to strike out in a new direction and live a new life after this dramatic do-over for the back from the dead character.

KEY SCENES

- the moment the "dead" character finds out he or she has been declared dead
- the love interest, or a major secondary character who knew the "dead" character before death, thinks for a moment that they saw the dead character alive
- the "dead" character spies on his or her former life, former lover, former friends, and family
- someone recognizes the "dead" character and has to be brought into the secret
- the big reveal of the truth to the love interest
- the big reveal of the truth to the other characters in the story (including the bad guy)
- the back from the dead character first steps back into his or her old life

THINGS TO THINK ABOUT WHEN WRITING THIS TROPE

Did the "dead" character actually come close to dying? If so, how? If not, how was he or she first presumed dead?

Who actually declared the main character dead? Why? Did this person genuinely and mistakenly believe the main character had died? Was he or she bribed to do it? Did he or she have an ulterior motive in declaring the main character dead?

How did the family, friends, co-workers in the "dead" character's former life react to the original news of his or her death?

How much time passes between the declaration of death and the "dead" character's return home? What did he or she do during that time? Why didn't he or she return home sooner?

What parts of the "dead" character's life will have been dismantled by the time he or she returns home? How have they been dismantled? Have they been sold? Demolished? Spent? Assigned to someone else?

Is the love interest in your story someone from the "dead" character's life before death or a new love?

If the love interest is an old part of his or her life, what relationship did this person and the "dead" character have before the alleged death? Was this relationship flawed? Failing? Over in all but name? Perfect?

Why does the "dead" character want to reset this old romantic relationship? How will he or she try to reset it? What will he or she try to reset it into—a repeat of the first time around or a different and better version of the first relationship?

If the "dead" character is meeting someone new who will become the love interest, how do they meet? Why doesn't the love interest recognize the "dead" character? What draws the "dead" character to this person?

When will the "dead" character reveal his or her true identity to the love interest? Why then? Why not sooner? Why not later?

If the love interest was in a relationship with the main character before he/she "died", what has the love interest been through in the interim of believing the main character is dead? What has his or her emotional journey been? How hard has it been? How much has he or she rebuilt his or her life or NOT rebuilt his or her life?

Will the "dead" character disguise himself or herself? Will he or she hide during the story? How will he or she pull either of these off? Will he or she have help?

Will the "dead" character tell anybody he or she is alive early on? If so, who and why? If not, why not?

What does the "dead" character learn about himself or herself as he/she observes the aftermath of his/her life and death? What does this character learn about how he/she lived life? Interacted with others? Left the world a better or worse place?

Was there foul play involved in the event that nearly killed the main character or appeared to nearly kill him or her? If so, what was it? Who did it? Why? What did this person expect to gain from killing the main character?

Was there foul play in the declaration of the main character's death? Did the person declaring him or her dead know the "dead" character was, in fact, alive? If so, how did the bad guy expect to keep the secret that the "dead" character was actually alive for the long term?

How hard is it going to be for the back from the dead character to reverse the dissolution of his or her old life and resume it? What obstacles stand in the way of that happening? How can you make those obstacles worse?

Does the love interest need to forgive the "dead character for a deception? Does the "dead" character need to forgive the love interest for anything?

Does justice need to be served to whoever pulled off the deception that the main character had died? What justice?

Why does the relationship between the "dead" character and love interest implode in the black moment? What conflicts rip them apart?

How will the lovers repair their relationship? Will one or both have to apologize or forgive? Will one or both have to make a major sacrifice or grand gesture to prove their worth or the veracity of their feelings?

Will the back from the dead character get his or her old life back? If so, all of it?

If the back from the dead character has a new love interest, how will he or she fit into the resumed, old life?

What lessons has the back from the dead character learned about how to live life going forward, about death, or about love? What lessons has the love interest learned?

TROPE TRAPS

The dead character using a lame disguise that any person with half a brain would see through.

Creating a wildly implausible scenario for how the main character is mistakenly declared dead.

The villain (who presumably knows the main character is not dead) fails to put a long-term plan in place to keep the "dead" character from coming back home.

Nobody suspects the villain of being a bad guy, or at least finds this person distasteful when he or she swoops in and usurps the main character's life in the wake of his or her death.

Failing to adequately portray the grief and loss the people left behind have suffered while believing the main character was dead and only focusing on the journey of the person trying to resume his or her life.

The "dead" character comes back too quickly in your story's timeline for the major consequences of his or her death to have plausibly unfolded.

The "dead" character is gone so long before coming home that he or she can't realistically expect loved ones or life to have waited around for him or her...and yet, he or she expects/demands exactly that.

The "dead" character is selfish—hence unlikable to your audience—by demanding his or her old life back at the expense of loved ones who've moved on and found happiness in their new lives.

The old love interest moved on way too fast from the death of the main character and comes across as shallow, insincere, or not capable of deep love.

You rely on a simple mistake that is far too easily correctable to set up the mistaken "death" of the main character.

The main character is a jerk for not telling everyone immediately upon his or her return home that he or she is alive.

The "dead" character has no good reason for taking such a drastic step as keeping being alive secret other than curiosity or a prank. Both are stupid reasons for torturing the people you love with grief and loss.

There are few or no consequences for the "dead" character failing to reveal that he or she is actually alive. In effect, he or she has compounded a mistake with a huge deception.

Everything goes back to exactly the way it was before the main character's "death." This has been a traumatic experience for many people. Things should change somehow as a result of all that pain, grief, and loss.

The love interest fails to learn any major lessons from this experience of believing someone he or she loved has died.

The main character fails to learn anything after seeing what would have happened in the aftermath of his or her death if he or she had actually died.

BACK FROM THE DEAD TROPE IN ACTION
Movies:

- Pearl Harbor
- Buffy the Vampire Slayer, season 3 (TV show)
- Return to Eden
- Brothers
- Cast Away
- The Martian
- Manifest (TV show)

Books:

- Wait for Me by Elisabeth Naughton
- Twice Loved by LaVyrle Spencer
- Hold You Against Me by Skye Warren
- Forget Me Not by Marliss Melton
- Everything We Keep by Kerry Lonsdale

2

BILLIONAIRE

DEFINITION

In the billionaire story, one main character is a billionaire, and the other main character is not. In its simplest form, they meet, have conflict, overcome obstacles, fall in love, and live happily ever after in the lap of luxury.

What truly defines this trope, however, is the non-wealthy character being swept into the billionaire's world of opulent wealth as the couple falls in love. Unlike a Rags to Riches story, where the focus is on a poor character's journey into wealth of their own or their journey into a world of wealth, the billionaire story concentrates on the love interest experiencing an existing world of extreme wealth held by the billionaire character and the billionaire's experience of sharing his or her special world with the love interest.

At its core, however, the billionaire story is ultimately less about money and more about safety and security. While some may argue that your audience craves the luxury, privilege, and power of wealth, I propose that it's the safety of never having to worry about money or the material aspects of life—food, shelter, bills, education, bad jobs, relatives or friends in need—that is the real draw of this trope to most people. Feel free to disagree with me, of course, and build some other core need into your non-billionaire love interest.

In most versions of this story the male lead is the billionaire, and the female love interest is not wealthy. In this gender arrangement, the billionaire is typically cast as the knight in shining armor who rides to the rescue, pulling the relatively poor heroine out of the struggles and difficulties of her life in part by throwing a lot of money at her problems to make them go away.

We frequently see billionaire male leads described not only as rich, but also as warriors or aggressively protective, so much so that the bodyguard-protector and fated mate tropes are often paired with this trope. Very often, the billionaire hero is an ex-soldier, professional athlete, supernatural hero, or some other form of uber-protective, alpha male.

Why is this, you ask? Because the billionaire hero is ultimately seen as a provider of safety. Whether it's financial safety and security or physical safety and security, audience members who gravitate to this hero type tend to crave a sense of being protected and taken care of, their worries and struggles wiped away by a strong, capable man who also loves them to distraction.

Implied in a main character being a billionaire is the suggestion that he or she is also highly intelligent, highly motivated, perhaps highly educated, talented at business and money management, probably a workaholic. Anyone who achieves billionaire status must be smarter, luckier, more disciplined, and more knowledgeable about their career field than most other people.

In other words, anyone who is a billionaire is typically portrayed as being exceptional—a perfect mate. It stands to reason that the fantasy of this perfect mate includes him or her being physically exceptional, too. Hence, most billionaire main characters are gorgeous, athletic, and outstanding in whatever career they've chosen. If nothing else, it's understood that money can buy good skin, straight teeth, the best hair, an outstanding personal trainer, great clothes, and that all billionaires will be attractive.

. . .

ADJACENT TROPES

- Rags to Riches
- Hidden Wealth
- Across the Tracks
- Bodyguard/Protector
- Fated Mates

WHY READERS/VIEWERS LOVE THIS TROPE

- they crave the safety and security that unlimited wealth can buy
- being swept out of one's mundane, hard, stressful, struggling life and completely taken care of
- all your problems are erased like magic
- you may live in humble circumstances, but you're worthy of a fantastic life...we all love to imagine ourselves as Cinderella being rescued by the rich prince, who also happens to be handsome and adore us
- who doesn't love the idea of being able to have whatever they want (no matter how expensive), whenever they want it, and to be waited on hand-and-foot

OBLIGATORY SCENES
THE BEGINNING:

The hero and heroine meet. The audience may or may not be clued in that one of the main characters is fabulously wealthy. You may choose to wait to reveal that to your audience and/or the love interest until later in the story...realizing that waiting too long to reveal this minor detail may turn your story into a hidden wealth trope.

If you choose to reveal the billionaire's wealth right up front, it's often done in a way that will set the tone for the rest of your story. If you're writing a comedy, the wealth will likely be revealed in a humorous way. If you're writing suspense, the billionaire's wealth or the love interest's lack of wealth is probably introduced in a way that creates danger for one or both of the main characters. For example, someone is kidnapped and a huge ransom demanded, a hostile corporate takeover is launched, or the love interest is thrust into devastating financial jeopardy in the inciting incident.

There may be a romantic spark right away between these characters, or you may begin your story with sparks of friction between these two characters who come from wildly different and potentially clashing worlds.

THE MIDDLE:

Because the two worlds of a very wealthy person and a non-wealthy person wouldn't necessarily intersect often or at all, the middle of your story must establish a reason why they're going to keep encountering each other over and over throughout your story, or at least often enough to fall in love.

The billionaire and love interest may have a shared problem to solve or project to complete. They may temporarily be working or living in close proximity. One of them may be in danger, and the other is providing protection. The reason they're thrust together is most likely a result of your story's external plot. Its tone will be driven by the genre of story you're writing.

The middle is when the billionaire's wealth and the love interest's relative non-wealth collide and cause problems for this couple. The pair's differing relationships with money may come into conflict.

They may have clashing values when it comes to using, sharing, or giving away money.

They may have clashing values simply because they come from very different backgrounds. In the case of a once-poor, now-rich character, he or she may have changed or left behind values the love interest still holds.

The billionaire character may have a very hard time trusting that the love interest loves him or her for himself or herself and not for his or her money. Particularly if the lovers meet after the billionaire has acquired his or her wealth, and even more so if the billionaire's wealth is known up front by the love interest, the billionaire will never really know if he or she is loved completely apart from all the wealth.

This is often a source of conflict between the lovers as the love interest struggles to prove that his or her feelings are genuine and have nothing to do with all that money. This becomes particularly challenging when the lover's feelings are, in fact, closely tied to needing safety and security or to their need for a rescue of some kind.

It's a good bet the friends and family of the love interest are going to have all kinds of strong opinions about this relationship. They may be all for it and expecting to get substantial financial benefits for themselves, or they may be violently opposed to the love interest selling out, marrying for money, or leaving behind the old neighborhood.

Either way, other characters' biases for and against wealth will tend to overshadow these people's opinions about the actual relationship and about the actual person behind the giant bank account. This is often a source of huge frustration for the love interest, who may already be struggling to see past the wealth to the person beneath the expensive clothing and lifestyle.

The personal values-based and morals-based conflicts between the lovers build to a crisis in the middle of the story. The external plot crisis that usually revolves around money or safety also builds toward a crisis.

·   ·   ·

BLACK MOMENT:

The trust between the billionaire and love interest breaks down. The relationship implodes. Worse, the threat to the safety and security of the love interest comes to fruition. The billionaire has failed to keep the love interest safe from financial or physical attack/harm. The love interest may feel betrayed, and certainly feels let down or abandoned. The "real world", meaning the non-wealthy world, comes crashing back in on the love interest, and it's even worse than before now that he or she has had a taste of another way of living where money is never a problem.

THE END:

Typically, it's the billionaire who makes a grand gesture to salvage the relationship. Given that this person is usually the one with the most trust issues to overcome, it's usually this person who must make the first move toward repairing the relationship. Any first move by the love interest to repair the relationship would logically be met with even more suspicion and distrust after the relationship has imploded.

Through one last effort to fix the problem, the love interest may solve his or her own safety/security problem. Or the billionaire may be the one to make one last big effort to secure safety for the love interest—a promise kept, or perhaps a parting gift.

In some stories, the lovers will have to work together, probably reluctantly, to overcome the big external plot threat or problem. They may reconcile in the course of working together to solve the problem.

That said, any reconciliation will require both of them to confront the billionaire's trust issues, the love interest's "proof of love issues" (proving his or her feelings for the main character to be genuine and not tied to his or her money) and resolving whatever conflict the wealth itself has caused between them.

The billionaire trope always ends with the lovers living in wealth and luxury—in a life that fulfills the fantasies of your audience.

. . .

KEY SCENES

- the moment the love interest finds out the main character is not only rich but *really* rich
- the love interest gives the billionaire a glimpse at his or her non-rich world
- the first time the love interest is exposed to the full extent of the billionaire's wealth
- a moment when the billionaire's money can't fix a problem
- a moment when the love interest makes a huge gaff or does something clueless in the billionaire's world
- the gesture in which the love interest proves his or her love is genuine and not tied to money
- the billionaire almost fails to protect the love interest in a close call with disaster

THINGS TO THINK ABOUT WHEN WRITING THIS TROPE

How did the billionaire get so rich? What special skills or talents did it take?

Just how rich is he or she? What trappings of this wealth does he or she own, for example a corporation, expensive art, private jet, yacht, mansion, penthouse, racehorses, casino, castle, private island, small country?

When does the love interest find out the billionaire is loaded? How does he or she find out? How does this event set the tone for the rest of your story?

When does the audience find out the billionaire is really rich? How? Does the revelation happen separately from the love interest?

How will you throw these two people together over and over through your story? What plot device will throw them into repeated contact? How does this plot device fit and help set the overall tone of your story?

What kind of jeopardy is the love interest in? What kind of help does he or she need from the billionaire?

What kind of jeopardy is the billionaire in? What kind of help does he or she need from the love interest?

What does the love interest think of the billionaire's wealth? How does the love interest feel about what the billionaire does with his or her money?

What about the billionaire's life does the love interest disapprove of? What about it does the love interest approve of?

What does the billionaire think of the world and lifestyle the love interest comes from? Is the billionaire familiar with that "normal" or "poor" world? If so, how? If not, why not?

How do the billionaire and love interest disagree about wealth, its trappings, how wealthy people behave, how the friends, family, and colleagues of the billionaire behave specifically?

How much trouble does the billionaire have believing that the love interest is genuinely attracted to him or her and not just to the money? What hoops does the billionaire make the love interest jump through to prove his or her feelings are genuine?

How willing is the love interest to make some sort of grand gesture to prove his or her feelings are genuine and not money induced?

What conflicts besides money and the external problem do these lovers have? Do they have personality conflicts? Habits that make each other crazy? Differing core values? Differing beliefs and opinions? Differing tastes?

What kind of person is the billionaire when all the wealth and external parts of him or her are stripped away? How will the love interest find or be shown this side of the billionaire? Is the billionaire freaked out by being metaphorically stripped bare or at ease with it?

What about himself or herself is the love interest hiding from the billionaire? How? Why? How will the billionaire finally see this secret side of the love interest?

How will this couple's two worlds collide, clash, and threaten to tear them apart?

How will you create a believable romantic spark between these two people? What about them first attracts them to each other? What about them keeps them together? What about them makes them fall hopelessly in love?

What is the wound each of these people carries around inside their heart? Whose pain or wound is the greatest? Will these wounds be part of what tears them apart? If so, how?

How does each of them heal the other's wound?

How will the people around this couple try to push them together or pull them apart? Why? What are these secondary characters' agendas and ulterior motives?

Who is the villain in your story? What does he or she want, and which of your main characters is the most threatened by this? Why does your villain believe he or she is doing the right thing?

What destroys the trust between the billionaire and love interest? How do they repair that trust? Does one of them make a grand gesture to try to repair the relationship? What is it? If it's not the love interest, how will the billionaire know for sure that it's a genuine gesture?

What last ditch, final effort will the couple make to overcome the external plot problem? Will the billionaire's money be necessary, or is all the money in the world useless in the face of this particular problem?

What lessons do the billionaire and love interest learn over the course of this story—about money, about love, about life?

What does happily ever after look like for this couple? How will you give your audience a glimpse of the couple's fairytale ending in a non-hokey way that fulfills your audience's fantasy of a perfect life?

TROPE TRAPS

Your billionaire doesn't appreciate his or her wealth or takes it for granted, thereby rendering himself or herself unlikable to your audience.

The love interest is too desperate to get his or her hands on the billionaire's money or too enamored of the billionaire's life and comes across as greedy, and hence, unlikable.

These two people would never plausibly cross paths, or there's no good reason for these two people to keep crossing paths in your story.

The billionaire's and love interest's worlds are so different that they could never plausibly be comfortable or learn to function comfortably in the other one's world. (See the trope traps section of the Hidden Wealth trope for some real talk about how billionaires actually live.)

The way the billionaire got rich wouldn't plausibly make him or her as rich as he or she is. A billion dollars (or whatever equivalent amount of currency you're using) is a LOT of money.

Your billionaire doesn't live even remotely like a billionaire actually would. Either he or she lives too opulently—there is a limit to what a billion dollars can buy—or he or she lives not opulently enough. People this rich almost always need security teams, privacy protections, financial planners, tax advisors, bankers, at least a little personal staff, and other necessary assistance to manage their wealth.

Your billionaire trusts the love interest too easily not to be after his or her money.

Your love interest is so uninterested in the billionaire's money that your audience finds him or her excessively naïve, unaware, or downright dim.

You fail to explain why the billionaire is dating, and potentially marrying way outside his or her social class. Billionaires do, in fact, live very different lives than most people. It is much easier to be with someone who is already familiar with that world.

Your non-wealthy love interest adapts seamlessly and easily to living in extreme wealth and magically knows all the ins and outs of living around that kind of money.

You fail to nail down your message about money and convey it clearly. Will you say that money can't buy love, that it can or can't solve all problems, that it's sure handy to have a lot of, that rich people have big problems too?

The reconciliation between the lovers isn't believable. Typically this results when you haven't adequately painted two people genuinely falling in love with each other at a deep and intimate level that has nothing to do with money.

BILLIONAIRE TROPE IN ACTION
Movies:

- Pretty Woman
- Crazy Rich Asians
- Sense and Sensibility
- The Great Gatsby
- Meet Joe Black
- The Ultimate Gift
- Sabrina
- Maid in Manhattan
- Pride and Prejudice

Books:

- Bared to You by Sylvia Day
- The Fine Print by Lauren Asher
- King of Wrath by Ana Huang
- The Stopover by T. L. Swan
- A Not So Meet Cute by Meghan Quinn
- The Wrong Bride by Catharina Maura
- Tease by Melanie Harlowe
- My Dark Romeo by Parker S. Huntington
- Praise by Sara Cate
- Beautiful Bastard by Christina Lauren
- Marriage for One by Ella Maise
- The Marriage Bargain by Jennifer Probst
- The Last Eligible Billionaire by Pippa Grant
- This Man by Jodi Ellen Malpas
- By a Thread by Lucy Score

3

BULLY TURNED NICE

DEFINITION

The hero or heroine in this story has been a bully in the past or is a bully to begin the story. In either case, over the course of the story, he or she has or has already had some sort of healing, epiphany, or lesson(s) learned that transform him or her and stop his or her bullying behavior for good.

Moreover, the bully becomes capable of a healthy romantic relationship with the love interest and finds his or her happily ever after at the end of this story.

Many people seem to believe that all bullies are victims of bullying themselves and are wounded souls, acting out their pain. If we only love them enough and forgive them, they'll change their ways.

This couldn't be further from the truth in most cases.

This is one of those misconceptions you may feel free to write into your story, but I exhort you to do your research and try at least in part or in an author's note to share more realistic information about how bullies can be treated and "cured" and what their prognosis is in general for recovery and change of behavior patterns.

To understand this trope, it's necessary to dig into what bullying actually is and where it comes from. The United Kingdom's National Centre Against Bullying defines it like this: "Bullying is an ongoing and deliberate misuse of power in relationships through repeated verbal, physical and/or social behaviour that intends to cause physical, social and/or psychological harm."

The NCAB goes on to say: Bullying is not

- single episodes of social rejection or dislike
- single episode acts of nastiness or spite
- random acts of aggression or intimidation
- mutual arguments, disagreements, or fights.

People (and it's worth noting adults are as likely to bully as children, and women are as likely to bully as men) are thought to bully for several reasons. They feel powerless, they suffer from insecurity, they need to control others, or they enjoy the rewards they get from bullying, to name a few.

Bullies often lack empathy, exhibit narcissistic traits, are emotionally unstable, or cannot regulate their own behavior. Controlling and intimidating others can be a means of feeling better about themselves or even self-soothing. Bullying is often a learned behavior and reinforced by past experiences.

Turning this person into a heroic, likable, relatable character is going to be a tough climb for you as a writer, but it can be done.

Keep in mind, many of your audience members have experienced bullying directly. They know for themselves that bullies don't just get hugged a few times and totally change. While you may be able to get away with writing a miraculous bully turn-around as a fantasy your audiences wishes were true, the reality is completely different.

In therapy, bullies first need to recognize they're doing something bad, which they may be reluctant to admit. Then, they need to be held accountable for it, something else they're likely to resist. But only then can they figure out why they bully, what triggers it, and how it negatively impacts them and others. This step presupposes that your bully is actually capable of feeling empathy for the suffering of those he or she has picked on—something a large percentage of bullies aren't capable of easily or possibly at all.

Then, the bully who truly wishes to change his or her behavior patterns must address the underlying trauma or mental health issues and change their thought processes, reactions to stimuli, and behaviors.

It's worth noting that most bullies are comfortable with their behavior, see their behavior as justified, like the results of their bullying—being seen as powerful or getting what they want—and don't feel empathy for their victims until some sort of intervention happens.

Typical steps in the healing process include:

- addressing trauma
- building empathy and/or conscience
- learning social skills
- learning to self-regulate impulsivity
- developing anger-management skills
- building ties with parents or other mentors
- feeling seen/loved/respected/understood
- developing healthier ways of thinking, behaving, and expressing emotion
- being surrounded by consistent, rational, non-aggressive authority figures who provide a stable environment, rational and graduated responses to relapses, and unconditional emotional support.

Bullies don't need to do ONE of these things to change their bullying behavior pattern...they typically need to do most or ALL of them.

> NOTE: This list of steps is by no means all-inclusive, and there may be other steps required to heal your bully.

Keep in mind, your story may be the only source of factual information on bullying recovery for some of your readers or viewers—and bullying is a devastating problem for its millions of victims and for bullies, themselves.

At any rate, the steps to healing give us a roadmap for this trope. For a bully to turn nice, some sort of healing or change must occur. It can have occurred before your story begins...although you may be passing up a great opportunity to explore character growth if you make your bully's transformation a fait accompli before your story begins.

It is possible, however, to sustain your entire story by following an ex-bully's apology tour of making amends for past wrongs he or she has inflicted on others.

As for the love interest in your story, for goodness' sake, don't make him or her the bully's therapist. It's unethical as heck for therapists to date their patients.

You have several choices to make regarding your love interest that will set the tone for your story—did he or she know the bully in the past, was he or she bullied by the main character, will he or she be part of the bully's healing process, how will he or she help the now-former bully move forward in a healthy way?

At its core, this is a story of huge personal transformation. Such fundamental changes in a person take huge commitment, don't come easy, and are hard to make permanent...so feel free to make this character really suffer or work hard for their happily ever after. For this character to learn a life-defining lesson that bullying is bad and he or she must stop doing it, your main character is probably going to need to experience a life-changing event that forces this lesson upon him or her.

Consider building your story around something on this scale if you want your audience to believe your bully has genuinely turned nice and will be able to stay nice in the long run.

ADJACENT TROPES

- Mafia Romance
- Bad Boy/Girl Reformed
- Forgiveness
- Redemption

WHY READERS/VIEWERS LOVE THIS TROPE

- there's great satisfaction in fixing flaws in a lover, polishing a diamond in the rough, as it were
- he or she loves me enough to do massive personal work to heal themselves, fix their problems, and completely overhaul their life, their thought processes, and how they deal with the world
- we relate to wounded souls because we all have wounds of our own. We love seeing someone overcome their wounds. It gives us hope that we can overcome our own traumas, hurts, and flaws
- finding the good person beneath the jerk...and the affirmation that, beneath the jerks we live or work with, there may actually be a good person
- the fantasy of being with someone who'll be rough with you, dominate you, tell you what to do while you're

helpless or at the bully's mercy, which is to say, a masochistic fantasy

OBLIGATORY SCENES
THE BEGINNING:

The hero and heroine meet in a way that will set the tone for your story, be it comic, dark, gritty, suspenseful, steamy, or something else. How you introduce your bully or former bully will take some thought about how you want your love interest (and more importantly, your audience) to react to this character initially. If your main character is not reformed as a bully yet, you'll need to show something interesting enough, likeable enough, or engaging enough about him or her that your audience will stick around to read or watch the rest of your story.

Keep in mind that many people have been the victims of bullies and suffered serious mental health issues, emotional damage, pain, and suffering as a result. Readers or viewers are not likely to be particularly empathetic, forgiving, or patient with a main character who has no strongly redeeming qualities to offset the enormous flaw of being or having been a bully.

The love interest's reason for not immediately walking away from a bully or former bully also needs to be established in the beginning of your story. Your audience is likely to worry that the love interest may be the bully's next victim, so you may want to consider establishing right away that the love interest is no way, no how, going to tolerate being pushed around by anyone. I'm not suggesting that the love interest can't be sweet, gentle, or compassionate. Rather, I'm suggesting that the love interest must demonstrate the ability to set healthy boundaries very early in your story lest your audience spend all its time fretting over this character's safety.

Whatever draws these two people together—an external plot device or strong attraction between them—must be established.

. . .

THE MIDDLE:

As the external plot problems mount in your story, the stresses upon the bully or ex-bully mount. If your main character is an ex-bully, pressures to relapse into old behavior patterns build. On his or her own, or with the help of the love interest, he or she must resist those temptations.

If you started your story with a bully still on the path to healing, the external plot problems grow until they provoke a crisis in the bully. He or she must, once and for all, face his or her behavior and deal with it, or else lose everything.

Through the middle of your story, personal conflicts between the lovers will also grow. The love interest may find out about the past bullying and be shaken by it. The bully may not trust himself or herself not to harm the love interest. The ex-bully may struggle with how far to go to protect the love interest as a threat grows worse. The ex-bully may be so passive now that he or she refuses to defend himself or herself.

The middle of your story may be taken up with the bully working through the healing process of learning not to bully, or with the bully facing the aftermath of past bullying, or with the new behavior patterns of a reformed bully being challenged. Regardless of which of these you choose, the bully/ex-bully's character arc builds toward a crisis.

BLACK MOMENT:

The bully falls off the wagon. He or she loses control of himself or herself and does something aggressive and/or emotionally hurtful to the love interest. The external plot problem may cause the bully to crack emotionally and explode. Even if said explosion is completely justified under normal circumstances by a normal person, the now ex-bully is devastated by it.

This loss of control devastates the love interest as well. He or she may be the target of the explosion. If the love interest merely witnesses the ex-bully's outburst directed at someone else, it may still destroy his or her fragile trust in the ex-bully's ability to move forward in a healthy emotional way.

As the external plot problem has reached a crisis point, the ex-bully does something radical to try to fix the problem—but it fails utterly. Not only does extreme action not work, but it also destroys his or her relationship with the one person who sees through the ex-bully's past problems and past bad behavior to the good, kind person beneath.

Both ex-bully and love interest are devastated. The ex-bully may fall off the wagon and revert to his or her old, worst behavior patterns. But beware of undoing all the good work this character has done. Correcting a pattern of bullying is typically a long-term process. You're already deep into your story by the black moment, and you probably can't afford to go all the way back to square one with this character and go through the entire healing process again.

THE END:

The ex-bully, having lost everything and everyone who matters to him or her makes one last, Herculean effort to solve the external plot problem through a non-bullying means and finally succeeds. Separately, or as part of this big effort to deal with a crisis in a healthy way, he or she recommits to moving forward as an ex-bully.

The ex-bully makes a grand gesture of some kind to prove to the love interest that he or she is done being a bully once and for all. And it had better be GRAND. It's a huge ask of the love interest to trust someone—and commit to a long-term relationship with that person—who has ever engaged in the extremely hurtful and harmful behaviors of a bully, even if it was a very long time ago.

The ex-bully convinces the love interest that he or she has REALLY changed, and in fact he or she really has. You must also convince your audience of the same thing, and that may be harder to do than convincing your fictitious love interest.

At any rate, the bully is fully turned nice and finally deserves the love he or she has worked hard through the story to earn. The love interest fully trusts him or her, and they find their happily ever after together.

NOTE: Every human being deserves to be loved. But in this trope, the bully turned nice is always required to earn the love of the love interest. And along the way, the bully turned nice learns to love himself or herself, as well.

KEY SCENES

- the bully/ex-bully encounters someone he or she has bullied in the past
- the bully/ex-bully encounters someone who bullied him or her. Often this is a parent, other family member, or authority figure from his or her past
- the bully behaves well or does something nice in a situation where, in the past, they would have bullied someone
- the love interest triggers or provokes the ex-bully (possibly intentionally)
- the love interest encounters someone who was bullied by the main character in the past
- the ex-bully almost, but not quite, succumbs to old behaviors when presented with a trigger from his or her past

THINGS TO THINK ABOUT WHEN WRITING THIS TROPE

Why was your main character a bully? What and/or who in his or her life triggered this type of behavior?

What kind of bullying did the bully engage in? (Physical, verbal, emotional, cyber or electronic, social, workplace, racial, religious, sexual, disability)

Who did the bully pick on?

Has the bully had counseling or therapy to deal with being a bully? Has he or she dealt with the source of it? If so, how?

Will the victim(s) of the bully be part of your story? If so, how? Who are they? How do they feel about the bully now?

Have the victims had counseling or therapy and dealt with the aftermath of having been bullied?

Is the love interest a past victim of the bully?

How does the love interest (and audience) find out about the past bullying? How does the love interest react?

What quality or qualities in the bully/ex-bully will make him or her likable, engaging, or heroic to the love interest and to your audience? How will you build upon this quality or add other positive qualities over the course of your story?

What does the main character think about having been a bully? How does he or she feel about it now?

Are you going to build your story around a Significant Emotional Event having just happened before your story begins or happening to the bully over the course of your story that will prompt him or her to turn nice by the end of your story? If so, what SEE? How will it force the bully to change?

Does your bully/ex-bully suffer the consequences of their past actions in your story? If so, how?

How does your ex-bully make amends for past bullying?

Will you show the bully actually bullying someone in your story? Why?—and your reason had better be fantastic. What makes this heroic to your audience and to the love interest? Keep in mind, bullying is not one incident of being mean. It's a repeated pattern of picking on someone.

Will you show your bully being mean to someone in a one-off incident? How triggering is this for the main character? For the love interest? For your audience?

How do friends, family, and coworkers of the love interest feel about him or her getting involved with the main character? Will they try to interfere? To protect the love interest? To warn off the main character?

Where in his or her journey of recovering from being a bully is your main character when the story begins?

How will the main character's healing from bullying behaviors be tested in your story?

How will your external plot problem set up a healing journey for your bully? How will this problem challenge your bully's healing journey? How will the plot problem turned crisis provoke a relapse by your bully?

How hard will your ex-bully fall off the wagon in the black moment and what form will it take?

What gesture from the ex-bully will it take for the love interest to trust him or her again in the end of your story?

How will you show your audience that the bully has really turned nice for good and can sustain this change for the long term?

TROPE TRAPS

The audience hates your bully. Full stop.

The audience has no respect for your love interest finding anything attractive about your bully/ex-bully main character.

Failing to give the bully/ex-bully a redeeming quality that's powerful enough to pull the audience through whatever healing or transformation your main character still has to go through.

Failing to convince your audience that the bully is truly committed to long-term change for the better.

Giving your bully a lame reason for having become a bully in the first place. If we're going to like this person, he or she should have some hardcore trauma in his or her past.

Your bully just "grew out" of being a bully. This RARELY happens without some sort of professional intervention. Most bullies aren't self-aware enough to realize they're bullying in the first place. They're surely not self-aware enough to fix their own trauma, social skills problems, or lack of empathy for others.

Depicting a bully who's not remorseful enough to satisfy your audience.

Creating a wet dishrag of a love interest who doesn't set boundaries with the bully or stick by those boundaries.

Creating a lame epiphany of how your bully figured out he or she was being a bully and behaving badly.

Failing to portray the real and hard work of stopping being a bully, or just skipping over it.

The bully depends emotionally too much on the love interest for self-esteem or to regulate or control their bad behavior for them. It's not sexy to replace bullying with codependency, kids.

Creating a main character whose bullying stems from narcissism, lack of empathy, or anti-social personality disorder, and having the love interest's "good love" cure it. Some personality disorders are not curable, no matter how much someone loves the person with one.

Misconstruing being mean to someone once with being a bully.

Failing to do your homework on what bullying is, what it does to victims, why people bully others, what it takes to stop bullying, and how much (or what kind of) therapy, counseling, and work is required to fix or recover from the causes of it.

Failing to address the victims of your main character's past bullying or doing it in an insensitive way.

The love interest forgives the ex-bully too easily for falling off the wagon in the black moment. In reality, trust, once destroyed, is darned near impossible to restore...and your audience knows that.

The ex-bully doesn't make a grand enough gesture or sacrifice at the end of the story to regain the love interest's trust and to prove himself or herself FULLY committed to a bullying-free future.

Failing to demonstrate to your audience that the ex-bully has what it takes to stay the course in the long-term, live in a healthier way, and never, ever bully the love interest or anyone else.

BULLY TURNED NICE TROPE IN ACTION
Movies:

- A Clockwork Orange (trigger warnings galore for violence and it's not a romance...but it's definitely about a bully who's cured)
- Mean Girls
- Beauty and the Beast (which treads dangerously close to Stockholm Syndrome)
- Pocahontas
- Not Another Teen Movie
- You've Got Mail

Books:

- Deviant King by Rina Kent
- Bully by Penelope Douglas
- Vicious by L.J. Shen
- Paper Princess by Erin Watt
- The Initiation by Niki Sloane
- Nash by Jay Crownover
- Fear Me by B. B. Reid
- Riot House by Callie Hart
- Rebellion by Siobhan Davis

4

BURNED BY LOVE

DEFINITION

In this trope one of the main characters has had a really bad experience with love in the past and has been left scarred, skeptical, and traumatized by love. Over the course of this story, he or she must overcome their distrust and heal their personal wounds enough to be able to fall in love once more.

This is a truly universal trope, given that almost everyone has been burned by love at least once in his or her life. It's an experience every single audience member will probably relate to on a very personal level. What's interesting, however, is how infrequently this trope is portrayed in literature or one screen. My guess is we also know universally that the journey back to trusting others can be a slow and painful one, and it's not a journey many of us relish reliving.

Your job then, is to write a story so engaging, so interesting, so engrossing, and characters so likable, relatable, and cheer-worthy that your audience will stick with them all the way through to trust repaired, faith in humanity restored, and the eventual happy ending for your lovers. In this trope, be especially wary of lags in pacing, sagging middles, excessively difficult to like love interests, or any drop-off in audience engagement. Particularly in the parts of the story where the romance isn't going well, your audience may be especially inclined to walk away from the story if their own wounds after being burned by love are not healed.

For the burned character, the bulk of this story will revolve around learning to trust in his or her partner and allowing themselves to love once more.

As for the love interest in this story, he or she has a great deal of heavy lifting to do. Not only must he or she be patient and understanding, but the love interest must be so good, so kind, so heroic, and so utterly trustworthy that the burned character not only can't help but fall in love with him or her but also learns to trust him or her completely. In this trope, it's not uncommon for the love interest to be the main character the story focuses on. It's the love interest who must usually take action and push the relationship forward.

The main character tends to be reactive as opposed to proactive in this trope. The burned character starts the story in a defensive crouch and only gradually comes out of that position. He or she probably returns to a full defensive position more than once over the course of the story and only at the end does he or she find the courage to fully open their heart.

At its core, this trope is more about trust than love. It's likely that the burned character doesn't dispute the fact that love can be good. But this character forcefully disputes the idea that one can find true love without being betrayed in the end.

ADJACENT TROPES

- Commitment Phobia
- Damaged Hero/Heroine
- Fear of Intimacy
- Couples Therapy
- Estranged Spouses
- Reconciliation/Second Chance

. . .

WHY READERS/VIEWERS LOVE THIS TROPE

- we've ALL been burned by love at least once. We've all experienced the trauma, the sense of being done looking for love, the despair of believing we'll never find the right person. And we all wish these things could be fixed
- wishing the right person would magically cross our path, take one look at us, know we're the ONE, and fight like crazy to convince us of the same
- being worth fighting for, even if we throw up every roadblock to love we can think of
- he or she took the worst I can dish out and STILL loves me. Which is to say, someone loves me unconditionally.
- who doesn't want their relationship wounds and scars completely healed by the love of my life?

OBLIGATORY SCENES
THE BEGINNING:

The burned hero/heroine and the love interest meet. Something about the burned character calls to the love interest. It might be the pain of the burned character, their isolation, their dark melancholy... or it might be their most lovable qualities. The love interest may see the burned character lavishing love on animals, children, a hobby, or a personal passion and may realize the burned character has a great deal of love to give a romantic partner...if only they would let himself or herself do so.

The burned by love character may register attraction to the future love interest but rejects the idea of falling in love. The burned character may be so closed off emotionally at the beginning of the story that he or she doesn't even register that. You can play with this character actually experiencing attraction subconsciously but rejecting it consciously.

It's also not uncommon for the burned character to engage in callous, unemotional sex in the beginning of stories. They'll go through the motions of courting, dating, and even having relationships, but they hold themselves aloof emotionally and never, ever let down their emotional walls.

This burned character is a common version the classic dark, dangerous hero/heroine who's unbearably attractive but unbearably remote emotionally. While other tropes may explain why a dark, dangerous character is emotionally shut down, this is perhaps the most common trope explaining that remoteness.

You'll probably establish just how lovable and trustworthy the love interest is right away. To earn the burned character's trust, this character must be so unwaveringly lovable and trustworthy that there's very little room for him or her to be anything else from the first moment of your story. (That said, it might be an interesting writing challenge to create a love interest who is neither lovable nor trustworthy at the beginning of your story or who isn't lovable or trustworthy to other characters in the story, but who is unswervingly both to the main character.)

OR

The person who burned your main character in the first is going to be the love interest in your story. Our love interest is probably following a redemption trope, or perhaps a reconciliation trope, and our burned main character is certainly going to have to follow a forgiveness trope as well.

But, if the main emphasis of your story is a character who's been burned by love learning to trust again and love again, Burned By Love is one of the tropes you should probably explore (and exploit).

When the love interest and burned character first meet in the beginning of your story, it probably goes very badly, indeed. The love interest has come back into the burned character's life for some compelling reason that you'll need to introduce and is determined to make amends for past wrongs. The burned character is likely to react with rage and want nothing to do with amends or forgiveness of any kind. Hence, the reason your love interest is back, and the reason he or she is allowed to stick around by the burned character has to be extremely compelling to both the burned character and the former love interest. It has to be strong enough to force two people, one of whom hates the other's guts, to stay in close proximity for the entirety of your story.

THE MIDDLE:

The middle of this tropes will be punctuated by approaches and retreats, starts and stops, moments of nascent trust followed by moments of return to distrust by the main character. The love interest may orchestrate many of the encounters in an effort to force the burned character to face his or her fears, wounds, trauma, and pain. The love interest is determined to prove himself or herself trustworthy.

The plot developments of your story should present opportunities and temptations to the love interest to betray the main character. The burned main character may, in fact, orchestrate some or all of these temptations to defect. If the love interest finds out the burned character is trying to force him or her to leave or betray the main character, this is probably going to cause substantial conflict between the lovers.

In the middle of your story, the attraction between the burned character and love interest grows and may take a physical form in the shape of dates, romantic encounters, and even love scenes. The burned character may start to let down his or her emotional walls, but it's a struggle for this person. Bit by bit, the love interest chips away at the burned character's fortress of solitude.

As for the plot, whatever has brought these two people together races toward a crisis where each of them will have to make a terrible choice. The love interest must choose whether or not to betray the fragile trust of the main character in some way, while the burned character must choose—under the most intense duress you can manufacture via your plot—whether or not to trust the love interest.

BLACK MOMENT:

The burned character can't do it. He or she can't bring himself or herself to trust the love interest. One last time, they give into their pain, trauma, grief, rage, and whatever other manifestations of their wounded heart you have given them. The love interest has given this relationship their all. He or she has done everything in his or her power to convince the burned character that he or she is not going to betray them...and the love interest has failed. This is the moment in which the love interest gives up on the relationship and gives up on the burned character ever being whole again. It's a moment of total emotional defeat for both characters.

Worse, the thing these two characters have come together to do in the first place has also failed. In the act of failing to trust each other, they've wrecked the external thing they've been working on together. It, too, is ruined by the burned character's lack of trust and the love interest's failure to break through to the burned character.

THE END:

One or both of your lovers decides to give it one last try. Where this hope and optimism comes from will depend upon which character makes the first overture to the other. It may be that their shared commitment to the external plot device they're working on together is enough to bring them together one last time for the sake of the problem or project they're working on.

It may be that the burned character, having been burned again, experiences true despair. In this despair, he or she finally realizes that this time, he or she has pushed away the love of his or her life. The first time someone burned them, the other person caused them pain. Now they, the burned character, have inflicted the same pain on someone else...someone whom they, in fact, love.

It may be that the love interest just can't bring himself or herself to abandon the burned character without one last try at reaching them. This character sees the good in the burned character, sees the wounded soul hiding inside, sees the burned character's desperate need for love and hears their silent cries for someone to help them out of their pit of despair. In this scenario, the compassion of the love interest overcomes his or her pain, and he or she reaches out one last time to the burned character.

From the utter despair of the black moment, the lovers find the strength to crawl out of their respective emotional pain and darkness and find each other once more. With this one last proof of trustworthiness and commitment to their love, these two find trust powerful enough to bind them together forever. They've found their true love, and now neither of them is ever letting go again.

The resolution of the plot problem may end up being quite secondary to the resolution of this dramatically fraught relationship finally resolving happily. Because of this, it's not uncommon to have a climactic scene that resolves the plot and a second, more important climax where the lovers finally prove their trust for each other once and for all and resolve their trust issues. In a particularly elegant ending, the dramatic actions necessary to resolve the plot problem force the hero and heroine to prove their love for each other. It's not uncommon for each of them to attempt to sacrifice their life for the other in the final scene. It can take literally being willing to die for each other to overcome the trust issues the burned character has cloaked himself or herself in.

The final moment of this story is typically a passionate declaration of their love for each other.

· · ·

KEY SCENES

- the meeting or scene in which we establish the burned character's complete lack of trust for anyone romantically
- the moment where the love interest sees something lovable about the burned character
- the first moment that requires trust from the burned character for the love interest the moment or scene after the first big romantic event (a love scene, a kiss, or some moment of passion shared) when the burned character pulls back sharply and wounds the love interest
- the moment when the burned character realizes he or she loves the love interest
- the moment when the love interest realizes he or she has failed and has lost the burned character to his or her own emotional dark night of the soul

THINGS TO THINK ABOUT WHEN WRITING THIS TROPE

What happened to burn the main character in the past? Who did it? How? How bad was it? Why did it hurt this character so badly? What Achilles' heel did this particular betrayal hit in the main character?

Who is your love interest in this story? Is he or she the person who burned the main character in the past or not?

- If so, why is this character back? What does he or she want? What is he or she hoping to accomplish—both externally in the plot of the story and internally in the emotional arc of the story? Is he or she looking for forgiveness, closure, redemption, a second chance?

- If not, why is this love interest exactly the right person to break through to the burned character? Why is he or she exactly the wrong person to break through to the burned character? What will be most attractive about this person to the burned character? What quality will be most necessary to break through the burned character's emotional walls?

What about the burned character irresistibly draws the love interest to him or her?

What good qualities does the love interest see in the burned character? Do others see these qualities, or does the burned character hide them from others?

How passionately attracted are these two people? Does their initial attraction revolve around physical attraction or something else? If so, what else?

What external problem, event, project, or other MacGuffin is going to throw these two people together often enough and closely enough that the burned character cannot just walk away from the love interest as a relationship starts to blossom?

How withdrawn is the burned character? Is he or she outwardly pleasant to those of the appropriate gender for romance? Is he or she out to take advantage of or punish others of the appropriate romantic gender? Is he or she only negatively reactive to those who remind him or her of the person who betrayed them? Is he or she totally unwilling to interact with others of the appropriate romantic gender?

Why is the love interest willing to stick around and put up with the burned character's distrust, caution, rudeness, or callousness? Will you portray this as a good quality in the love interest or a flaw in the love interest?

How do the people around the couple perceive their interactions? Do the burned character's friends want to protect him or her? See him or her come out of their shell? Do they promote a romance with the love interest or try to interfere with it?

How do the love interest's family and friends perceive the burned character? Do they see his or her potential? Do they think the love interest should dump him or her? Do they help or hinder the relationship?

Does the burned character set up situations to test the love interest's loyalty, to tempt him or her to betrayal, or to drive away the love interest?

Does the love interest orchestrate situations to desensitize the burned character to romance or emotions, to push the burned character to trust the love interest, or to prove his or her trustworthiness to the burned character?

If either character finds out the other is setting up these sorts of situations, how does he or she react to that?

What about these two draws them together romantically? Do they have shared interests? Do they share core beliefs or morals? Are they unusual among the other people they both live with in some unique way that draws them together? What do they each see in the other that's admirable, lovable, fascinating, or irresistible?

What causes conflict between these two (other than the obvious trust issues the burned character brings to the relationship)? What pulls them apart? What drives them crazy about the other one? What thing(s) do they see in the other that niggles at the back of their mind, nibbling away at the trust they're trying to grow between them?

Does the love interest have a secret that, if revealed to the burned character, would destroy his or her trust in the love interest? If so, what is it? And of course...when is it revealed to the burned character and how? Vice versa, does the burned character have a secret that, if revealed to the love interest, would destroy his or her trust/love/respect/feelings for the burned character? If so, when is this secret revealed to the love interest and how?

What crisis in the external plot will force an emotional betrayal between the lovers? Which lover will betray the other? Will they both betray each other? Will the betrayal be real or merely perceived as betrayal?

What does complete failure of this relationship look like to each character? What does it feel like? How does each character react? Do they shut down? Rage? Become reclusive? Go on a drunken bender? Try to destroy themselves? Something else extreme?

After it has all gone to hell, which character(s) will decide to give it one last try? Why? Does someone else give them a swift kick in the butt, or is it a personal decision?

If the conscious decision to give it one last try is based on the need to solve the external plot problem, what personal, private, emotional elements will contribute to that decision to move ahead with trying one more time to solve the plot crisis?

How will resolving the plot problem force the lovers to confront their relationship? To confront their trust issues? To confront the fact that they love each other?

TROPE TRAPS

Creating a burned by love main character who crosses the line into mean, genuinely hurtful, or cruel to others of the appropriate romantic gender, and who is so unlikable that he or she cannot be redeemed in the eyes of your audience.

Creating a love interest who has so little self-esteem, self-respect, or self-love that he or she will put up with bad behavior from the burned character that no heroic character should tolerate, making him or her unredeemably unlikable.

Creating a love interest who's so perfect as to be unlikable to your audience.

If you're using the person who originally burned the main character as your love interest, creating a past betrayal or harm by him or her as to make any renewed relationship completely unbelievable.

Leaving the burned character so stuck in his or her pain that he or she seems immature, whiny, selfish, or generally annoying for their total failure to move on from past hurts. Remember, most of your audience has been burned by love and managed to move on in part or in whole. They'll have little respect for a character who remains totally mired in pain, rage, betrayal, or state of injury...

...unless, of course, you've burned the main character so badly in the past that he or she can do nothing but live in a state of trauma and inability to heal. In which case, the trope trap here is creating a character too wounded to ever plausibly heal enough to find trust and love again.

The burned character orchestrates temptations to the love interest to betray him or her that are truly mean and unlikable.

The love interest (selfishly) manipulates the burned character into romantic situations that are well beyond what the burned character is ready to handle.

One or both of your main characters aren't honest with themselves or self-aware about their wounds, motives, or goals. NOTE: This trope requires a certain amount of personal growth and self-awareness in each main character to be plausible to your audience.

Not creating lovers likable and interesting enough to hold your audience's attention even if your story is triggering old wounds in the audience members themselves.

Creating a lame or implausible external problem, or one that doesn't force your burned character and the love interest together closely enough or long enough for them to form a real relationship and fall in love.

The burned character heals too easily.

The burned character trusts too easily.

The love interest sticks around too loyally.

The thing that breaks the lovers apart isn't devastating enough.

The reason the lovers decide to give their relationship one last try isn't powerful enough.

Relying on hot sex (which is to say physical attraction and passion) to pull these characters past truly deep emotional wounds and to heal their souls.

Failing to have one or both of the lovers make a grand sacrifice... one that's really hard for them to do.

Failing to give your audience the deeply satisfying moment of the burned character's heart breaking open, of him or her finally truly trusting their lover, and the burned character committing fully to love.

BURNED BY LOVE TROPE IN ACTION
Movies:

- The Break-Up
- Forgetting Sarah Marshall
- Legally Blonde
- What If
- Hope Floats
- The Holiday

Books:

- To Seduce a Sinner by Elizabeth Hoyt
- Prince Charming by Julie Garwood
- Bittersweet by Sarah Ockler
- A Broken Heart Mended by Jenna Hendricks
- Always Something There to Remind Me by Beth Harbison
- The Bucket List to Mend a Broken Heart by Anna Bell
- How to Mend a Broken Heart by Anna Mansell

5

DANGEROUS PAST

DEFINITION

In this trope the main character clearly has a dangerous past. That, in and of itself, does not a trope make. This title is a common shorthand name for a longer trope name, something along the lines of Hero/Heroine's Dangerous Past Comes Back to Threaten Them, Their Present Romance, or Their Present Lover.

Got all that?

Dangerous Past. Present romance in progress. Something or someone dangerous from the main character's past returns to cause problems for the lovers.

What the nature of that past danger might be is up to you:

- The main character can have done something dangerous.
- The main character can have been dangerous.
- The main character can have been in danger.
- The main character can have known someone dangerous.
- The main character can have been surrounded by danger (that wasn't dangerous to him or her at the time but is dangerous now).

. . .

The main character may or may not have any idea that a past danger could show back up in his or her life. He or she may have spent enough time in hiding, changed identity, or made peace with the dangerous people in his or her past to believe himself or herself safe from any danger now. This may be naïve, or this may have been true...until something changed.

The main character is living his or her best life, meets the love interest, and a relationship commences developing. It's into this happy chain of events that the past danger comes back to bite the main character and probably to endanger the love interest.

This danger may freak out the love interest, who may have no idea that the main character has a dangerous past or may naively believe the main character when he or she says their dangerous past will stay firmly in the past.

The love interest in this trope is almost always in jeopardy, and the main character almost always is cast as a protector of the love interest.

Because of his or her dangerous past, the main character usually has survival skills for navigating danger, skills that he or she must use to protect his or her true love.

The love interest may feel betrayed by the main character for not confessing his or her past, or for putting the love interest in danger the love interest did not bargain for. The love interest may want out of the relationship and/or out of danger...but may have no choice about sticking around, close to the main character who is the only person who can keep him or her safe.

The danger from the past puts an unbearable strain on the romantic relationship, eventually forcing the lovers apart. Then, it's up to the lovers to find a way to evade, flee, or defeat the danger so they can be together safely forever.

At its core, this trope is a version of the knight in shining armor/damsel in distress archetype. The knight errant has retired from his or her wandering fight against evil, hung up his or her spurs and sword, and put the white horse out to pasture. But then the dragon finds him or her and brings the fight to the (now rusty) knight. The knight must take up sword, shield, spurs, and white horse one last time to protect his or her true love.

ADJACENT TROPES

- Dangerous Secret
- Mafia Romance
- Bad Boy/Girl Reformed
- Fresh Start
- Ex-Convict Hero/Heroine

WHY READERS/VIEWERS LOVE THIS TROPE

- who doesn't love a tall, dark, and dangerous stranger
- getting to be part of a secret and special world or be in on the secret
- feeling utterly safe and protected
- no matter what life throws at us, my partner can handle it and I'm not on my own to deal with it
- he or she loves me enough to stand by me even if I put his or her life in danger
- my lover trusts me with his or her life

OBLIGATORY SCENES
THE BEGINNING:

This is one of the rare romance tropes that may not necessarily begin at the beginning, meaning the lovers may already know each other and may already be in a romantic relationship when this story begins. Of course, you can always begin your story with their first meeting, but it's not required.

It's entirely possible that the meeting with the love interest is an innocent meet cute. It's also possible that the main character and love interest are total strangers when the past danger shows up and endangers them both. In this case, the love interest may be a bystander who was simply in the wrong place at the wrong time and gets sucked into the main character's danger completely by accident.

Regardless, once the danger from the past shows up and puts the love interest in danger, the main character must stay close to the love interest to protect him or her until the danger is past once more.

All that's truly required to get this story rolling is a main character with a dangerous past meeting and commencing a (potentially romantic) relationship with the love interest who is put into danger.

The main character may or may not share details of his or her past with the love interest when they meet. Both of them may believe this danger will stay firmly in the past and poses no threat now.

But, once the danger shows up, romantic conflict ensues. The love interest may want to leave the relationship but has no choice. The only person who truly understands the threat and can keep him or her safe from the danger is the main character.

The couple may have some external plot reason for being in physical proximity within your story, or their attraction to each other and a budding romance may be the thing that draws them together. Or it may be the danger itself that forces the couple into proximity in the beginning of this story.

Regardless, by the end of the beginning, the danger from the past shows up, and present danger is clearly established.

THE MIDDLE:
Whatever the danger or dangerous person from the past has

planned for the main character and love interest becomes clear in the middle of the story. The dangerous element always wants something —perhaps revenge or perhaps some action from the main character that he or she is reluctant to take.

Sky's the limit on your imagination when you create villains, so have fun with what the danger from the past wants. The only requirement is that the main character is dead set against doing the thing, handing over the information, or dying. And he or she is even more dead set against letting harm come to the love interest.

Romantic conflict builds as the love interest feels unsafe, betrayed, lied to, endangered, unfairly targeted, and a host of other negative emotions while at the same time he or she is falling in love with the very person who has put them at such terrible risk.

The love interest is deeply conflicted internally, and the emotional turmoil spills over into the relationship with the main character.

For his or her part, the main character may feel guilt, shame, rage, fear, uncertainty, temptation, and a host of other negative emotions about the return of this aspect of his or her past that also spill over into the romantic relationship and cause havoc.

On top of all of this emotional upheaval in and between the lovers, there's a tangible threat, a clear and present danger to both of them, that absolutely must be dealt with.

While writers will occasionally take a light, humorous tone in a story such as this, most of the time this is a taut, suspenseful, fast-paced tale of barely managing to stay one step ahead of the bad guy(s).

By the end of the middle, the danger has caught up with them and the main character fails to protect the love interest from it. Disaster strikes. The dangerous element appears to win and the love interest's life, freedom, or safety is forfeit. The main character may walk or run away from the love interest in a desperate attempt to draw the danger away from the person he or she loves...but whatever last-ditch gambit the main character tries, it fails.

The lovers are torn apart.

The love interest's trust in the main character to keep him or her safe has been betrayed.

The main character has let down the love interest, broken his or her promise to keep the love interest safe, and has lost the love interest for good.

BLACK MOMENT:

The main character has failed to protect his or her true love. And the main character has failed to defeat the danger from his or her past. While the main character got away from it before (or even thought the danger to be destroyed), the danger has come roaring back into the main character's life.

The danger is bigger and badder than before, and this time gets the best of the main character. That would be bad enough on its own, but now the main character has dragged his or her true love into the fight and the lover has paid the price for the main character's failure to defeat the danger.

In his or her despair, the main character sees no way forward to defeating the danger or rescuing the love interest. The failure of the knight in shining armor is complete. He or she is broken. Finished. Utterly defeated. Without the resources or will to continue the fight.

The deeper the main character's defeat and despair, the deeper the sense of betrayal to the love interest, who was counting on the main character to win the fight and protect him or her.

The dangerous person or element has won and all is lost for the good guys.

THE END:

The main character has some sort of epiphany, learns a lesson, gets a new tool or piece of information, is given a pep talk by a mentor or maybe even by the love interest, and the main characters gather himself or herself for one last go at vanquishing the danger once and for all.

The main character is resolved to save the love interest or die trying...and he or she may come very close to dying physically or metaphorically before the danger is finally defeated.

The love interest may help the main character in the final battle, or the love interest may offer one last bit of encouragement to the main character when the main character is on the verge of losing or dying.

With one last, Herculean effort, sacrificing everything, the main character saves the love interest and defeats the danger (usually completely).

If you plan to continue this saga and need the danger to survive, you may do so. But be sure to give your audience a satisfying win for the main character. You must badly wound the danger, nearly defeat it, or take a satisfyingly big chunk out of its hide for your audience to feel as if the main character got a win commensurate with his or her effort and sacrifice.

KEY SCENES

- the returned danger reveals itself to the main character
- the returned danger first threatens the safety of the love interest
- the love interest tries to talk the main character into fleeing with him or her and the love interest refuses
- the love interest nearly dies or is harmed in some way because the main character failed in some way
- the main character bargains with the danger for the love interest's safety
- the love interest wants to fight alongside the main character, but the main character refuses the offer

- the desperate final romantic moment before the main character goes into battle...and loses

THINGS TO THINK ABOUT WHEN WRITING THIS TROPE

What is the main character's past? How did he or she become involved with danger? What's his or her relationship to it?

How did the main character's past involvement with danger end? How did he or she extricate himself or herself from it?

Does the main character start your story believing the past danger is fully gone, or does he or she have some inkling that it might come back one day to bite him or her?

How has the danger from the past changed? Has it taken a new form, has a new person taken up its cause, have a new goal, new resources, and new threat?

How vigilant is the main character to possible danger (past or a new, present one) when your story begins?

How do the main character and love interest meet?

Does the love interest have some connection to the main character's past and/or to the past danger? If so, what? How? When?

When does the love interest find out about the past danger in the main character's life? How? Who tells him or her? Why?

When is the love interest first put into danger from this past danger? How? Why?

What does the danger from the past want? Does this dangerous person or element want it only from the main character or also from the love interest?

How can you make what the past danger wants worse for the lovers? Much worse? Truly terrible?

What attracts the lovers to each other? What do they find fascinating about each other? Irresistible? Admirable?

What do the lovers find frustrating about each other? Irritating? Infuriating?

What's the external plot problem in your story? Is the entire plot the past danger's quest for what it wants from the lovers and the lovers' efforts to stay alive/defeat the danger, or is there some additional plot you'll hang your story on?

How does the plot problem get worse? Much worse? Truly awful?

How do the actions the past danger takes get more and more dangerous and hard to defeat?

What does the confrontation look like where the main character loses to the past danger? How is the love interest involved in this confrontation? How is the love interest harmed by it?

How does the main character fail the love interest? What happens to the love interest because of the main character's failure to vanquish the past danger? How can you make that worse? Much worse? Truly horrific?

What lesson does the main character learn, what epiphany does he or she have, or what gift does he or she receive (a weapon, information, a helper) that makes the main character willing to have one more go at the past danger?

What's different about the final conflict/confrontation/battle that makes the main character able to win this time?

Does the love interest help the main character in the final battle? If so, how? When? Why?

Will the past danger be permanently defeated now or will you let the danger live to return another day and try again? How will you show this outcome to your audience? What outcome to the past danger will you show to your lovers?

If you're not completely finishing it off now, do the lovers know this danger might be back one day?

When does the love interest forgive the main character for putting him or her in danger? For losing to the past danger in the black moment?

Does the main character make a grand gesture of apology or of true love? If so, what? When? How?

What does the reunion between the lovers after the final battle look like?

What does happily ever after look like for the lovers? Will you show your audience a glimpse of this or is it not necessary in your story?

TROPE TRAPS

Your audience thinks the main character is a jerk. He or she really should have told the love interest about his or her dangerous past, especially if the main character knows it might be back one day.

The love interest is unlikeably naïve for not understanding just how much danger he or she might be in if he or she sticks around to have a romance with the main character.

The love interest is too stupid to live for not running away when the main character tells him or her to go.

The main character is too stupid to live for not running away at the first sign of the return of the past danger.

The past danger is so dangerous there's no way the main character can plausibly take on this threat by himself or herself...and yet he or she sticks around to go solo against this overwhelming threat... like the idiot he or she is.

That past danger isn't dangerous enough to force the main character to truly do something heroic. Remember, the goodness of your good guy is defined by the badness of your bad guy.

The past danger is so likable and without fatal flaw(s) or the audience is so sympathetic to him or her that the audience roots for the bad guy to win.

The love interest isn't mad enough or is too mad at the main character for dragging him or her into danger and isn't believable to your audience.

This couple should totally go to the authorities for help, and yet they don't. Worse, you don't give them a good reason not to go to the authorities.

You fail the ratchet up the threat from the danger, or fail to ratchet it up enough, over the course of the story. You just have danger lurking, then a big fight, then the good guy wins.

The danger from the past is lame, hokey, silly, or not that dangerous.

You fail to give a good reason why the danger from the past still exists. Why didn't the main character eradicate it in the past?

You fail to explain why the main character doesn't realize the past danger is still coming after him or her.

(If you plan to do a sequel with the same bad guy/danger) you fail to explain why the main character doesn't successfully eradicate the danger this time around.

You don't give your audience a satisfying reunion between the lovers after the final battle. Your audience has earned a good one.

DANGEROUS PAST TROPE IN ACTION
Movies:

- Solo: A Star Wars Story
- The Batman
- Robin Hood
- True Lies
- Echo (TV show)
- The Flash
- Terminator 2: Judgment Day
- Deadpool
- Kill Bill
- Thor

Books:

- Dark Lover by J.R. Ward
- Fourth Wing by Rebecca Yarros
- Alpha's Temptation by Renee Rose & Lee Savino
- Lord of London Town by Tillie Cole
- Beautifully Cruel by J.T. Geissinger
- Rebirth by Belle Aurora
- The Scarlet Pimpernel by Baroness Orczy
- Taking the Fall, Vol 1 by Alexa Riley
- Blind Faith by Rebecca Zanetti

6
ENEMIES TO LOVERS

DEFINITION

Ahh, the enemies to lovers trope...this is perhaps the most widely misunderstood and mislabeled of all the romance tropes. In the enemies to lovers story, two people who are actual enemies ultimately overcome their enmity and its source to fall in love. Seems simple, right? But where this one gets tricky is in understanding what enemies are.

Most writers and audience members label as "enemies" any characters who despise each other, rub each other the wrong way, antagonize each other, or exchange ongoing rat-a-tat attack dialogue. This couldn't be farther from the truth.

This trope is not hate to love, instant and intense dislike to love, snark to love, or constant bickering to love.

Actual enemies are not even necessarily unpleasant to each other in a true enemies to lovers trope. In fact, as a result of working on this trope, I've added a Hate/Snark to Love trope into the Hook Tropes book, Vol.4 in the Universal Romance Tropes series, to differentiate Enemies to Lovers and Hate to Love from each other.

So, what is the enemies to lovers trope, then?

In this trope, two people are simultaneously working toward opposing goals. The success by one of them in achieving his or her goal precludes the possibility of the other person achieving his or her goal. Within this context, the two main characters still manage to fall in love.

The external, plot-based challenges for the enemy main characters are to set aside their opposition to each other (or for one of them to give up the fight) and/or to separate their external enmity from their personal feelings for each other.

Where this trope gets really interesting, however, is in the internal character conflict side of your story. When two people hold personal loyalties or deeply held beliefs that are in direct opposition, overcoming these—or at least reconciling them—to fall in love is a huge challenge for your characters and for you as a writer.

Let's start with an extreme example to make this concept crystal clear: A Union officer falls in love with a Confederate spy during the American Civil War. They are committed to opposing sides in a war only one side can win. But what if the northerner is also deeply, morally opposed to slavery, and the southerner is deeply supportive of it as an economic system that supports his or her family. Not only does their external story make them enemies, but their internal beliefs make them mortal enemies.

The challenge with writing a couple like this is reconciling their opposing core beliefs in a believable way. Is it even possible to love someone whose beliefs are so different from your own? How will one of these people convince the other one that one of their core ideologies, that defines who they are as a human being, is *wrong*?

Remember, people *rarely* change their core beliefs after these are fully formed. It usually takes a life-changing event—something shattering, devastating, or life altering—to get anyone to change a core belief.

Let's look at another slightly less fraught example: Two executives at different companies are maneuvering to take over a third company that's failing. Only one of their firms can succeed at buying out the target company. Only one of the lovers can win at convincing the third owner to accept his or her offer, and the other lover will necessarily fail.

If we were going to be cliché and saccharine, we might have the lovers' two competing companies form some sort of consortium to work together to buy the third company.

But what if the heroine's company intends to corporate-raid the third company, lay off all its workers, sell off its assets, break it apart, and make a lot of money for its shareholders? Meanwhile, the hero's company plans to update facilities, retrain workers, keep everyone's jobs, and revitalize the dying town the failing company is in, even knowing doing this will wreck the stock price?

Furthermore, what if the hero and heroine are fully on board with their own company's plan for the failing company? One believes in duty to shareholders; one believes in duty to workers. This story isn't interesting because we care who gets to buy the troubled company. It's in the conflict of core beliefs between these two enemies that this story becomes powerful. The fact that they're falling in love while they wrestle over their differences is almost frosting on the cake.

In the enemies to lovers trope, one or both of your characters will probably have to change their loyalty or their deeply held beliefs for the couple to end up together. This, then, is the core of the enemies to lovers trope—a transformation of one or both enemies so they can be together.

Many other tropes contain elements of opposition, being on opposite sides of a conflict, or interpersonal conflict, but what they lack that differentiates them from Enemies to Lovers is the one must win-one must lose scenario.

ADJACENT TROPES

- Rivals/Work Enemies
- Hate/Snark to Love
- Love-Hate Relationship
- Opposites Attract
- Grumpy-Sunshine
- Feuding Families
- Forbidden Love

WHY READERS/VIEWERS LOVE THIS TROPE

- being on an equal footing with one's love interest and perceived as a worthy opponent
- transforming (typically male) aggression into love, and turning the language of aggression into expressions of affection
- he or she loves me enough to sacrifice EVERYTHING... their loyalty to an important cause, their core beliefs, even their life to be the person I need them to be
- he or she saw past our enmity to see the real me and love me

OBLIGATORY SCENES
THE BEGINNING:

The hero and heroine meet, often in a clash of values, beliefs, or opposing sides of a conflict. This is one trope where the meet is rarely cute. It's typically the conflict they're engaged in that brings this pair together.

Because these characters start out on the opposite sides of a serious conflict, they usually don't know each other before the story begins.

The conflict itself has to be established in the beginning of the story along with which side of the conflict each of the future lovers is aligned with. The stakes of winning or losing in this clash need to be laid out for your audience, as well. The higher the stakes, the more your audience will typically engage with your story.

The types of stakes will set the mood and tone for your story, whether it's a war with the survival of nations at stakes and thousands or millions of lives on the line, or it's a corporate takeover battle with vast sums of money at stake, or it's a fight over who gets to buy the only bakery in a small town and live out their dream.

Trickier to pull off in the beginning of your story will be establishing the attraction between these two enemies. It's not uncommon for this to be a slow burn romance that develops gradually. These two characters may not like each other at all to begin with and may feel little or no attraction at first.

However, before you get too far into your story—this trope is a romance, after all—you'll need to show what about each character the other one finds appealing, interesting, fascinating, unexpected, or irresistible enough to pursue getting to know him or her better.

Somewhere along the way, you'll have to establish the beginnings of romantic attraction between them, as well. I'm personally skeptical of relying purely on physical attraction between two people to launch a love story, but that may be all you have to work with initially. Regardless of what pulls them together in the first place, they must begin to develop a real, emotional connection.

. . .

THE MIDDLE:

The external plot problem that the main characters are working on against each other gets bigger and bigger and builds toward a crisis. The moment of one of them winning and one of them losing draws nearer, and as it does so, the stakes mount higher and higher and comes closer and closer.

As the conflict intensifies, the main characters' conflicts in beliefs, morals, and loyalties will rear their ugly heads and become ever larger problems between them. As they fall in love, their intractable differences become more and more of a looming disaster lying ahead of them. These personal conflicts are going to have to be dealt with sometime...but not now. The lovers try to hold off the reckoning as long as they can, stealing moments of happiness whenever and wherever they can.

This is often a secret relationship because they must hide the fact that they're consorting with the "enemy." There very well might be terrible consequences if they're caught fraternizing with anyone from the opposing side of the conflict.

Indeed, in the middle of the story, friends, family, and co-workers may become significant obstacles to the romance, either because they're strongly opposed to it or because they're a constant threat to discover and expose this forbidden relationship.

It's not uncommon that a love scene (or whatever approximates it in your story, depending on the heat level) acts as the climax to the middle of your story and precipitates the black moment. The lovers may have finally consummated their love but have not faced their ultimate, unsolvable conflict. And in the aftermath of coming together romantically, this becomes achingly, tragically clear and usually precipitating the internal, emotional aspect of the black moment.

. . .

BLACK MOMENT:

The confrontation between the two opposing forces comes to a head. The lovers are ranged against each other in a climactic conflict where they're forced to choose between the love for each other and their loyalty to their own side in the conflict. One or both of the lovers chooses badly in this moment (at least for the romance).

Either the conflict between them tears them apart, or their own personal conflicts in beliefs do the job, or some combination of both breaks up the lovers.

This can be a very difficult black moment to recover from in a plausible fashion, particularly if there's not a towering love already established between these enemy-lovers.

THE END:

The conflict that has pitted the lovers against each other as enemies resolves. One side wins or loses, or some other solution to the conflict is found that ends it. The consequences of this outcome happen to your main characters. One of them may celebrate victory while the other mourns defeat. The winner may take no joy in having won. The loser may be simultaneously glad for the person he or she loves and sad for himself or herself.

If you're going to pull some sort of compromise, merger, peace talks, or other solution out of a hat where both of your main characters win or sort of win, you're going to have to make it clear why this solution wasn't available earlier in the conflict than the end of your story. Something significant will need to change that suddenly makes this compromise outcome possible now.

If the conflict was so intractable before that this compromise solution wasn't possible at the beginning of your story or even earlier than that, the nature of the conflict must change plausibly over the course of your story to allow for compromise now. Often in a romantic story, the catalyst for this change is one or both of the lovers.

Which begs the question: how will one or both of your main characters be in a position to affect the very nature of the conflict, shape it or change it to make a compromise outcome possible? Are they in a position of sufficient power, responsibility, or access to leadership to reasonably be expected to affect the outcome of the conflict?

As for the personal aspect of these enemies turned lovers' relationship, there are three broad categories of possible outcome:

1. they can try one last time to make the relationship work despite their differences (and the conflict may rage on around them while they choose to live with their differences)
2. one or both of them chooses to lose personally and professionally to be with the person they love and/or giving the win to the person they love
3. one or both of them actually changes a core belief that clears the way for the lovers to be together

The action of your story between the black moment and the resolution typically centers around some dramatic crisis that's so personally significant to one or both of the main characters that it changes one or both person's core beliefs.

This drastic action is usually what breaks the external stalemate and resolves the conflict one way or the other. There's a definite end to the conflict, even if there's not a decisive win or loss.

The lovers have overcome the final hurdles keeping them apart. Crisis/conflict/battle over, they can return to one or both of the lovers' normal worlds and begin to build a forever relationship free of conflict.

KEY SCENES

- the first time the main characters' differing beliefs cause a fight between them

- the first time their attraction to the other main character causes them to question an order or instruction from whomever they're normally loyal and obedient to on their own side of the conflict
- a stolen romantic moment in which they're nearly caught with the "enemy"
- the moment they are caught consorting with "the enemy" by a friend, family member, or coworker
- one or both of the lovers is accused of being a spy or traitor either unofficially by a friend or officially by a superior
- the morning after...which is to say, in the aftermath of their first big romantic joining (depending on the heat level of your story) the moment of realization that they can never be together forever or possibly again, that what they've done is wrong, that they've both made a terrible mistake by given in to their feelings
- the moment after the drastic, climactic crisis where one or both of the main characters learns a life-changing lesson that changes his or her core belief(s)

THINGS TO THINK ABOUT WHEN WRITING THIS TROPE

What is the conflict that pits your main characters against each other as enemies?

What side of your main conflict does each main character fall on?

What does each main character believe about their side of the conflict that they believe to be right and good and worthy of their loyalty?

Are each of these sets of beliefs true? Is one or both sets of beliefs actually a misbelief? If so, which one(s) and why?

Will either of your eventual lovers start the story as a "bad guy" to your audience? If so, which one?

What core beliefs do the main characters have in common? What core beliefs of theirs clash?

How violently do their differing beliefs, ethics, morals, or value systems collide? Is this difference plausibly possible to overcome at all? How will one or both of them actually see the other character's point of view and accept it?

Why does the main character believe the love interest's loyalty and beliefs are misguided or wrong? Vice versa, why does the love interest believe the main character's loyalty is misplaced and beliefs are misguided or wrong?

How will your future lovers meet? Is it an accident? Part of the action of the conflict? Completely separate from the conflict?

Do the lovers realize they are enemies when they meet or do they meet first and learn that they're enemies later?

How do the main characters react to figuring out they're on opposing sides of a conflict and to each other in that moment?

What about your main characters draws them powerfully to each other romantically? How will they discover this about each other?

How will your main characters be thrown together to meet frequently (so that, as a story mechanic, they can fall in love)?

Will the main characters meet periodically in secret or encounter each other primarily in public as part of the conflict itself? Will they do both?

Does either lover confess to anyone about this budding romance? If so, who?

When and why do friends, family members, or coworkers suspect that there's some sort of hanky-panky going on between these two supposed enemies? What do those people do about their suspicions?

Will the lovers pretend to remain enemies in public situations? Do they find this amusing, or do their public clashes upset or anger them when they're next together in private?

How do the conflicts in their loyalties to organization, boss, country, liege lord, play out in private between them? Do the lovers argue about their conflicting loyalties? Does one try to talk the other out of continuing to be loyal to someone on the other side of the conflict?

Do they argue about which side of the conflict is better or more correct? What do they do in the aftermath of these arguments? Do they make up? Set the arguments aside unresolved? Storm out of a tryst? Refuse to speak to or meet with the other one for a period of time afterward? Revert to the party line of their own side of the conflict?

Does anyone help this couple spend time together in private or in secret? If so, who? How? What is this character risking to help them?

When do they nearly get caught?

When do they get caught together? By whom? Are there serious consequences, or does the person who catches them agree to keep their secret for now? If this person agrees to keep the secret, how do the lovers convince him or her to do it?

How do you plan to resolve the external plot conflict? Is one of the lovers going to win and the other lose? Is so, which one will win and which will lose?

In this win/lose scenario, how will each of the lovers react, both in public and in private with their lover?

Is there a way to set up a partial win (and corresponding partial defeat) prior to resolving the larger conflict, such that your lovers do have to deal with one of them winning and one of them losing, mid-story? How does that moment between your lover go? Does it increase the tension between them, cause one or both of them to learn anything, or cause the beginnings of any epiphanies in one or both of them?

How will one or both of your main characters change their mind(s) about their side of the conflict, change their loyalties, and/or break oaths or promises to their employer and coworkers? How will they still be heroic, honorable, and likable in the eyes of your audience? Which is to say, how will you make your main characters suffer before they change? What price(s) do they have to pay for stepping away from promises or commitments to their side of the conflict?

Is one of your characters right or wrong? There is no right or wrong answer to this question. The theme of your story and the type of conflict you chose to work with will determine this. Also, you may choose to let your audience decide who they think is right or wrong, in which case, you'll probably make compelling arguments for each side of the conflict. Or you may choose a conflict with no right or wrong side. Or, you may choose to have your characters believe that both sides or neither side of the conflict is better than the other.

Are either or both of the lovers tempted to betray their side of the conflict by the other lover? What form does that temptation take? How do they each feel about it?

Does one of the lovers actually betray his or her side of the conflict to their lover? How do each of them feel about it after it happens?

What will precipitate the black moment between your lovers? Will it be primarily a personal conflict of beliefs, or primarily and external moment of being forced to choose loyalty to their side of the conflict over their lover, or will it be both?

Which of your lovers chooses badly in the black moment? What does he or she choose? Do both of the lovers choose badly or just one of them? How do they each feel about their own choice and how do they feel about their lover's choice? Do they understand it? Revile it? Feel betrayed? Understand why the other chose as he or she did?

What causes your broken-up lovers to decide to make one last effort to put the relationship back together?

What is the dramatic, big crisis in the conflict at the climax of your story? This is the moment of decision, the moment of win or loss, for both the external conflict and the personal conflict between your lovers? How will both of these conflicts be brought to a head by this crisis?

How does this big crisis resolve? Does one of your characters win while the other loses?

Will you introduce another solution where neither fully wins or loses or where they both win? If so, how do the lovers make this new solution possible? How is this solution not cheesy, contrived, saccharine, or eye-rollingly cliché? Why is this solution possible now when it wasn't possible before your story began, at the beginning of your story, or somewhere in the middle of the story prior to now?

What does reconciliation and forgiveness look like between these two characters? What sort of scene will this be? A love scene? A conversation? A proposal? Will it be public or private? Will there need to be a grand gesture by one or both of the lovers to get over the conflict between then?

What does life look like for this pair after the conflict ends? Will they live in one character's normal world with the other lover having to move into that world? Will they leave both of their homes and go somewhere new?

Will you show your audience a slice of peace between this pair or not at the end of your story?

TROPE TRAPS

The conflict between your main characters is not strong enough to hang an entire story on. Your audience finds it lame, dumb, or ridiculous for these two people to fight for an entire story over the conflict between them.

There's an obvious solution to the external conflict or an obvious compromise that the main characters don't avail themselves of or argue for with their superiors. If the audience can easily see this solution, they perceive the main characters as TSTL (too stupid to live) and dislike them.

One side of the conflict between these characters is so obviously wrong or bad that the character supporting it at the beginning of the story isn't likable as a main character in a love story.

Setting up a conflict of the main characters' core beliefs that is so huge that these two people could never plausibly overcome it and the audience doesn't buy it when one of the main characters suddenly changes at a deep, fundamental level

If one character starts the story supporting a bad or wrong cause, you fail to give them a good reason for initially believing the way they do, or you fail to give them likable, honorable, kind, decent, or at least fascinating enough traits to keep your audience rooting for them or at least interested in them long enough for you to start redeeming the character's misbelief.

One or both of your main characters change loyalties or their opinion too easily. They come across as having no real loyalty to their cause, or to their side of the conflict. Changing sides too easily makes them seem untrustworthy—a trait that the audience will extend to their relationship going forward. If they'd betray their boss or their beliefs, they'll betray their lover.

The characters argue or snipe at each other so much that it's not plausible they'd ever actually fall in love.

Failing to build a big love between these two characters. They'll need it to survive the black moment.

Their friends, family, and coworkers unrealistically don't or can't spot the sparks and romance between these two and never suspect a thing.

Whichever character(s) who ultimately change their beliefs don't agonize over it a realistic amount (either they wrestle with their decision too much or too little)

Failing to create real and serious consequences to each of these characters for breaking a promise, betraying an oath, or being disloyal to their side of the conflict—or heaven forbid, betraying their side of the conflict.

If one or both characters is going to change a core belief over the course of the story, you fail to create a traumatic/significant enough crisis in that person's life to provoke an actual, permanent change in a fundamental, core belief, ethical code, or deep understanding of self.

After the black moment, when this couple has broken up, you

haven't already created a powerful enough love between them to plausibly pull the lovers back together in the end.

Chickening out as a writer on having one of your main characters lose big in the resolution of the story's external conflict. It's possible the genre you write in will require you to give each of the lovers a happy outcome, but not all genres and not all stories require that.

Shortchanging your audience by not giving them a grand reunion of these two characters in the end. This trope requires a lot of suffering on the parts of your main characters, and your audience will have been through the emotional ringer by the end of your story. The audience deserves a big emotional payoff in this trope.

Sending your happily ever after lovers off to live in one of their normal worlds after building two characters from such diametrically opposed worlds that there's no way for one to live happily in the world of the other.

Failing to create appropriately serious consequences for each of the main characters for consorting with the enemy.

Failing to execute those consequences in full on the lovers once they're caught.

ENEMIES TO LOVERS TROPE IN ACTION
Movies:

- You've Got Mail
- Beauty and the Beast
- How to Lose a Guy in 10 Days
- Shadow & Bone (TV series)
- Laws of Attraction
- Allied
- The Last of the Mohicans

Books:

- The Cruel Prince by Holly Black
- Fourth Wing by Rebecca Yarros
- The Hating Game by Sally Thorne
- A Court of Thorns and Roses by Sarah J Maas
- Serpent & Dove by Shelby Mahurin
- From Blood & Ash by Jennifer L. Armentrout
- The Bridge Kingdom by Danielle L. Jensen

7

ENGAGED TO/MARRYING SOMEONE ELSE

DEFINITION

When the hero and heroine in this story first meet, one of them is already in a committed relationship with someone else. Nonetheless, when this hero and heroine are thrust together by the events of your story, they are intensely attracted to each other. While they probably fight hard not to fall in love—it's wrong, after all—they fall in love anyway. This version of the trope is, at its core, a love triangle.

This trope differs from a traditional love triangle in that one leg of the triangle—the pre-existing engagement is already in place when the main characters of this story meet.

The love interest may or may not initially know that the main character is engaged to, promised to, or expected to marry someone else. In this scenario, the main character is keeping a whopper of a secret, and it's this dangerous secret that becomes the core of the story.

In this scenario, your audience may have a big problem with the main character keeping such an important secret from the love interest. You will have to overcome that distaste for and distrust of the main character by your audience—and by the love interest when he or she eventually finds out the main character is otherwise committed already and has been keeping that secret.

The main character may be unwillingly betrothed or promised to someone else, or family members may expect the main character to marry the person whom they've chosen for him or her. In this case, the act of falling in love with a person of his or her choosing is an act of defiance at its core.

Obviously, the "other" relationship with the third-party fiancé(e) isn't perfect, or your main character wouldn't be in an emotional space to up and fall in love with someone else when your love interest comes along. The reason this engagement is flawed will be critical to determining the tone and mood of your story and how the audience and love interest perceive the main character.

Is he or she a schmuck for two-timing their fiancé(e), or is he or she someone to be pitied for being stuck in a terrible arrangement he or she never asked for? Is the main character strong for resisting an engagement he or she hates or is the main character weak for going along with an engagement he or she doesn't want?

You will have to explain at some point why the main character didn't break the first engagement before falling in love with your story's love interest. This explanation will determine a great deal about how your audience perceives your main character.

While this story is technically a love triangle at its core, I propose that it's more a story of fated mates than anything else.

Regardless of the main character's prior engagement to another, the love between the main character and your love interest is so great and so perfect that it's meant to be.

The whole problem of your story is this couple coming to realize they're meant to be together and then doing what it takes to be together in the end.

ADJACENT TROPES

- Love Triangle
- Arranged Marriage
- Dangerous Secret
- Left at the Altar
- Rebound Romance
- Fated Mates

WHY READERS/VIEWERS LOVE THIS TROPE

- who doesn't fantasize about stealing the hot boyfriend/girlfriend of someone whom you think doesn't deserve him or her
- he or she is strong and brave enough to admit they didn't get it right the first time and to take the heat for getting out of another relationship to be with you
- finding your true love late...but not too late...
- not settling for a "second best" partner
- you're the perfect partner for someone, so much so that he or she will leave someone else they've agreed to MARRY for you

OBLIGATORY SCENES
THE BEGINNING:

The hero and heroine meet and there's enormous attraction. It may not be instantaneous, but as these two get to know each other, it's clear that they've got something very special developing between them. The main character may or may not admit there's someone else in his or her life to begin with.

If the main character DOES tell the love interest immediately that he or she is already engaged to someone else, your challenge will be to build a love interest that your audience likes and doesn't perceive as a selfish man- or woman-stealer. It's not cool to move in on someone else's fiancé(e).

If the main character DOES NOT tell the love interest immediately that he or she is already engaged to someone else, your challenge will be to build a main character that your audience likes and doesn't perceive as a selfish, disloyal, playboy or playgirl who's destined to serially cheat on whomever they eventually marry.

If the main character is involuntarily engaged or has been coerced into an engagement with another person, while your audience will have sympathy for both your main character and the love interest, the reason that the main character has been forced into an engagement is probably going to be the main plot problem in your story. Which means you have to create a really compelling reason for the main character having allowed his or her arm to be twisted. It has to be a big enough reason that it'll sustain much or all of the action of an entire story.

It's not enough for a meddling mama to have decided who her child should marry and having bullied her child into it. Mama has to be dying and it's her final wish to see her child marry the person she's chosen. Or Mama is worth millions and will only give her estate to her child if he or she marries the person Mama chose. You get the idea. It has to be a BIG coercion. Your audience won't respect your main character if he or she has meekly gone along with a lame coercion tactic.

By the end of the beginning, the audience surely knows there's a fiancé(e) out there, somewhere…and that all hell's going to break loose when said fiancé(e) shows up. Your love interest may or may not be aware of the third party in the relationship as soon as the audience knows. But because this isn't a "Secret" trope where the main character is hiding the existence of a fiancé(e), this third party is probably revealed to the love interest in the first act of your story.

You may want to consider whether your love interest has already fallen in love with the main character before finding out about the fiancé(e) or whether love grows between the two main characters after that revelation.

THE MIDDLE:

The existence of a fiancé(e) is certainly revealed by the middle of the story, and the problems really get rolling for your lovers, now.

You'll probably want to build in some sort of forced proximity between the main character and your love interest, meaning an external plot reason why they have to keep bumping into each other. They're working on the same project, they're neighbors, their children are best friends—something to force them to have to keep seeing each other. Otherwise, one or both of them will undoubtedly try to do the right thing—breaking up and stopping seeing the other person at all.

The fiancé(e) may show up in the middle of your story and demand an explanation from the main character. Or the person who forced the prior engagement upon the main character may show up to demand that the main character abide by his or her earlier promise.

Through the middle of your story, you'll need to build a terrific romance between the main character and love interest. A love for the ages. A relationship that's clearly better and more right than the relationship between the main character and the old fiancé(e).

But this romance will be tinged with tragedy—they got the timing wrong, they found each other too late, the main character is trapped in a future, a duty, that will make him or her deeply unhappy forever. Having now known true love with the love interest, there's no way the main character will ever be truly happy with the earlier fiancé(e).

There is likely to be increasing conflict between the lovers as the black moment approaches. The love interest may be fighting to convince the main character to break the other engagement. The main character may be fighting with the person who coerced him or her into the first engagement. The old fiancé(e) may be fighting with the love interest to back off of his or her fiancé(e).

Whatever problem has drawn the main character and love interest together is heading for a crisis as well. Perhaps the tension between the lovers is affecting the problem. Perhaps others around this pair are getting suspicious. Perhaps the lovers are struggling to work well together as the tension between them continues to rise.

Everything and everyone in your story is headed toward a cliff.

BLACK MOMENT:

The main character is finally forced to choose—the prior fiancé(e) or their true love. Obviously, he or she chooses the fiancé(e) in this moment of all being lost for your lovers. The love interest is devastated. He or she has given it their best shot to convince the main character to choose happiness for himself or herself but has failed.

Whatever external problem the main character and love interest were working on falls apart or implodes without the two of them able to cooperate (or probably even able to be in the same room together).

The old fiancé(e) or person who forced the main character to get engaged to the old fiancé(e) triumphs.

The main character is probably devastated as well. He or she is well and truly trapped in a relationship with someone he or she doesn't love or loves much less than the love interest.

THE END:

The easy way out of the black moment in this story is for the old fiancé(e) or the person who forced the engagement to relent. They see how unhappy the main character is and release him or her from his or her promise.

Don't take the easy way.

Make the main character (possibly with help from the love interest) find a way out of the marriage trap. Have your main character give up whatever gigantically valuable thing he or she was going to get in return for marrying the fiancé(e). Let the main character get disowned.

Or, have the main character and/or love interest blackmail the fiancé(e) or arranger of the engagement into letting the main character out of the engagement. Have the love interest confront the fiancé(e) and show the fiancé(e) he or she doesn't know the main character at all and won't be happy with him or her. Expose the fiancé(e) as a gold digger. Have the love interest confront the main character and demand that he or she do the right thing and break the engagement.

What I'm suggesting is that having a third party, either the fiancé(e) or person who arranged the marriage relent and fix the whole problem for your lovers, you're making your main character and love interest too passive. They don't take direct action to fight for their love and their future together if someone else gives them permission to be together.

Give your main character and love interest agency. Let them solve their own problem. Make them actively find a way to be together. This is the ending that will truly satisfy your audience in this trope.

KEY SCENES

- the moment when the audience finds out there's a fiancé(e) waiting in the wings
- the moment when the love interest finds out there's a fiancé(e) waiting in the wings
- the moment the fiancé(e) shows up and announces who he or she is to the love interest
- the farewell love scene between the main character and love interest (the heat level of your story will determine what happens in this farewell)

- the main character confesses his or her love to the love interest
- the main character and love interest are caught together by the fiancé(e) or person who arranged the engagement
- the moment the main character tells the love interest of his or her decision to marry the fiancé(e)
- the moment the love interest makes his or her case to the main character of why he or she should choose to be with the love interest forever.

THINGS TO THINK ABOUT WHEN WRITING THIS TROPE

What is the nature of the relationship between the main character and his or her fiancé(e) before the story begins?

What caused the main character to propose to the fiancé(e) in the first place?

What will be the consequences to the main character if he or she doesn't go through with the wedding?

Did the main character think he or she was in love with the fiancé(e) before he or she met the love interest?

What about the love interest is completely fascinating and attractive to the main character?

What about the main character is completely fascinating and attractive to the love interest?

How will you demonstrate a love between your main characters that's so powerful, so romantic, that your audience will root for them to be together even though it's totally unethical for them to be falling in love?

What external story element or plot problem will throw your couple together over and over again so they have a chance to fall in love?

When does the main character reveal the existence of the

fiancé(e) to the audience and to the love interest? Are they separate events or the same one?

Does your couple fight their attraction for each other?

Why doesn't the main character immediately break up with his or her fiancé(e) when he or she realizes he or she's falling in love with the love interest?

How does the love interest fight for the main character? Does he or she argue with the main character directly? Use subterfuge? Pretend not to care who the main character chooses? Launch a campaign of perfect dates or romantic encounters?

How does the fiancé(e) show up in your story and reveal himself or herself?

How does the fiancé(e) fight to keep the main character?

How do the love interest's friends, family, and coworkers find out that he or she is in a romantic relationship with someone who's engaged to a third party? What do they think about it? What do they do about it?

What do the main character's family, friends, and coworkers think of him or her getting into a second relationship with a new person after already being engaged? What do they do about it?

What do the fiancé(e)'s family, friends, and coworkers think of the main character cheating on him or her? What do they do about it?

What or who pressures the main character into going ahead and marrying the fiancé(e)? How does the main character feel about it?

How does the love interest react to finding out the main character has chosen the fiancé(e) and plans to go through with the original marriage?

Will the main character actually go through with marrying the fiancé(e) in your story or not? Side note: this makes for a heck of a black moment.

What event or epiphany gives the main character the fortitude—or spine—to break up with the fiancé(e)? When and how does this break-up finally happen?

What consequences actually land on the main character when he or she breaks up with the fiancé(e)? How does the main character react to these?

What grand gesture of apology does the main character make to the love interest that's grand enough to convince the love interest to give the main character one last chance?

What does the main character and love interest's happily ever after look like when they're finally together forever? Your audience and your lovers have been through a LOT to get to this point. Give all of them a glimpse of this couple finally happy and finally able to be together.

TROPE TRAPS

Your main character comes across as a schmuck for cheating on his or her fiancé(e).

Your love interest comes across as a jerk for being willing to date someone who's already engaged to another person.

Your main character comes across as a liar if he or she doesn't immediately tell the love interest about his or her fiancé(e).

If your main character is willing to cheat on his or her fiancé(e) before they're even married, how on earth is he or she not going to be a serial cheater once the main character and love interest finally get together? Which is to say, you don't make your main character agonize enough about cheating on their fiancé(e).

If he or she is being forced into a marriage, you don't create a big enough or plausible reason for the main character going along with it.

The main character looks weak and spineless for allowing himself or herself to be forced into a marriage he or she doesn't want.

The main character looks clueless about relationships or un-self-aware for having gotten into an engagement with someone who wasn't exactly right for him or her in the first place.

The fiancé(e) is so awful and flawed a character that the audience doesn't buy the main character would have proposed to this person in the first place.

The fiancé(e) is such a perfect and wonderful character that the audience is mad with the main character for cheating on him or her and for choosing the love interest.

The people around the main character and love interest interfere too much or not enough. (Real friends would have something to say about either of these people getting into a relationship while one of them is engaged to someone else).

Failing to build a love story so romantic and epic that your audience is fully on board with the main character jilting his or her fiancé(e) to be with the love interest.

The reason the main character chooses to stay with the fiancé(e) in the black moment is lame or unreasonable given that he or she is fully in love with the love interest by this point.

The love interest forgives the main character too easily for having chosen the fiancé(e) in the black moment. Why should the love interest trust this lying, cheating, schmuck who apparently used him or her?

Relying on the fiancé(e) or person who arranged the engagement to let the main character off the hook and out of the engagement.

ENGAGED TO/MARRYING SOMEONE ELSE TROPE IN ACTION
Movies:

- Burlesque
- Midnight in Paris
- Something Borrowed
- His Girl Friday
- Bringing Up Baby
- Sleepless in Seattle

Books:

- Sinners Anonymous by Somme Sketcher
- The Saint by Monica McCarty
- The Heiress by Jude Devereaux
- Thoughtless by S. C. Stevens
- The Gamble by Kristen Ashley
- Captured by the Highlander by Julianne MacLean
- Silver Lining by Maggie Osborne
- An Irresistible Bachelor by Jessica Bird
- Love and Other Words by Christina Lauren

8

ESTRANGED SPOUSES/ON THE ROCKS

DEFINITION

As its name implies, this is a story about a married couple on the verge of ending their relationship. Over the course of the story, they find their way back to each other again.

Where this trope differs from, say, the Couple's Therapy trope, is the couple in therapy wants to save their relationship and is willing to work at it. The estranged couple is well past that. They are broken up in all but name and legality.

Where this trope differs from a Reconciliation/Second Chance Romance is they have not already broken up and gone their separate ways. In a reconciliation story, the lovers have totally separated, emotionally and physically disengaged, and consider themselves single. These estranged spouses still retain the baggage of being legally married. They're not quite single and have not 100% disengaged emotionally and physically...yet. But they're about to.

This couple will probably have to be forced back into proximity with each other—both physically and emotionally. Unwillingly and over the course of your story, they must rediscover why they fell in love in the first place or find a new reason to love their spouse. The core of this trope is two-fold: it's a story of forced proximity and it's a story of forgiveness.

By the time a married couple has reached the stage of being completely estranged, they've already done a lot of emotional damage to each other. They've probably fought a lot, and deeply hurtful words have undoubtedly been exchanged. This couple is so damaged they don't even consider themselves a couple anymore, and they're both on their way out of the relationship.

Your story isn't even the last-ditch effort by these two to save their marriage. They're already past that when your story starts. They're going to fight the idea of spending any time together, or at a minimum, they'll resent bitterly whatever circumstance forces them back together (unless of course their child is dying, in which case they'll probably still resent having to be polite to each other in front of their sick child).

This couple is going to fight you, as the writer, tooth and nail not to reconcile, and they're going to have a lot of old baggage to sort through before they find their way back to each other.

Your challenge will be two-fold. You have to make us like these angry, distant, hurt people and root for them to get back together, and you have to make both the reason they're estranged plausible, but not make us hate one of them, and the reason they get back together plausible.

It's common for this story to resolve with a grand apology by one or both spouses. It typically takes a major change/lesson learned by one or both spouses, big enough to be provoked by a life-changing event and constitute a life-defining lesson, to convince these two people to forgive each other and give their marriage another try.

You may spend your whole story walking your characters through a life-changing event and how it changes them, or you may fill your story with unresolved conflict and then drop in a life-changing event at the big climax to change everything all at once.

. . .

ADJACENT TROPES

- Couple's Therapy
- Forgiveness
- Reconciliation/Second Chance
- Redemption

WHY READERS/VIEWERS LOVE THIS TROPE

- we would like to think if our own long-term relationship ever got to this point, we would find a way back to our spouse somehow
- most of us have lost someone we love in our life, and we fantasize about getting a do-over and getting it right the second time around, which includes figuring out before it's too late that we still love him or her
- love wins in the end. No matter how strained it is by mistakes and hurts, it finds a way to survive and thrive
- we'd all like to think we're capable of changing for the better
- we definitely would like to think our significant other can, and eventually will, change for the better

OBLIGATORY SCENES
THE BEGINNING:

This story usually opens with a bang. The hero and heroine are forced into proximity with each other by the inciting event in your story, and all hell breaks loose the moment they come into each other's presence.

You'll have to establish that they're married at some point but you don't necessarily have to do that in the opening scene. It's enough to throw the hero and heroine together and have them all but try to kill each other.

You'll have to set up the reason why this couple is going to continue to be forced together as your story progresses. It should be crystal clear to your audience that there's no way these two people would voluntarily spend a single minute in each other's presence.

A great deal of this couple's story has happened before your story begins. They met, fell in love, got married, and something went terribly wrong—all before your story begins. Hence, a fair bit of backstory and flashbacks are usually employed in telling this couple's story while you catch up your audience on the past events that have brought your couple to this point of estrangement.

Remember: Backstory, by its very nature, slows down the forward movement of your current day story. You're asking the audience to stop everything as you put your story on a literal pause to bring them up to speed on something that happened a long time ago.

Backstory often feels like an instructional lecture from the writer to the audience. It's an, "Oh, by the way, there's this thing you need to know. I'm not going to show you what happens next, which is what you really want to experience. Instead, I'm going to tell you this historical information first."

Overused, backstory will KILL your story's pacing. Your job, then, is to minimize the amount of backstory you force your audience to sit through, particularly in the beginning of your story when they're not terribly invested in your characters and their story, yet. Your audience needs to be fully engaged with these two people, curious to know more about them, and very curious about why they're estranged now before you can get away with dropping in much—or any—backstory.

I play a game with myself in this type of story of seeing how far into the story I can actually go before I absolutely have to include any backstory or flashbacks so my audience won't be lost or won't understand the current situation. Keep in mind almost all of your adult audience has been through at least one relationship that went south and eventually fell apart. They can fill in the blanks pretty well for themselves with surprisingly few clues about what might have gone wrong between these people.

THE MIDDLE:

The middle of this trope is going to be all about conflict. This is where all of the past mistakes and hurts are going to come out. You'll hang all this argument, accusation, confrontation, and ongoing damage to each other on the scenes in which they're forced together by the external plot problem.

Because these people have no desire to be in the same room with each other, that plot problem has to be big. It must be serious, consequential, dangerous, or absolutely necessary for both of these people to be part of addressing it and part of solving it.

As the middle of your story unfolds and the plot problem rises toward a crisis, the personal stakes for each of your characters must go up exponentially. The longer they're together and the more they're in conflict, remembering all the reasons why they became estranged, the more powerful the problem has to become at forcing them to remain in proximity to each other.

It's very easy (and not necessarily wrong) to hang this story on a very sick child or loved one, on a will or pre-nup that must be executed, or a house or business that must be liquidated before they can divorce. But I encourage you to think outside the box and come up with a creative problem that forces them together.

As the middle of your story unfolds, all the dirty laundry between these two is going to come out. Again, I encourage you to be creative in devising why this couple is estranged. Your audience is going to assume they're estranged for all the usual reasons that married couples break up—cheating, money, interfering family, over- or under-working, drinking, and the like. Feel free to throw your audience a curve ball and ultimately reveal that there's a unique or unexpected reason these two have become estranged.

If you're slow-rolling the big, life-changing event that's going to change one or both of your main characters or teach one or both of them a huge life lesson that will allow the couple to get back together and forgive each other, you will need to build toward that event's climactic conclusion. It can be a ticking time bomb counting down, or it can be a crisis that gets worse bit by bit. Either way, you should build the pressure of this impending or unfolding event until it's unbearable for your main characters and for your audience.

BLACK MOMENT:

The worst happens. If you've been slow-rolling a life-changing event, it concludes now, and all the terrible consequences of it happen. If you've chosen to let your couple argue and fight continuously (and perhaps obliviously) until you drop a bomb on them, this is the moment when that bomb drops.

Emotionally, this is the moment when the couple gets to the crux of the estrangement between them. If they've been avoiding talking about the 600-pound gorilla in the corner of their relationship, this is the moment when it roars out of the corner and demands to be addressed.

The trauma of the life-changing event strips away the last artifice, deception, or denial, and the couple is forced to face the true reason for their estrangement. And, because this is the black moment, it doesn't go well. If they were estranged before, they're finished now.

THE END:

It's not uncommon for the end portion, Act Three if you will, of this story to be longer than normal. This is a couple with a LOT to work out, or if not a lot, a very LARGE issue to work out between them. In this section of your story whatever life-changing lessons are to be learned from the life-changing event will happen.

It's worth noting that people often initially learn an incorrect lesson from a life-changing event. For example, if someone is the victim of a violent crime, the first lesson they may take away from it is never to leave their house again. It may be only later, after therapy, counseling, facing their fear, and lots of hard work, that they unlearn that initial lesson and learn a larger lesson of caution but continuing to live their life.

So, your third act may include learning an initial lesson, unlearning it, and learning the ultimate life-changing lesson.

Next, your main character(s) will have to translate that lesson into real and lasting change in their own beliefs and values.

Then, your changed main character will have to translate their change into action. It's this action that will ultimately resolve the estrangement between your main characters.

In the meantime, your main characters also have to resolve the implosion or explosion of the life-changing event. They may have a fair bit of plot-based clean-up or problem solving left to do before the story can end.

Last of all, your couple needs to forgive each other and reconcile. You will need to consider if and how you want to show your audience that the couple is going to be okay, that they're able to sustain the changes that made their reconciliation possible, and that they're going to be happily married for the long term.

Given the length of this list of things that have to happen in the third act, it becomes clear why, in this trope, the ending often runs longer than normal.

KEY SCENES

- the first time the hero and heroine are together alone and can really rip into each other

- the moment when they lose control of themselves in front of other people and conflict erupts between them
- nostalgia sex (or a romantic encounter of some kind, based on your story's heat level)
- angry sex (or an angry romantic encounter, based on your story's heat level)
- one character breaks down emotionally and the other comforts him or her
- the main characters reminisce about when their relationship was good
- individually or together, they reflect on why they once loved each other and those qualities still exist in the other person
- individually or together, they recall the thing that was the last straw that tore them apart, the mortal wound, as it were.

THINGS TO THINK ABOUT WHEN WRITING THIS TROPE

What's this couple's entire backstory? How did they meet? What attracted them to each other? How did they fall in love? When did they know this person was the one they wanted to marry? How did the proposal go? What was their wedding like? How was their early marriage? What soured it? What estranged them? (You'll probably need to add other details and backstory to this list to support your front story.)

Since most marriages don't dissolve because of a single event or single mistake, what are the many mistakes each of your main characters made during their marriage? Did a series of small mistakes lead up to one big mistake that was the final straw?

How long has this couple been estranged? Are they talking about divorce?

Does one of your main characters consider himself or herself single already? Which is to say, is one or are both of them dating outside of the marriage?

What event forces your main characters back together?

What plot problem that spans most of your story will keep your couple in proximity to each other and having to interact frequently?

Do you plan to use some sort of life-changing event to change one of your main characters such that the couple can get back together, or will their reconciliation revolve around forgiveness for some past transgression(s)? Depending on which you're choosing, what is that life-changing event, or what past transgression(s) will their reconciliation hinge upon?

If you plan to use some giant, life-changing event, will it unfold slowly over the course of your story, or will it be a shock relatively late in your story that precipitates the black moment and sets in motion the resolution to the couple's estrangement?

What do friends and family think of this pair being back together, even if unwillingly? Do they machinate to push the couple back together or to pull the couple apart?

What past mistakes will your couple argue about in your story? Typically, you want them to confront their problems from least important to most important.

What event—a betrayal, something that was said, something that was done—was the final straw, the mortal wound, that estranged the couple for good?

What form(s) will this couple's conflicts take? Will their arguments be quiet and restrained? Funny? Sarcastic? Screaming matches? Destruction of property?

What critical backstory information is absolutely necessary for your audience to know to understand why these characters feel and act the way they do over the course of your story?

What pieces of that backstory can be revealed in front story instead? Are there ways you can recreate that backstory event in the now so your audience can see the couple react to it (again) in real time?

Can some of the backstory be revealed in "now" dialogue or argument between the main characters?

How short can you possibly make the backstory intrusions you have to keep?

What is still good between these main characters? What do they still like about each other? Do they still find each other, or at least aspects of each other, attractive? If so, what?

What is the foundation stone of their relationship that you will build their reconciliation upon? For example, have they always been honest with each other, or has one of them always been great about protecting the other, or have they always made each other laugh?

What life-changing lesson will one or both of these people learn that's profound enough to change their partner's mind about them? Or what apology will one or both of these characters make that's sincere enough to make their partner forgive them and give the marriage another chance?

How will this couple not repeat the same mistake again in the future? Even if you're choosing to structure the reconciliation around forgiveness, the person(s) who made the critical mistake(s) that destroyed the marriage needs to learn a hard lesson about not doing the same thing again and learning that lesson needs to be shown to your audience.

How will you convince your audience that this couple is going to be okay for the long-term?

TROPE TRAPS

Failing to create a fully-fleshed out backstory for this couple and they come across as cardboard characters who only hate each other and fight.

Failing to create a complex and layered relationship between the main characters that includes years of shared history and experiences, both good and bad, and includes deep and intimate knowledge of each other...also both good and bad.

Creating unlikable main characters who only snipe, scream, and fight with each other.

Creating a hero and heroine who are so different and share so little in common that the audience thinks they'll never be happy together and shouldn't be together.

Creating so much constant tension and unrelieved conflict that it turns off (and exhausts) your audience.

Failing to give the couple at least occasional moments of peace, cooperation, humor, nostalgia, or understanding.

Creating a reason for forcing the couple into proximity that's not high-stakes enough for them to plausibly continue to deal with each other through the whole story.

Creating a lazy or cliché reason for your couple to be forced back together.

Creating a couple so ill-suited for each other that your audience doesn't want them to reconcile and is angry when they do.

Setting up emotional abuse as the norm in this marriage, let alone physical abuse.

The couple's arguments and conflicts are emotionally abusive or so disrespectful that they should never forgive each other or end up back together.

Failing to craft a grand enough apology or a large enough lesson learned for one spouse to plausibly forgive the other spouse.

Blaming just one of the partners for the collapse of the marriage. Your audience knows full well that it takes two people to wreck a marriage and both partners will have contributed to its collapse in some way, even if that means one partner tolerated bad behaviors by the other for too long or didn't walk away from bad behaviors when they first started.

Rushing the reconciliation. It may take a *while* for one or both partners to finally trust the other enough to give the marriage another try.

Reconciling this couple without strong enough lessons having been learned for them to avoid repeating the mistakes of their past in the future.

Failing to convince your audience that this couple can stay together happily for the long term.

ESTRANGED SPOUSES/ON THE ROCKS TROPE IN ACTION
Movies:

- Die Hard
- Sweet Home Alabama
- The Parent Trap
- Fatal Attraction
- Indecent Proposal
- Frida
- Cat On A Hot Tin Roof

Books:

- The Unwanted Wife by Natasha Anders
- Wild Card by Lora Leigh
- Any Man of Mine by Rachel Gibson
- Private Arrangements by Sherry Thomas
- Almost Heaven by Judith McNaught
- Redeeming Love by Francine Rivers
- What Alice Forgot by Liane Moriarty

9

EX-CONVICT HERO/HEROINE

DEFINITION

As the title suggests, the main character in this story is an ex-convict. He or she is starting or has started a new life, which includes falling in love. The complications from his or her past typically rise from the ashes of his or her past to cause problems in this new romance. These old problems or traumas must be overcome before the ex-con and love interest can be happy, and possibly safe, together.

The specific problems that arise from your main character's past can vary widely. The main character may have been wrongly convicted of a crime he or she didn't commit and may be working to clear his or her name.

The main character may have committed the crime for which he or she was convicted, but there may have been extenuating circumstances...which must be reckoned with now that he or she is out of prison.

The main character may have done a bunch of growing up in prison and may be trying to turn over a new leaf in life or make a new start, in which case, problems or people from his or her past may show up to tempt or threaten the main character back into a life of crime.

The simple fact of being an ex-con may complicate the main character's life so much that it threatens his or her ability to find true love and keep a happily ever after. He or she may struggle to obtain a place to live, find a job, vote, or do certain kinds of work. The terms of his or her parole may prevent the main character from living in certain places or associating with certain people.

It's not uncommon in this trope for an ex-con to go to a new place, make a new start, often without revealing his or her criminal past, and then have said past show up to ruin everything he or she has built.

At its core, this is a trope of redemption. Although in reality, the ex-convict has served his or her time and paid back his or her debt to society in full. He or she has already redeemed himself or herself, so perhaps it's more accurate to say this this is a trope of getting other people to accept and recognize one's redemption.

ADJACENT TROPES

- Bad Boy/Girl Reformed
- Redemption
- Fresh Start
- Coming Home
- Dangerous Past

WHY READERS/VIEWERS LOVE THIS TROPE

- all the danger of a mafia hero but having learned his lesson—a dangerous man walking on the straight and narrow
- he loves me enough to stay out of trouble, go clean, do the hard work to stay straight

- I see his worth/heart/true self when nobody else does. Finding a lover who sees my worth/heart/true self when . nobody else does
- what's sexier than a heart of gold beneath that rough, scary exterior
- a taboo lover (who will infuriate your straitlaced family and friends) and do taboo things with you
- the fantasy of rebelling with a bad boy or bad girl

OBLIGATORY SCENES
THE BEGINNING:

We meet the ex-convict hero or heroine. You may or may not reveal to your audience right away that he or she is an ex-con. We may see this character going to a new place to start a new life, or we may meet this character already living in his or her new life.

The ex-con and love interest meet...and this is a prime candidate for some sort of extreme meeting, either a totally cute meet-cute or a very dangerous meeting where the love interest is in serious jeopardy and the ex-con protects or saves the love interest.

In many cases, the love interest contrasts sharply in personality and life with the ex-con. It's very common (approaching cliché) to pair the dark, dangerous, hardened ex-con with a naïve, innocent, openhearted love interest.

There's no law saying your ex-con has to be any particular way, however. Not all prisons turn convicts into tough, violent, gang-savvy warriors, and some prisons provide counseling, education, job train- ing, and help reintegrating former inmates into society.

Some inciting event or problem throws the ex-con and love interest together in a way that will keep them in proximity with each other for long enough in your story to become romantically involved.

At some point, the main character reveals to the love interest (and possibly to your audience) that he or she is an ex-convict, or someone else in the story reveals it. This may be the first big crisis to the relationship...or it may be no big deal at all to the love interest.

Whatever problem you plan to throw at your main character rears its ugly head, typically provoking the first major crisis or turning point of your story.

THE MIDDLE:

The complications of the main character's past occupy the middle of this story. If he or she is trying to prove their innocence, the investigation proceeds and encounters setbacks, dead ends, and just enough progress to keep your story moving forward. New revelations will drop that change what the love interest and your audience think, sending them both on an emotional roller coaster through the second act.

If outside forces are trying to drag the main character back into a life of crime, those threats or temptations get ever stronger as your story progresses. Will the power of the love interest's love be enough to keep the main character from going back to his or her old ways?

If there's a threat to the love interest that the main character is using his or her old skills or skills learned in prison to protect, that threat grows exponentially through the middle of your story.

All the while, the main character and love interest are growing closer emotionally. Their relationship may have to overcome issues of trust, honesty, past misdeeds, naïveté, or a host of other emotional conflicts you choose to throw at them.

As both your external plot problem and the couple's relationship build toward crises, one or both will finally explode to send your story to the black moment.

BLACK MOMENT:

The main character's past comes back to haunt him or her in the worst possible way and tears apart the main character and love interest. This destruction of their relationship can come from any number of possible sources. The love interest's family finds out the main character is an ex-convict and insists that the love interest break off the relationship. Past criminal associates of the main character's force him or her to commit another crime. The main character is forced to walk away from the love interest to protect him or her. The main character commits a crime to protect the love interest and is caught, arrested, and thrown back in jail. I could keep going, but you get the idea. Some combination of the ex-convict's past, present problems, and the flaws in the main character and love interest's relationship conspire to break up the lovers and implode the ex-con's new life.

THE END:

The main character, with or without the help of the love interest, has to face the crisis from his or her past and overcome it once and for all. This may mean finding the proof of the ex-convict's innocence. It may mean turning in past criminal associates. It may involve stopping a crime. It may include saving the love interest in some way.

The main character probably does something that involves great self-sacrifice, once and for all proving that his or her heart is pure and good and that, faced with an impossible choice, he or she will choose to do the right thing.

It's also possible that the love interest steps way out of his or her comfort zone to do something heroic to protect, save, or exonerate the main character. While this is wildly romantic, be careful not to steal the main character's agency to make right his or her own life.

This is often a couple that does not need a big apology and forgiveness scene, given that the forces tearing them apart are typically more external than internal in nature. However, this couple probably does need a grand apology from external people or forces that have doubted the ex-convict all along.

Having once and for all redeemed himself or herself, the main character is now free to move forward into the future with his or her true love and have happily ever after with him or her.

KEY SCENES

- the moment the love interest finds out the main character is an ex-convict
- someone from the ex-convict's past shows up to cause havoc in the main character's new life
- the love interest throws the main character's past in his or her face
- the main character acts out some or all of the love interest's worst fears about the ex-convict in an effort to drive away the love interest for his or her own good
- the ex-convict's criminal past comes back to haunt him or her in some way
- the love interest publicly and fiercely defends the main character
- the main character does something or acts in a way that's completely unexpected to the love interest and seems out of character for an ex-con

THINGS TO THINK ABOUT WHEN WRITING THIS TROPE

Why was the main character incarcerated? Did the main character commit the crime he or she was convicted of?

What kind of prison was he or she in and what kinds of programs did it or didn't it have for rehabilitation?

For how long was he or she there? Why, when, and how did he or she get out of prison?

In what way did the experience change him or her?

What's your main character's primary goal after leaving prison? Prove his or her innocence? Avenge some wrong? Catch a bad guy from his or her past? Avoid past criminal associates? Forget the past altogether and start a new life? Look up a past love? Make amends to someone?

When does your story begin? At the point of the main character's release from prison? As he or she starts a new life? Well after he or she has started a new life?

Do the people around the main character know he or she is an ex-convict? Why or why not?

How is your main character's day-to-day life impacted and made more difficult by his or her past?

When will you reveal to the audience that the main character is an ex-convict?

How do the main character and love interest meet? How does this meeting start a chain of events that become the main plot problem of your story?

Does the main character tell the love interest right away about his or her past? Why or why not?

Is the reveal of the main character's past the first crisis or turning point in your story (and it doesn't have to be)? Who reveals it? How does the love interest react to finding out this information?

How will the main character's past come back to haunt him or her? Who from his or her past represents this return of the past to mess up his or her life?

How is the love interest threatened physically or emotionally by the return of the main character's past to the picture?

How do the love interest's friends and family react to finding out he or she is involved with an ex-convict? Will they support or sabotage the romance?

How are the main character and love interest completely different? What do they have in common? What do they find most attractive about each other?

How can you make the plot problem worse? How can you make it much worse?

How will the problem from the ex-convict's pass first threaten and then destroy his or her relationship with the love interest?

While the external problem is tearing the main character and love interest apart, what problems between them will also tear them apart?

What event, dilemma, trauma, or choice forces the main character and love interest to break up?

How will the lovers overcome the insurmountable problem between them so they can get back together? Who will sacrifice what? How? Why? Will they work together to solve the big plot problem, or will one of them work proactively and alone to fix everything? If so, which one? What will he or she do?

How much will the lovers both risk to be together? What form does that risk take? Can you make the risk even riskier, more dangerous, more deadly, more impossible?

What lessons do the main character and love interest learn when they break up, while they're apart, when they risk everything to get back together...or at least to save the other person?

Who has to apologize to whom in the end? Do one or both of the lovers have to make an apology? Do friends and family have to apologize? Does a bad guy have to apologize?

Who forgives whom in your story?

Does everyone around the ex-convict see him or her as fully redeemed by the end of the story or not? Does it matter to your main character and love interest?

Where do they settle at the end of your story? Do they go someplace new or stay where they've been? What does happily ever after look like for this couple?

TROPE TRAPS

Creating a cliché ex-convict who had a cliché prison experience and behaves in a cliché way. Did I mention not doing cliché characters?

Creating a love interest who's so naïve, trusting, and unaware of personal safety that the audience finds him or her TSTL (too stupid to live)

Failing to acknowledge any of the difficulties facing ex-convicts in rejoining society, finding housing and jobs, and the like.

Creating overly predictable bad guys who do obvious bad guy things…like insist the ex-con help them commit a crime.

Creating overly judging secondary characters who condemn your ex-convict out of hand or wax excessively preachy at your ex-convict.

Automatically reaching for a main character who's innocent of the crime and was wrongly convicted. While this surely happens in the criminal justice system, the vast majority of convicted criminals did what they were convicted of.

If I see one more bad cop who framed an ex-convict and now is out to kill him or her to silence the ex-con, I'm going to throw that book or my TV remote against a wall…along with a lot of your audience. You can do better than that. Or at least make the bad cop really interesting and not just a beer-gutted, tobacco-chewing, southern sheriff whom everyone knows is a crook and who's in cahoots with the rich businessman in town.

Failing to address issues of trauma in your ex-convict and trust in your love interest.

Creating such a purely good ex-convict that we don't believe this person ever was capable of committing a crime and hence isn't believable.

Creating such a bad main character that he or she isn't plausibly redeemable and doesn't have any heroic qualities for your audience to fall in love with or root for.

The main character gets away with committing another crime to fix the big plot problem in your book, destroying their heroism and goodness in one fell swoop.

The people who need to apologize to your main character never do.

EX-CONVICT HERO/HEROINE TROPE IN ACTION
Movies:

NOTE: I was unable to find any movies or TV shows featuring an ex-convict with a story primarily about him or her falling in love. I did, however, find any number of movies featuring ex-convicts re-starting their lives or dealing with their pasts that might be of some use to you in researching your stories.

- The Informer
- Buffalo '66
- Blood Father
- Desperation Road
- Double Jeopardy
- Stolen
- Jackie Brown
- The Drop
- Bound
- Baby Boy

Books:

- Edge by Cora Brent
- The Highwayman by Kerrigan Byrne
- King by T.M Frazier
- The Groom Says Yes by Cathy Maxwell
- When She's Ready by Ruby Dixon

- Morning Glory by LaVyrle Spencer
- All Chained Up by Sophie Jordan
- Beneath These Lies by Meghan March
- Do or Die by Suzanne Brockmann
- Reaper's Fall by Joanna Wylde

10

FINDING A HOME/FOUND FAMILY

DEFINITION

At first glance, it might seem that finding a home and finding a family are two entirely separate stories, but at their core, both of these revolve around a person who is alone to begin with ultimately finding safety, acceptance, and love.

While a home might technically be a physical place, I would argue that what makes a home is not the walls and roof but the people in it. It's people who fill a physical space with a sense of comfort, security, and love that we associate with "home." It's fair to say most people consider "home" to be defined by people rather than physical structures.

With that understanding in place, let's proceed with the trope.

In this trope one or both main characters begins the story alone, unloved, untethered to any particular place, without a sense of belonging to any particular group of people he or she considers to be family. As the main character meets the love interest and falls in love, the family-less main character finds the sense of family and home that he or she has been missing all along.

I don't know about you, but reading that paragraph just bored me to death. No trope, no *story*, is interesting without a conflict, barrier, obstacle, or problem of some kind in it. So we must ask ourselves, where's the conflict in this trope?

The homeless, family-less main character may resist the idea of having a family or home. Perhaps he or she fears the commitment or responsibility of maintaining a long-term relationship. Perhaps he or she worries that being part of this family will endanger it. Perhaps he or she is terribly traumatized by past family and struggles to trust this one.

OR

The love interest may be the source of conflict. Does he or she dare bring the love interest home to his or her family, based on how different, dangerous, or disruptive the main character might be to the family? Does the love interest trust the main character enough to make him or her part of their family? Does the love interest want to share his or her family with anyone else?

OR

The family itself is yet another source of conflict. Do the family members want anyone else to join the family? Do they want control of choosing who the love interest brings into the family? Do they approve of the main character specifically? Is the family willing to adapt and change to accommodate a new member, particularly this new member?

Once you know what obstacles stand in the way of your main character finding a home and family, the rest of your plot will probably unfold for you in a fairly straightforward fashion.

This trope is often layered with other tropes. They can be complimentary tropes like Lone Wolf Tamed, Across the Tracks, or Newcomer/Outsider/Stranger to name a few. Or you can layer this trope with less obvious tropes, for example, Fake Fiancé(e), Secret Identity, or Stranded Together.

. . .

ADJACENT TROPES

- Fresh Start
- Insta-Family
- Coming Home
- Outsider/Newcomer/Stranger
- Running Away From Home
- Lone Wolf

WHY READERS/VIEWERS LOVE THIS TROPE

- everyone—EVERYONE—desires a family/place they can call their own
- having ride-or-die friends or family who will always have our back
- having somewhere to go for holidays and big occasions in our lives and having people to share those times with
- not being alone
- being safe
- being accepted exactly as we are
- being loved unconditionally by our family
- getting to choose our own family, with whom we get along great and with whom we don't have conflict (often replacing the crappy family we were born into)

OBLIGATORY SCENES
THE BEGINNING:

Your main characters meet, and you'll probably establish that the love interest has a home and family the main character is envious of, or you may establish that neither of your lovers has a family/home.

What you will establish for certain is that one or both of your characters has a hole in their heart left by a lack of family and home. Often the opening of this type of story serves to make one or both of your main characters aware of this hole in their heart.

You may or may not want to reveal why this person is without family or home in the opening of your story. Which is to say, beware of bogging down the pacing of your opening with backstory. Also, a mystery clinging to a character only adds to your audience's intrigue about them.

At any rate, whatever conflict or obstacle you choose to put between your main character and his or her attainment of a family/home also needs to be introduced in the first act of your story.

If you're going to create some other external plot or problem—perhaps what brought your main character to this place, what brought your main character into the life of the love interest, or some threat to the family the main character will eventually join—this also needs to be set up in the beginning.

THE MIDDLE:

Complications ensue. Whatever personal issues the main character has regarding families, his or her family (or lack of one), and around the idea of having a solidly rooted home rear their ugly heads.

As the hero and heroine fall in love, the main character's issues with not having a family or home become even more problematic and urgently in need of confronting and solving. Odds are great that the love interest is part of the family/home the main character craves or will become the family/home the main character so desperately needs.

If the main character was not aware of the hole in his or her heart left by not having a family or home before, it definitely becomes clear to him or her, now. The main character glimpses what having an accepting, loving family and a safe place to call home looks like, and the main character realizes he or she wants that worse than life itself.

But whatever's standing in the way of your main character having that family/home grows in complication, power, or danger, standing in the main character's way. Every time he or she tries to go around or overcome one obstacle, another even bigger one rises up to block his or her path to safety, acceptance, and love.

Whatever external plot problem stands in the way of your main character finding a family/home gets worse and worse until a crisis looms.

Whatever has been preventing the main character from having a family or home of his or her own may show up to complicate matters even further. This can be a person (typically an authority figure or companion of some kind to whom the main character owes allegiance), an organization (an employer or official agency of some kind), or an event (something that happened in the past to cost the main character his or her family, a past crime, a past commitment).

Let's clarify this with a few examples.

1) A bodyguard with no family is hired to protect the love interest's family from a string of attacks. While working to stop any more attacks and figure out who's behind them, the bodyguard falls in love with both love interest and his/her family.

But then the bodyguard's boss calls to ask when he's finishing up this job and moving on to the next one. Now our bodyguard has a dilemma. Does he stay with this new family and home he's found, or does he go back to his nomadic, rootless, lonely life, moving from job to job?

2) An orphan with no family and no home is hired to work in a family business. She's sucked into the big, raucous, warm family and falls in love with the love interest, who's one of several brothers about to inherit the business. She wants nothing more than to settle down in this place with this family.

But then, she's contacted by her birth parent...who's a dangerous criminal. Or perhaps her past in the juvenile justice system is revealed by another employee, maybe who wants to marry the brother themselves and live a cushy life. Does the orphan run away? Face her past? Does the brother accept her past and believe she's not a gold digger or does he walk away from her?

3) A soldier who's been injured and forced out of the military has no home to go to. He finds a small town and gets a job. He moves into a ramshackle house and begins repairing it. As he builds a life for himself, he faces suspicion and ostracism by the locals.

One local gives him a chance and falls in love with him. But then, a rumor about why he left the military threatens to drive him out of town. He and the love interest have to prove the rumor wrong so he can stay.

Or maybe the rumor is true, and he has to clear his name before he can stay in his new home and be accepted by the locals and the family of the woman he's fallen in love with.

BLACK MOMENT:

For the character desperate for family, home, safety, acceptance, and love, losing these is the blackest moment he or she can imagine.

So, just as the main character finds a true love that comes with a ready-made family, or will be a family, it's all snatched away from the main character. The brewing external plot problem explodes, ruining the main character's shot at having a home or family and ripping the thing he or she desires most right out of his or her grasp.

The brewing personal conflicts between the main character and the love interest also implode—possibly as a result of the external crisis or possibly from building internal pressures and disagreements. Either way, the love interest turns his or her back on the main character and they break up.

Not only did the main character lose his or her shot at a home, the main character has lost the one person who actually loved him or her.

The love interest is similarly devastated, having just lost the love of his or her life. While the love interest may still have a family and a home, it now feels incomplete or empty without the main character in it.

THE END:

The main character is so desperate to have the family and home that just slipped through his or her grasp that he or she musters the courage and wherewithal to give getting it one last, Herculean effort.

The main character is willing to sacrifice everything, up to and including his or her life to solve the problems (external and internal) that stand between him or her and having a family and home.

The love interest, having now lost the main character realizes how desperately he or she wants to share family and home with the main character. The main character's absence now leaves a giant hole in his or her heart.

The main character may solve the big problem(s) alone, or the love interest may join in to help. Even though estranged, they may agree to work together to solve the external plot problem that poses a threat to the family and home they both love.

It may be through working together to save the family and home that they reconcile or at least open a dialogue with each other that can lead to reconciliation.

The main character may make a grand gesture or apology to the love interest or they may finally find a way past their conflicts, having learned how much they miss each other and how much being part of the same family and sharing the same home means to them.

With forgiveness earned, the main character finally finds the safety, acceptance, and love that he or she craves. The love interest's family and home are complete with the addition of the main character to them. The family is now complete, the home is finally established.

KEY SCENES

- the main character first gets a glimpse from afar of the family or home he or she doesn't have
- the main character's internal mental or emotional block to letting himself or herself have a home or family rears its ugly head
- the main character pulls away from the love interest out of fear of blowing it, fear of actually getting a family/home, or whatever other fear stands in the way of the main character being happy
- the love interest confronts the main character about why he or she has no home or family
- when the main character's past shows up to cause yet another obstacle to finding a home or family of his or her own, this person, organization, or event threatens the love interest in some way
- if the main character has an estranged blood family, some or all of it shows up unannounced to interfere with his or her chosen family or new home

THINGS TO THINK ABOUT WHEN WRITING THIS TROPE

Why does the main character have no home or no family? What happened to his or her blood family?

Has the main character ever had a home and family? If so, what happened to them? If not, why not?

Why has the main character not found a (new) home or (found) family before now?

Is the main character aware of wanting a home or family when the story begins? If so, what does he or she envision when imagining a home or family of his or her own? If not, what triggers the main character's desire for home and family and what does he or she envision then?

How do the main character and the love interest meet? Is it a meet cute? Accidental? Does the external plot problem introduce them?

How will the main character and love interest continue to be in each other's presence often enough to develop a relationship and eventually fall in love?

What first attracts them to each other?

We all know what the main character stands to gain from this relationship...but what does the love interest stand to gain from it? What does he or she see in the main character that's fascinating, fabulous, lovable, or irresistible?

Will the love interest's family be the one the main character joins, or will the love interest alone become the main character's found family?

Will you give the main character's desire for a home a physical representation in an actual place to live, or will "home" be a metaphorical concept of safety and roots in your story?

What emotional, or mental obstacle from the past has been blocking the main character from finding a home or family before now? This is the internal obstacle to finding home and family.

What in the main character's past has happened to make him or her be alone and without a family or place to call home now? This is the external obstacle to finding home and family.

What external plot problem will throw the main character and love interest together going forward? Will this problem keep throwing them together all the way through your story or will the main character's attraction to the love interest and to the idea of finding a family be what draws them together for the most part?

What about the external plot problem will interfere with or work to block the main character from finding a home and a family?

What conflicts develop between the main character and love interest that threaten the survival of their relationship? Are these conflicts external in nature, internal in nature, or both? (both being the optimal set-up in most stories)

What do the love interest's family and friends think of the main character? Do they pose an obstacle to him or her having the home and family he or she dreams of? If so, what kind of obstacle?

Does the main character have any colleagues or friends? Do they serve as a partial found family? Why don't they meet the main character's need for home and family? What's missing?

How does the plot problem the main character and love interest are trying to solve go from bad to worse? Worse to terrible? Terrible to disastrous?

How does the plot problem interfere a little, then a lot, then disastrously with the lover's relationship? With the main character's quest to build a home and a family?

What's going to break up your lovers in the black moment? There may be both an external plot reason and an internal, relationship, or personal reason.

How will the found family members prove to the main character that they really consider him or her to be family? What are they willing to do or sacrifice for him or her? How can you make that thing bigger, more difficult, more costly...and make them do it?

How will they fix the external plot problem? What changes that finally allows them to overcome it?

How will they fix the implosion of their relationship? Will one or both of them make a grand gesture or big apology? If so, what does it look like?

Will one or both of them learn some lesson or have some epiphany that clears the way forward for a long-term relationship? If so, what lesson or epiphany? What causes it, and how does it happen?

What does the main character look like settled into his or her home and family at the end of the story?

TROPE TRAPS

Creating a main character who's whiny and self-pitying in his or her loneliness and desire for home and family. Which is to say, everyone in your audience understands the craving for both, and no character needs to harp on it.

Creating a love interest that is cardboard and not fully developed, who is overpowered by and acts only as a prop to the main character in the story.

Creating an implausible back story to explain why the main character has no family and no home.

Failing to explain why the main character hasn't filled the home and family void in his or her life already.

Never explaining why the main character is stopping his or her wandering (physical or metaphorical) at this exact moment in this exact place and finally putting down roots.

Creating an external plot problem that in no way relates to the main character's search for home and family and doesn't function as an obstacle to that search in some way.

Creating a found family that's too perfect to be plausible.

Not making the main character earn acceptance in place to call home or earn acceptance into a found family but at least proving himself or herself to be reliable and trustworthy (at a minimum).

Failing to make the search for home and family interesting to your audience. If it's ultimately as simple as moving to a new place and meeting new people who accept you, where's the conflict and struggle in that?

Failing to develop a plausible trauma or internal, personal block in the main character to allowing himself or herself to be safe, happy, or loved.

Failing to challenge the found family to act like actual family to the main character. Family members typically would die for each other. But if you never make them prove it to the main character, how will the main character or your audience believe they're truly family?

Relying on a fix to the broken romantic relationship that could have happened earlier in the story...hence, it's lame as a climax to your story.

Not involving both the main character and love interest in fixing the external plot problem (which is to say, the love interest is too passive and relies on the main character to do everything for him or her).

Failing to teach the main character and love interest a big life lesson or give them big epiphanies that make a happily ever possible (when it wasn't possible before).

Failing to give the audience at least a glimpse of the main character finally getting the home and family that he or she craved and worked so hard to get.

FINDING A HOME/FOUND FAMILY TROPE IN ACTION
Movies:

- Dune, Part 2 (Denis Villeneuve version)
- The Quiet Man
- Wakefield
- Lilo & Stitch
- The Peanut Butter Falcon
- Boogie Nights
- Paddington
- The Grand Budapest Hotel

Books:

- A Place to Call Home by Nora Roberts
- A Place to Call Home by Carole Matthews
- Six of Crows by Leigh Bardugo

- One Last Stop by Casey McQuiston
- Raybearer by Jordan Ifueko
- The Gilded Wolves by Roshani Chokshi
- The Very Secret Society of Irregular Witches by Sangu Mandanna
- We Hunt the Flame by Hafsah Faizal
- The Dream Thieves by Maggie Stiefvater
- Happy Place by Emily Henry

11

FIRST LOVE

DEFINITION

Ahh, first love. I'll bet we all remember our first love vividly—the ecstasy and the agony, the uncertainty and excitement, the bad poetry and drama. ALL the drama. Which is a defining feature of this trope. First love is dramatic. It's a life-changing event all by itself. The whole world looks different through the eyes of first love.

Most of us experience first love relatively young. If you're telling a young adult or new adult story, you're right in the sweet spot for characters to experience their first love. But what about characters who've made it to adulthood before Cupid's Arrow first pierces them? First love may be quite a disruptive shock to the adult character with a fully established life.

In this trope, two people fall in love, and for one or both of them, this is the first time he or she has ever fallen in love. They overcome whatever obstacles to being together litter their path forward, and they end up together happily ever after.

Seems pretty straightforward, doesn't it? Which is where you the writer will have to do the heavy lifting of creating an engaging and interesting story with enough twists and turns to pull your audience forward all the way to the "will they or won't they end up together" cliffhanger and eventual happily ever after.

As I discussed in this book's introduction, you need to plant a lot of questions in your audience member's minds to pull them forward into your story. The simple act of two people meeting offers very little of great interest that would suck a reader or viewer into a story. Hence, something about these main characters' meeting needs to be intriguing, surprising, funny, vaguely alarming, or something else that causes us to wonder what will happen next between these two people.

Because of its simplicity, this trope is almost always layered with another trope or multiple tropes. Often the secondary trope explains why the main character has never been in love before—he or she is oblivious to love, has a fear of intimacy, or is clumsy, awkward, or bumbling, for example.

But it's entirely possible to write a story purely about first love and make it work. Just prepare to torture your lovers a lot before you let them have their happily ever after.

For what it's worth, studies show that about one in four people end up with their first love. People who commit to a long-term relationship with their first love typically worry that they settled too quickly for the first person who came along, that by not dating around more and waiting to commit, they might not be with the right or best person. They also cite curiosity about what sex and intimacy with other people might be like and worry that they might not have grown as much as they otherwise might have had they experienced a few more relationships.

Something you're likely to address in an adult character experiencing first love is why they haven't fallen in love before now. Was something different about them in the past that made them unprepared to fall in love, undesirable to fall in love with, or in some way prevented them from having experienced first love before now?

Likewise, you'll need to figure out why the conditions have changed or are right now for love to blossom. Has something about the main character changed, or is it a timing thing, a right person finally coming along thing, or something else?

This is as simple a romantic relationship as a trope can be. Boy meets girl (or some other gender combination of your choosing), boy and girl fall in love, boy and girl overcome various problems or obstacles. Boy gets girl and girl gets boy. End of story. At its core, this trope is exactly what it says it is: finding the right person and falling in love.

ADJACENT TROPES

- Virgin Hero/Heroine
- Celibate Hero/Heroine
- Straight Arrow Seduced

WHY READERS/VIEWERS LOVE THIS TROPE

- for the audience member who has already gone through it, who doesn't love reliving the rush of first love and experiencing it again through the eyes of the main characters
- for the audience member who has yet to experience it, imagining what our own first love will be like and vicariously experiencing it along with the main character
- what if our own first love had worked out? What would it be like to have stayed with that person? Studies show 64% of people keep track of their first love to some degree and one in six people actually get back together (briefly) with their first love at some point
- imagining that our current love has all the heightened drama, anxiety, newness, and epic memorability that our first love had

- first love is just so darned romantic and swoon-worthy

OBLIGATORY SCENES
THE BEGINNING:

The main character and love interest meet, are attracted to each other, and begin the process of falling in love. This trope is strongly associated with meet cutes and intense attraction at first glimpse vibes, but neither is obligatory.

As soon as these characters do realize they're attracted to and interested in each other, feelings tend to develop quickly and go big.

That said, a person experiencing first love may find it very scary. For the first time, he or she is emotionally vulnerable in a new way, risking getting hurt worse than they've ever been hurt before. The main character probably experiences heightened anxiety, fear of rejection, insecurity about his or her own lovability, frets about his or her physical appearance, clothes, job, financial status, and anything else that might be a turn off to the love interest.

If the love interest is also experiencing first love, he or she will be going through the exact same process. However, if the first love has been to the love rodeo before, he or she may find themselves guiding or mentoring the main character through the maze of new and scary thoughts and feelings. Or, of course, the first love may not let the love interest in on what a mess they are, and the main character may have to navigate this new emotional landscape alone or with the help of a close friend.

Because "two people meet and they commence falling in love" is such a straightforward relationship path, your external plot is likely to be your main source of complications initially. Your other option for keeping the beginning of your story interesting and moving along briskly is to layer other tropes on top of and around this First Love story.

. . .

THE MIDDLE:

Somewhere in the middle of your story, the main character and love interest will realize they're hopelessly, completely, passionately in love. First love tends to move very fast and this realization may mark the end of your beginning. Or you may hold off the realization that the couple is in love to later in your story...even as late as the end of the middle. In this case, the realization that the main characters are in love may precipitate the break-up of the black moment.

The middle of your story is punctuated by the idea that into the romantic ointment, a fly must land. The first flush of attraction, crush, and goo-goo eyes is giving way to doubts, conflicts, and obstacles to true love. The external plot problem is getting worse with every scene, and the couple's doubts, insecurities, individual flaws, and whatever else they have to overcome to be together is becoming more and more of a problem.

The trope lends itself to a three-pronged plot structure. There's an **external plot problem for the hero and heroine to solve**—Superman has to stop General Zod and companions from taking over Earth.

The **hero and heroine each have internal problems within themselves to overcome** before they can love healthily —Clark has to overcome his shyness and figure out how to tell Lois he's really the Superman she has a wild crush on, and she has to overcome her insecurity about being merely human in the face of Superman's amazing abilities and overwhelming goodness.

And **the couple may have an external relationship problem to overcome** before they can be together—she's obsessed with work over personal life and finds Clark boring and too naïve for her. He has a responsibility to protect everyone in the world and cannot focus only on protecting Lois.

In the middle of your story, the friendly people around your couple—friends, families, coworkers—and the unfriendly people around them—frenemies, enemies, and nemeses—are starting to interfere in the relationship.

These secondary characters may want to help your couple in the most awkward possible way, hinder them in an underhanded way, slow down the budding relationship, speed it up, and destroy it outright. It's common to have some secondary characters working to advance the romance while others work to sabotage it.

If this is a comic story, shenanigans really get silly in the middle of the story. If this is a suspense, the danger really ratchets up. If it's mainly a relationship story, the relationship really gets messy and complicated.

Because of the simplicity of this trope, you risk losing momentum and audience interest in the middle of the story, particularly if the romance advances too slowly or the external plot action of the story drags.

While a specific audience still exists that enjoys a slow-roll or leisurely unfolding of love that's chock full of beautiful imagery, poetic dialogue, long, lingering looks, descriptions or images of sunlight off water, dragonflies in flower-dotted meadows, and dappled sunlight through leaves, this particular audience is NOT going to be the majority of your readers or viewers.

In today's insanely fast paced, technology-driven world, most people consume story at extremely high speed. We fast forward through commercial breaks, movies have shortened from two hours to barely 90 minutes in many cases, and we listen to music, news, and more on the go.

Beware, beware, beware of boring your audience in the middle of your First Love story. Keep it moving along briskly. Keep the twists and turns coming. Keep your audience wondering what's coming next, and for goodness' sake, don't make it easy for your main character experiencing first love to get his or her happily ever after with the love interest.

The old writing mantra holds true for this type of story. Make things go from bad to worse, from worse to much worse, and from much worse to terrible.

. . .

BLACK MOMENT:

Something goes catastrophically, horribly wrong in the couple's relationship that causes them to break up. This can be an abrupt event that strikes out of the blue, or you can have been building to this crisis for a while before it finally implodes.

The main character has lost his or her first love and plunges off the cliff of agony, loss, grief, despair, rejection, self-blame, self-hatred and whatever ever other dark and terrible emotions you choose to torture him or her with.

If the love interest has lost love before, he or she may be a bit more prosaic or prepared for this moment of having lost the one person who matters most to him or her.

But it's probably not the love interest who reaches out with any wisdom, advice, or support for the devastated main character. That job will probably fall to a trusted friend or family member.

This is your moment to really make a character suffer. Losing a first love is possibly one of the most painful events in any person's life up until that point and you should feel free to really unleash your inner writer-sadist upon your unlucky lovers.

Additionally, whatever external plot problem the couple has been wrestling with over the course of the story goes completely off the rails at the same time.

This plot crisis may precipitate the lovers' break-up, or the lover's break-up may provoke the plot crisis to explode. Either way, the main character's world falls apart in every possible way, all at once.

THE END:

In the ending of your story, you have both an external plot problem to resolve, and a broken relationship to repair.

In a perfect world, you would find a climax to your story that allows for both of these plot lines to be resolved at the same time, in the same

event or series of events. This is generally considered to be the most elegant way to end a story with multiple, simultaneous plot lines.

In Superman, Lois has died (the blackest of all possible black moments in a First Love story!) and Superman has allowed the world to be terribly damaged before he commits to sacrificing Lois and confronting the bad guys, which doesn't go well. He solves both of these problems—dead girlfriend and triumphant bad guys—by flying around the planet fast enough to reverse time so he can save Lois and defeat the bad guys decisively.

In some stories, it may take two completely separate climactic events, one to resolve an external plot problem and another to fix and resolve a relationship problem.

If you have more than two major plot lines to wrap up, you may have even more climactic scenes to deal with. Which leads to the question, which plot line should climax and resolve first and which should climax and resolve last?

In some stories, the two (or more) big climactic scenes must happen in a specific order. For example, if a character must be freed from the bad guys, that has to happen before he can return home and reconcile with his true love.

But what about the story where you could end your big plot lines in any order? The common wisdom in writing is to resolve the most important plot line last. Make your audience wait for the most satisfying moment in your story and leave your audience with a final impression of the biggest win to take away with them.

So, if your story is primarily a romance with an external sub-plot, you will solve the external plot problem first and get the lovers back together last.

If your story is primarily an action-adventure, mystery, sci-fi/fantasy, superhero story or some other type of fiction, you'll solve the love story first and the big plot problem last.

· · ·

KEY SCENES

- the moment when the main character clocks that he or she might be falling in love with the love interest
- the love interest realizes the main character is falling in love with him or her. This may be a wonderful realization or a terrible one, or something else entirely
- the couple's first touch, first kiss, first intimate encounter, first date, first dance...so many firsts for the main character(s)
- the couple's first time going out in public as a couple
- the first argument
- the main character's first ever declaration of love

THINGS TO THINK ABOUT WHEN WRITING THIS TROPE

How old is your main character?

If your main character is an adult, why didn't he or she experience first love any sooner than this? How will his or her age now affect how he or she relates and reacts to falling in love?

Is this also the love interest's first love, or is he/she a veteran of first love and first heartbreak? How will this decision impact this person's relationship with the main character?

How do the hero and heroine meet? How does this set the tone for the rest of your story?

Will you layer any other tropes into your story in addition to this trope? Will you use a trope to explain why the main character has never been in love before?

Is the main character relieved to finally find someone and start falling in love? Terrified? Apprehensive?

What has the main character heard about love or what does

he/she believe about it that will pose an obstacle to falling in love now? Where did this belief come from? Is it true or not?

What big misbelief does the main character have about himself or herself that's going to pose a huge obstacle to falling in love (aside from his or her misconceptions about love)?

What about the main character attracts the love interest?

What about the love interest attracts the main character?

Will these two people have passionate chemistry from page one or will it develop more slowly?

Are the hero and heroine obviously and instantly compatible or not? If so, what do they first connect over? If not, how do they first find common ground and over what?

Who is the initiator in the relationship? Meaning, who approaches whom first? Who starts the first conversation? Who asks whom out? Who takes the relationship to the next romantic level? Is it always the same person in the relationship, or does it go back and forth?

What's the external plot of your story? How does it function to throw the couple together? How does it act as a wedge between them, keeping them apart?

Does the external plot in some way mirror or parallel the development of the love story and the romance's ensuing complications?

What conflicts or problems will come between the main character and love interest? Will these reveal themselves early—before they've fallen in love, or will they show up later—once the couple is fully involved in a romantic relationship?

What obstacles do the couple have to overcome to give themselves permission to fall in love? What obstacles do they have to overcome once they are in love? What obstacles to they have to overcome to stay in love?

What doubts, fears, insecurities, and anxieties does the main character have about falling in love or being in love? Same question for the love interest. Do they share the same issues or different ones?

If the main character and love interest share the same anxieties, fears, or insecurities, do they respond the same or differently? How can their reactions come into conflict with each other or drive each other crazy in a bad way?

What's perfect about the couple's relationship?

What's less than perfect about it?

What is a deal breaker for the main character in a relationship? How about for the love interest?

What's something the main character would never, ever do? Is there a way for him or her to be forced to do that thing...by the love interest? What's taboo to the love interest? Is there a way for him or her to be forced to do that thing...by the main character?

NOTE: I'm not talking about breaking personal sexual boundaries, committing a crime, or debasing oneself. I'm talking about things like stopping going to church or never setting foot in a church, wearing a suit or putting on make-up, dancing in public or giving a speech—things that push the characters out of their comfort zones and teach them they can be more and do more than they previously believed.

I'm suggesting this as a means of counteracting the common regret among people who marry their first loves that they could've grown more as a person if they had dated more widely before settling down with the first person they ever fell in love with.

How do the friends, family, coworkers, and other secondary characters feel about this pair being a couple? Do they support and try to help the relationship along or do they hinder or try to sabotage it?

What in the external plot and in the couple's relationship goes from bad to worse to terrible, and rises to the level of a crisis?

Will the main character get cold feet at some point? Does this happen before or after he or she first declares their love to the love interest? What does the main character do about his or her cold feet?

What breaks up the lovers?

What does their break-up look like?

Just how devastated is the main character after the breakup?

How about the love interest? What do each of them do or not do in their misery?

How will you resolve each of your plotlines—external plot problem, internal character problem(s), external character/relationship problem(s)? Is there a way to resolve them all at once in a single, big, climactic scene or series of scenes? If not, in what order will you resolve them?

Is there a big lesson one or both characters must learn or an epiphany one or both of them must have to be deserving of another chance in the relationship? If so, what lesson or epiphany? What event will trigger him or her or both of them to learn this?

Does one or both of your lovers have to make a grand gesture or apology to the other? Why?

Who forgives whom? What does the forgiver actually have to forgive?

What does happily ever after look like for this couple?

Have you painted a relationship strong and resilient enough to last for a long time...at least in the eyes of your audience? Does your audience walk away from your story satisfied that this couple has fully earned their happily ever after?

TROPE TRAPS

Creating a main character who's so awkward, oblivious to love, or unlovable that your audience doesn't buy the love interest falling for him or her.

Creating a love interest who's so jaded or cynical that he or she doesn't seem capable of falling in love and isn't believable as an object of the main character's love.

Creating a couple so opposite in every way that the two of them falling in love is completely implausible to your audience.

Creating a romance that's too perfect to be real. While fiction is meant to be escapist and/or aspirational, you can only push the bounds of believability so far before your audience snorts and declares, "No way."

Failing to create enough or big enough flaws, problems, insecurities, misbeliefs, and other obstacles to challenge your lovers or to make them earn their happily ever after.

Failing to put in enough conflict, both internal and external, to keep your story interesting to your audience.

Slow pacing. While in reality, a person in love for the first time may sit around daydreaming for hours and hours ad nauseum about their new love, your audience doesn't want to experience it in real time, ad nauseum.

Failing to surprise the audience or give your audience any twists and turns to what is an otherwise extremely straightforward relationship arc.

Failing to create any meaningful connection between your external plot problem and the romantic relationship in your story.

Failing to flesh out this first romance with all the myriad firsts that come with it (first touch, first kiss, first dance, first date)

Being cavalier about the newness of first love and glossing over or ignoring how romantic it is.

Failing to give both romantic leads as deep and powerful emotions and feelings as their partner. Their feelings and emotions may be different at different places in the relationship but beware of short-changing one of your lovers in his or her development as a character.

A lame breakup. They break up for a stupid or implausible reason. While people surely can and do breakup over ridiculous things, don't tick off your audience by cheating them out of a good tragic breakup scene.

Failing to make your lovers suffer to earn their eventual happiness.

Failing to appropriately devastate the lovers after their breakup.

A lame make-up. Once they've gone through the agony of a breakup and the emotional devastation to follow, failing to have them make a grand enough gesture or apology, or making an apology insufficient to win back the heart of their lover.

Failing to win back the hearts of your audience members with the grand gesture or apology. If you don't convince *them* that the love interest should give the main character one last chance, your audience will never buy that the characters should have gotten back together in the end, and they'll be mad if the love interest takes back the main character.

Failing to give your audience a satisfying reunion kiss or romantic moment at the end. Your audience wants one last romantic swoon before the story ends, darn it.

FIRST LOVE TROPE IN ACTION
Movies:

- Superman
- The Notebook
- The Perks of Being a Wallflower
- The Man in the Moon
- The Fault in Our Stars
- Tuck Everlasting
- A Walk to Remember

Books:

- Eleanor and Park by Rainbow Powell
- It Ends With Us by Colleen Hoover
- The Fault in Our Stars by John Greene
- Love and Other Words by Christina Lauren
- The Summer I Turned Pretty by Jenny Han
- If I Stay by Gayle Forman

- Every Summer After by Carley Fortune
- Twilight by Stephanie Meyer
- Where the Crawdads Sing by Delia Owens
- The Selection by Kiera Cass
- Pride and Prejudice by Jane Austen
- Outlander by Diana Gabaldon

12

FORGIVENESS

DEFINITION

Before we dive into this trope, let's get one thing straight—straight from the mouths of professional therapists—**some things should not be forgiven. Ever**.

Forgiveness is not the be all and end all in moving on from a terrible or tragic event. It's fine never to forgive someone for something they've done to you or to others if, in your eyes, it's an unforgivable thing.

Yes, some people's religious beliefs suggest that one must forgive every transgression against oneself. And this is a perfectly fine thing to believe, with the caveat that everyone's religious or spiritual beliefs are also a completely personal and individual choice.

To the idea that all transgressions must be forgiven in all cases, psychological professionals respond that forgiveness can take many forms. Forgiveness, particularly complete and unqualified forgiveness, is neither necessary nor healthy for everyone in every situation.

What constitutes forgivable or unforgivable is a purely personal and subjective decision, individual to each of us. Before you jump into a story about someone seeking forgiveness, first ask yourself if you're comfortable writing a story about forgiveness being granted for the mistake or transgression perpetrated in the past that you've chosen to write about.

Then, ask yourself if your audience is likely to think some past transgression is forgivable or not. The answer to that may determine how you handle the subject in your story.

You may choose to have different characters react in different ways and to different degrees when asked to grant or accept forgiveness. You may choose to outrage your audience and provoke discussion. Or you may choose to write about not forgiving an event if doing so is likely to offend a lot of your audience members.

That said, let's dive in.

Sometime in the past, typically one or both of the main characters, has or have done something for which they feel a need to obtain forgiveness from someone, grant forgiveness to someone, or forgive self before becoming worthy and deserving of true love.

Usually what precipitates this search for forgiveness is meeting someone with whom they start falling in love. It's also possible the person seeking forgiveness has finally arrived at an emotional place where he or she feels ready to forgive or be forgiven, that he or she feels lonely and wants to be able to love.

In point of technical fact, forgiving self, forgiving someone else, and seeking forgiveness from someone are separate tropes. But they're so similar and deal with such identical issues that I went ahead and mashed them into a single entry for the sake of brevity in this volume, which is already longer than I wanted it to be.

In all cases, a transgression—perceived or real—that calls for forgiveness has happened in the past that currently blocks the main character's path to love. Before he or she can allow self to love or be loved, this transgression must be resolved.

The good news is it's ultimately an emotionally healthy path to true love. Clearing one's most pressing emotional or psychological trauma before diving into one of the most important relationships of one's life is an excellent strategy for success.

Where this trope gets interesting is what the main character did or had done to them that precipitated this search for forgiveness and why the main character is seeking to resolve it once and for all, now.

At its core, this is a story of redemption (as many of the backstory tropes are), of fixing a past wrong, of making the past right so it won't ruin the future.

ADJACENT TROPES

- Redemption
- Bad Boy/Girl Reformed
- Ex-Convict Hero/Heroine
- Reconciliation/Second Chance

WHY READERS/VIEWERS LOVE THIS TROPE

- we all crave forgiveness for some past mistake that haunts us
- the generosity and magnanimity of being able to forgive is love in one of its purest forms
- he or she loves me enough to do this incredibly difficult and painful thing to be with me
- we wish those who've wronged us would truly apologize and try to make amends (either because we secretly want to make them suffer and pay or because we can't bring ourselves to forgive until they first seek forgiveness)

OBLIGATORY SCENES
THE BEGINNING:
Typically, this story begins with the main character and love

interest meeting. It's often a meet cute or accidental meeting and looks pretty normal. Your main characters are thrown together in some way, there's a spark of attraction or at least interest, and they'll develop a relationship from there.

As it turns out, most people don't lead with, "Hi, my name's Joe. You're hot, and I can't have a meaningful relationship with you until I'm forgiven for X past tragic mistake." Which is to say most writers introduce the hunt for forgiveness relatively slowly. Even though it's the underpinning of your whole story, it'll usually fester beneath the surface for the early part of your story.

The issues of guilt, absolution, apology, and forgiveness are deep and tend to be very personal. Their wounds are not visible to the naked eye, and we don't share them freely with others. As your main characters get closer and start to fall in love, the issue of sorting out forgiveness will become more pressing and become the focus of your story.

The external plot of your story may be the thing forcing your main character to confront past events now. If this is the case, it's probably tied in some way to the event(s) that have provoked a need for forgiveness.

It's typical to drop hints and veiled references of there being a deep problem the main character is wrestling with well before the big, tragic thing that the main character needs forgiveness about is actually revealed.

All of that said, it's also entirely plausible to open your story with your main character arriving in a place, people taking one look at him or her, and all hell breaking loose.

At any rate, in the beginning of your story, you need to put the main characters together, launch your external plot story/problem, hint at a big, tragic past mistake that needs forgiving, and by the end of the beginning, probably reveal at least some of what happened that has provoked the main character's search for some version of forgiveness.

· · ·

THE MIDDLE:

A life-wrecking, tragic mistake or terrible transgression is rarely a simple event. There are typically layers to the whole story that you'll reveal in stages to the audience and other characters in the story. Often each new layer of information about what happened causes the audience's perception of the terrible event to twist, turn, and change. What initially seemed straightforward may not be simple or clear at all.

In the forgiveness story, it's normal to mess with the audience's loyalties, likes, and dislikes. They may start the story convinced one person is at fault for whatever happened, and by the middle be convinced of something else—or several somethings else—entirely.

Unreliable narrators are sometimes used in this trope. We start out thinking the main character is a good guy...but this may not be entirely or even partially the case.

Who needs to be forgiven for what, who should forgive whom, who's really guilty, who should feel guilty...all of this can be played with, misdirected, change completely, and keep readers guessing as to what really happened as you gradually reveal more and more details.

In the midst of this changing landscape of guilt and what really happened, your main characters are trying to fall in love. They may have on-again, off-again trust issues. Should I trust this person or not? Do I dare love him or her? Am I setting myself up for something terrible or not?

The external plot is probably also tied up in some way with the terrible thing from the past, and it, too, will get messier and more tangled as the past unravels and the truth comes out.

If there's one last, big explosive piece of information to be revealed to your audience and to the characters in your story, it probably is the thing the middle of the book leads up to and climaxes with that provokes the black moment.

If your story isn't structured that way, the strain on the budding romance of all the secrets, lies, guilt, shame, and whatever else your couple has been wrestling with finally comes to a head by the end of the middle.

The external plot problem also arrives at a moment of crisis. Whatever the main characters were trying to accomplish fails utterly and usually in some sort of crisis.

BLACK MOMENT:

Which brings us to the moment of complete failure. The main character has finally arrived at the crux of the event he or she is seeking forgiveness for or for which he or she must forgive. And whoever must grant forgiveness doesn't do so.

The problems and trusts issues in the romantic relationship have overwhelmed your couple and they break up. There may be one last, terrible misunderstanding, one last revelation that changes everything and makes your main character appear unforgivable.

If the external plot problem and past events in need of forgiveness are linked in your story, they finally crash into each other and blow each other to smithereens. In this trope, the black moment is usually a shocking or spectacular one.

Because of the scale of black moment this story tends to build to, it's not uncommon for it to happen far enough before the ending of your story to give you time and space to sort out the mess that's been made of everything and everyone.

THE END:

In the final act of your story, your main characters have to finish figuring out what really happened in the past, see it clearly, and find a way forward to forgiveness. It may be that the mere fact of knowing the truth makes forgiveness possible.

This last, big push to solve the plot problem and get over the final hurdle to forgiveness usually takes a Herculean effort from your main character and love interest. If it were easy, they would have done what's needed to make things right long before now.

Or it may be that a new villain must be forgiven now. At any rate, the act of resolving the huge mistake in the past and the current external problem act as catalysts to make forgiveness possible and happen.

Depending on how complex your story has been, you may need to insert some sort of summary or rehash of the entire twisty truth once it's fully revealed to help your audience see the entirety of it. The challenge in writing such a summary is making sure it doesn't come off mechanically and that it fits organically into your story.

If you're relying on a single, big surprise that changes everything or makes everything clear in one fell swoop—a big reveal that everything else hinges upon—this revelation may happen only a few pages from the end of your story. You may have a very tight space to unwind all the many tangled plot threads you've been spinning throughout your entire story.

While there may still be some sort of grand gesture(s) between your lovers to put their relationship back on course, this may take the form of a grand apology and/or a grand absolution.

Don't skimp on the main character's reaction to finally achieving forgiveness. It's a profound moment that has been a long time coming.

Once the forgiveness your main character has sought for so long is finally granted, the path is now clear to love. Your couple can finally trust each other and go forward into their happily ever after.

KEY SCENES

- the moment when the person who needs to forgive the main character first sees the main character (or the moment when the main character first acknowledges to your audience his or her need to forgive self)

- the moment when the love interest figures out who the main character is in relation to past events or in relation to the current plot problem
- the moment when the main character confesses what it is he or she is seeking forgiveness over
- the moment when the love interest refuses to grant forgiveness to the main character (or refuses to extend grace to the main character, who still can't forgive himself or herself.)
- a moment when the main character almost, but not quite, reveals a big secret to the love interest
- moment when the love interest seriously doubts and doesn't trust the main character
- the new development that happens immediately after the first romantic scene to change everything (usually for the worse)

THINGS TO THINK ABOUT WHEN WRITING THIS TROPE

What happened in the past that your story ultimately revolves around?

Is this a forgivable transgression or not? How do you plan to handle this question in your story?

How do you expect your audience to respond to the past mistake? Will they think it's forgivable or not? Are you okay with your audience disagreeing with you?

How do you plan to have all the characters in your story respond to the idea of forgiving the past transgression?

How does the current plot problem you plan to write about relate to that past tragic mistake or transgression?

How do the hero and heroine meet? How are they both involved with the plot problem? Are they both involved in the past event that provoked this search for forgiveness?

Who needs to forgive whom?

Why now?

At what point do the main character and love interest, individually or together, figure out they can't be happy together as a couple until forgiveness is achieved for the one(s) seeking it?

When in the new romantic relationship does the character seeking forgiveness tell his or her partner about it? How much or little of past events that provoked the need for forgiveness does he or she share with the love interest?

What attracts the love interest to the main character?

What makes the love interest doubt the main character? What makes him or her distrust the main character?

What really happened in that tragic past event? How does the truth differ from what the main character(s) believe to have happened when the story begins? Map out the facts that will be revealed, the order they'll be revealed in, how each will come to light, and how each new fact will change the main characters' perceptions of each other.

How do the secondary characters react to each new revelation? Will these people try to help along or sabotage the growing romance between the main character and love interest? Why? What's their relationship to each of your main characters—both in the past and the present?

What's the emotional journey you plan to take your audience on? For each of the new facts revealed that relate to either the plot problem, the past event, or both, how do you want your audience to react? Who do you want them rooting for now? Who do you want them to distrust? Dislike? Worry about?

How will you convince your audience that the character seeking forgiveness has both earned it and deserves it? Will you change the audiences' mind about either of these at any point in the story? If so, how, when, and why?

When and how will you implode the romance between your main character and love interest? What issue between them blows up? How will the main plot problem and past transgression come together to tear them apart?

How will your main characters overcome the utter failure of the black moment? In the absence of trust, why does each of them decide to make one last try to fix everything anyway?

How will the plot problem finally be solved?

How will the full truth about the past event finally be revealed? Does this truth make your main character seem innocent of a past wrong or guilty of it? (Either is okay as long as he or she faces up to it honestly and owns it.)

Now that we're at the end of the story with all the facts revealed, who needs to forgive whom? Is this different that your answer to this question at the beginning of the story?

How will the character in need of forgiveness earn it? Have they truly earned it in the eyes of the other character? How about in the eyes of your audience?

Will the character whose trust has been broken be able to restore that trust for their partner? (The answer to this must be yes if they're to be a couple and get their happy ending.) How?

Will someone need to make a grand apology or some sort of grand gesture to ask for or grant forgiveness? If so, what is it?

Who ultimately forgives whom? Why? How?

Who else needs to grant forgiveness before everyone's satisfied?

Will the lovers stay in this place once they've reconciled or will they leave? If they leave, will they ever be back or not? Why?

What does happily ever after look like for this couple?

TROPE TRAPS

Royally pissing off your audience by asking them to forgive an unforgivable transgression...without intent to piss them off or create controversy.

Stomping insensitively on audience members' religious, spiritual, or personal beliefs about forgiveness and offending them.

Failing to acknowledge that there may be different ways to respond to the past transgression at some point in your story.

Judging your characters' (and indirectly, audience members') opinions about whether or not some past event is forgivable or not.

Creating a character so consumed with guilt or shame (and darkness, brooding, and depression) that he or she can't possibly manage to love anyone else, which makes them not lovable or attractive as a romantic lead.

Creating a love interest who's a glutton for punishment by falling for someone totally devoid of light or joy.

If your story revolves around two totally broken souls, why then, is one or both of them seeking forgiveness and healing? This dichotomy comes across as too jarring to your audience and they don't buy into the love story.

The past event that your tortured main character is seeking forgiveness for isn't gigantic enough to merit all of his or her angst and woe or a quest for forgiveness.

The past event is too simple and straightforward, which makes your audience wonder why it takes an entire story to forgive that thing.

Your main character is racked with guilt over an accident and can't let go of any of their guilt. At some point, we've all done something bad accidentally...and we all know that you eventually have to forgive yourself for it. Your audience won't buy a character who can never find any peace at all over something they truly didn't mean to do. Accidents happen. Regrets are fine. But total inability to move on? Not great. Your audience won't like it.

The past event turns out to be rather dull, boring, and straightforward when all is revealed...and your audience feels robbed of a decent story.

You never make the audience question who actually needs to be forgiven.

You create something unforgivable and expect your character in a position to grant forgiveness to actually forgive it. You expect your audience to forgive something unforgivable.

FORGIVENESS TROPE IN ACTION
 Movies:

- Schindler's List
- The Fisher King
- Dead Man Walking
- No Great Love
- Mass
- Moonlight
- Chateau Christmas

Books:

- The Perfect Husband by Lisa Gardner
- Dreaming of You by Lisa Kleypas
- Deadline by Sandra Brown
- Lord of Scoundrels by Loretta Chase
- Key of Knowledge by Nora Roberts
- Lover Awakened by J.R. Ward
- The Love of My Next Life by Brit Benson
- Frisco's Kid by Suzanne Brockmann

13

GUARDIAN/CARETAKER ROMANCE

DEFINITION

In this trope, the main character falls in love with his or her guardian (as in a legal, parental substitute) or primary caretaker. By its nature, the main character in this trope is usually much younger than the love interest, who has assumed a parental role in the main character's life at some point, past or present.

The potential for the main character not to be old enough legally or emotionally to consent to such a relationship can make this a tricky trope to write ethically.

Let's be clear. It's squicky at best and illegal at worst for adult caretakers to become romantically involved with their minor wards. NOTE: In the context of this trope, minor means the main character is under the legal age of consent to engage in an adult relationship in the jurisdiction your story is set in.

Teachers, for example, are legally forbidden from having romantic or sexual relationships with minor students. Breaking this rule will most certainly cost them their job and possibly mean they're facing jail time depending on the age of the student. Prison guards may not legally be involved with their prisoners. Medical staff at care facilities may not become involved with patients.

The key to this trope not crossing the line into unethical is the age and maturity (not OR. That's age AND maturity) of the main character and his or her personal and legal ability to consent to a relationship with his or her guardian or caretaker.

Even if the guardian or caretaker is relatively close in age to the main character, there's still an assigned parental role that comes with certain responsibilities—like safeguarding the physical, emotional, and psychological wellbeing of the main character and acting as a parent to that young person. Parents do not sleep with or seduce their children. Full stop. Incest is not only illegal but wildly immoral, destructive, and deeply unhealthy.

Let's say you create an eighteen-year-old main character, who is considered adult in most places and able to consent, and this teen main character falls in love with his or her legal guardian. This will *still* raise serious questions in your audience of when the relationship crossed over from platonic/parental to romantic/sexual in nature. Your audience will wonder if and for how long the guardian or caretaker groomed this young person and will question whether or not this young person truly consented to this relationship at all.

A work-around is to have a main character raised in part or in whole by a guardian or caretaker, have the main character leave home for a long time, have the main character return home much later, fully an adult, and only then begin a romantic relationship with his or her former guardian.

For what it's worth, this isn't an uncommon trope in the historical romance space, largely because young women weren't allowed to manage large estates by themselves and inherited a male guardian anytime they inherited substantial property or wealth. Additionally, young women who were left without means or family were often placed in the care of a guardian to provide a dowry and get them safely married off.

At any rate, the responsibility is going to fall on your love interest —the guardian or caretaker—to stay completely away from the main character romantically until the main character is of an age and maturity to be able to decide for himself or herself if a romantic relationship is of interest to him or her.

It almost always needs to be the main character who initiates a change in the relationship from parental to romantic to avoid the appearance of having been manipulated into a relationship by an older, more experienced adult.

This, then, leaves you with the problem of explaining why your main character isn't attracted to someone closer to himself or herself in age, and why he or she finds a parental figure romantically and/or sexually attractive.

This sort of attraction generally signals massive emotional trauma or psychological wounds in your main character that need to be healed...not indulged in and acted out. Psychologists are unanimous that there is rarely healing to be found in leaning into a deeply self-destructive behavior.

Freud's Oedipus complex suggests that a male child may, at around the age of four, be sexually attracted to his mother and resent his father. (Freud called the female equivalent where female children feel sexual attraction to their father an Electra complex.)

The key point here is that Freud was talking about *four-year-olds*. Not adults. You're going to have to address why your adult or nearly adult main character retains this early childhood impulse and furthermore, acts upon it...with the complicity of the adult parental figure in his or her life.

At a minimum, your couple is going to have to navigate the complicated emotional, psychological, and social taboos regarding their obliteration of parental boundaries that forbid sexual or romantic involvement with one's children.

Again, I get that in historical stories, the guardian or caretaker may be a total stranger the main character, and they've never established any kind of relationship, let alone a parental-style relationship.

While the guardian or caretaker is not the actual parent of your main character, this trope has potential to tread perilously close to incest given that the guardian or caretaker may have already stepped into that parental role for your main character before falling in love with the younger main character.

Of course, it's entirely possible to write a relationship of this type in an ethical, believable, sympathetic, ultimately healthy (or at least healing) way. I'm also sure it's not easy to pull off.

This is one of those tropes where writers may legitimately be describing lived experience and its traumas, and audience members may be revisiting lived experience or learning about such an experience.

It's also entirely possible that this is a fantasy or wish fulfillment story where your audience members are looking for someone to take care of them, guide them, teach them, or take responsibility for initiating a romantic relationship.

That said, it is not okay to normalize adults taking advantage of children nor to normalize the trauma of a parental figure crossing a strongly taboo line with a child who is completely dependent upon that adult and relying on that adult to keep him or her safe from exactly that sort of harm.

At its authentic core, this is a story of acting out a deeply damaged and unhealthy relationship with one's parent figure and with love and sex in general. At its fantasy core, this is a story of being taken care of and having decisions made for you, a return to childlike freedom from agency or responsibility for one's actions.

The key, then, is to find a way to handle this story in an ethical way that models healthy avoidance this type of trauma or healthy healing from it. Or, of course, to write a thorough disclaimer and include trigger warnings in your packaging materials.

ADJACENT TROPES

- Stepsibling/Stepparent Romance
- May-December Romance

. . .

WHY READERS/VIEWERS LOVE THIS TROPE

- it plays out a deeply taboo fantasy that some readers or viewers may have regarding a parental or caretaker figure in their life
- it explores a lived experience some readers or viewers may have and, ideally, models recovery from the trauma of an adult violating this ironclad parental boundary
- someone else older and responsible for me makes all the decisions. A return to childhood when I had no responsibilities and didn't have to make any major decisions

OBLIGATORY SCENES
THE BEGINNING:

The main character was probably in the care of the guardian or caretaker before your story begins, but it's possible that the moment of the main character coming under the care of the guardian/caretaker may be where you start. At a minimum, this moment is probably included in backstory fairly early on in your story. Just be careful not to interrupt your forward pacing by dropping in this information. It's okay not to explain how the main character got a guardian or caretaker immediately. Your audience will be curious, but they'll wait to find out how it all happened if the opening action of the story needs to move forward quickly and seamlessly.

Having established the guardian/caretaker relationship between your main character and the older guardian or caretaker, a spark of romantic attraction is necessary to get your love story rolling. In some cases, this moment of realization, of the shift from parent/child to romantic interests may be where you choose to start your story.

Typically, as soon as the spark of attraction is recognized by one or both of your main characters, whichever one of them spots it (and it can be both of them) will reel back hard from the idea and absolutely refuse to consider such a taboo thing. Act One often ends with a second moment of attraction, perhaps one that crosses another line —a look, a touch, a romantic moment like an embrace or kiss—and causes the first crisis to this wannabe couple.

Your couple may choose to keep their relationship completely secret precisely because they know how everybody will react to it. In this case, Act One may end with the pair nearly being discovered in some sort of compromising situation. This brush with near discovery causes a crisis of "What are we doing? We have to find a way to stop."

THE MIDDLE:

The plot thickens considerably in the middle of this story. All the reasons NOT to get romantically involved rear their ugly heads. The overall wrongness of it, age differences, legal prohibitions, the reactions of everyone around the couple, and so on.

In the middle, you will probably begin to address the traumatic events in the past of both of these characters that have wounded them so badly that they're willing to engage in a violently taboo relationship with each other.

Absolutely everyone around this couple is going to hate this relationship and do everything in their power to break it up. Family members, friends, health professionals, law enforcement—feel free to throw all of them at your couple. For the couple keeping their relationship secret, they have ever closer brushes with being found out. Likewise, the danger of being caught also ratchets up as they continue to learn more of the consequences waiting for them if they're found out.

The more we get to know these two people, the more their traumas, wounds, and pasts will unfold as you peel away layer after layer of emotional and psychological complexity that explains why these two people are falling in love and what they hope to get out of this relationship.

If they've been keeping their relationship secret, Act Two generally ends with the couple being discovered.

If they've been out and proud about their romance, this act usually ends with some terrible consequence of their forbidden relationship being unleashed up them. The guardian/caretaker loses a job or is arrested. The main character is removed from the guardianship or care of the love interest. Some threat is leveled at one of the lovers that forces them apart.

Or, of course, the building release of trauma, emotional pain, and psychological damage finally reaches a crisis point and explodes. Either or both of your lovers may be triggered into a crisis.

BLACK MOMENT:

The lovers are torn apart or have blown apart. Everything they've feared happening has now happened to them. The whole world knows about their taboo romance and is judging them. Everyone around them cannot wait to tell them how bad they've acted, how terrible a choice they've made, and how damaged they both are.

They're physically separated in a way that seems impossible to overcome. One of them may be sent to jail or one of them may be sent away, for example.

Everything they thought they knew about their love for each other seems to have been a lie.

THE END:

The lovers find a way to overcome their physical separation. One may wait for the other to be released after serving a jail sentence. One may find where the other one is and find a way to join him or her.

But most importantly, they must convince each other and the

people around them that they truly, deeply, healthily love each other. They must show themselves, the people around them—and your audience—that this relationship is not based on trauma and unresolved personal issues any longer, that both characters are healed from whatever trauma drove them into this unnatural relationship, and that they have, indeed, found an enduring and real love between two consenting adults.

In most cases, enough people around this pair will never accept the relationship that the couple is likely to move to a new place where nobody knows about their past relationship as guardian/caretaker and ward. Only there, can they find a measure of peace and happiness.

KEY SCENES

- the moment where one or both characters acknowledges that it's both wrong and a terrible idea to get involved and they agree not to pursue any kind of romantic relationship
- the couple is nearly caught by someone who would have a fit if he or she found out the two of them are getting involved
- a quiet moment together where they discover how much they have in common, age difference notwithstanding
- a moment of humor or laughter between the main character and love interest that breaks up the ongoing stress and drama of this relationship
- the first big romantic scene between this couple
- the aftermath of that big romantic encounter, be it guilt, recriminations, secret exultation, even greater fear of getting caught
- some giant complication from outside the couple or between the lovers that neither of them saw coming (for

example, a pregnancy, a physical threat to the guardian,
an investigation, or arrest warrant)
- a moment of emotional healing as a result of this
relationship
- the moment when these two forgive each other for the
hurt they've caused each other

THINGS TO THINK ABOUT WHEN WRITING THIS TROPE

Oy. Where to start...

How did the main character come under the guardianship of the love interest? What past event made the main character parentless? Why was this person appointed as the guardian or caretaker?

Did the guardian/caretaker have a past relationship with the actual parents? If so, what kind? How well did they know one another?

What does the main character think initially of having a guardian/caretaker? What does the main character think of this person specifically?

What kind of relationship do the main character and guardian/caretaker have before any romantic element enters into their relationship?

How old is the main character when your story starts? How old was he or she when the guardian was appointed?

For how long has the guardian/caretaker had a romantic interest in the main character before he or she first expresses it in any way? Has he or she kept it secret from the main character or not? Why?

Has the main character had a secret crush or romantic interest in the guardian/caretaker before the first romantic spark? For how long? Has he or she kept it secret from the guardian or not? Why?

What moment triggers the first romantic spark between these two people? Why now? How do they each react to it?

Who declares it wrong and a terrible idea first? Does the other character agree or not?

What moment triggers a second romantic spark? How do they both react to this? Do they keep fighting the attraction?

When does one or both of the main characters start to give in to the mutual attraction?

Will they keep their relationship secret? Why or why not?

Who around this couple knows about the budding romance? How do they react to it? Do they tell others? Why or why not?

How enraged are the people around this couple as they find out about the taboo romance?

What consequences await one or both of these characters if their relationship is discovered? How can you make those potential consequences worse? How can you make them even worse than that?

What personal conflicts between these two people cause them to disagree, argue, or have friction between them?

What do they legitimately have in common?

What do they find attractive in each other?

How far apart are these two characters in age? What disconnects does this cause between them? How will they overcome their age difference and disconnects?

What breaks up this couple? What external plot problem becomes a crisis that tears them apart? What relationship problem between them builds to a crisis that tears them apart?

What consequences land upon them both when they're found out? Will they avoid suffering those consequences or will they have to go all the way through those consequences before they can be together?

What lessons do they learn from being together? What lessons do they each learn after being torn apart?

What lessons do they each need to learn before they can engage in a healthy, consensual relationship as two adults? How will they learn these lessons?

How will they overcome the last remaining obstacle(s) to being together?

Do they have things to forgive each other for before they can be together? If so, what?

Will one or both of them make some sort of grand gesture to the other to demonstrate their love? If so, what?

Will any or some of the people around them ultimately accept their relationship? If so, who? Why? What changes to make the relationship acceptable to those who do come around to being okay with it?

Will the couple go to a new place to start their long-term life together? If so, where? Why that place?

TROPE TRAPS

Skirting too close to incest.

Not addressing how truly different people are when their ages are very different and not addressing the disconnects between them.

Creating a love interest that has secretly desired the child main character in a gross and inappropriate way for a long time before coming out and admitting that he or she is attracted to the main character.

The love interest has groomed the main character and taken away the main character's consent.

Creating a guardian/caretaker your audience despises for being a creep.

Creating a main character who's so horny for a much older adult parent figure that your audience despises him or her for being a predator, narcissist, or worse.

Creating a main character who's not old enough or mature enough to make an informed decision regarding engaging in this relationship.

You, the writer, not realizing what grooming is and having your guardian/caretaker engage in it without realizing you're doing so.

Not addressing why the main character is attracted to a parental figure. Not addressing the trauma or mental health issues implicit in this attraction.

Not addressing why the love interest is attracted to a minor or at least a much younger person whom they've assumed a parental role toward. Not addressing the trauma or mental health issues implicit in this attraction.

Normalizing incest or near incest.

Normalizing abuse of a child by the person responsible for keeping him or her safe.

Failing to create appropriately awful consequences for the guardian/caretaker for violating the parent/child relationship boundary. Failing to enforce those consequences.

Failing to create real and lasting consequences for the main character entering into a forbidden relationship and staying in it once it's made clear to him or her that it's wrong on every level.

Failing to in any way address the traumas and emotional damage of these wounded characters.

Failing to do your research on how such wounds are treated and healed by psychological and medical professionals and incorporating ethical and healthy techniques and means of healing and growth for these two characters.

Having the characters around your romantic couple accept the taboo relationship far too readily.

GUARDIAN/CARETAKER TROPE IN ACTION
Movies:

- I was unable to find any movies that explored a guardian falling in love with his or her ward or vice versa

Books:

- Unconditional by Q.B. Tyler
- Castles by Julie Garwood
- The Protégé by Brianna Hale
- Minx by Julia Quinn
- Regency Buck by Georgette Heyer
- Once and Always by Judith McNaught
- Forbidden Love by Karen Robards
- Dangerous Temptation by Giana Darling
- Seducing My Guardian by Katee Robert

14

IN LOVE WITH THE WRONG PERSON

DEFINITION

This trope is a specific variation upon the classic love triangle story (in which your main character meets two possible love interests relatively simultaneously, builds parallel relationships at the same time, and then has to choose one over the other).

In this version, the love interest is already in love, or at least thinks he's or she's in love with someone. Small problem: a second potential lover enters the picture to give competition to the existing romantic relationship and to challenge the notion that the love interest is with whom he or she is meant to be with, or whom he or she is best-suited to be with, or whom he or she loves the most.

Over the course of this story, two people fight for the love of the third person. One of them has a distinctive advantage over the other by being in an existing relationship.

In this version of the love triangle, the interloper has a tough job to do to convince the love interest to dump an existing lover and to take a chance on a newer, less established relationship with him or her.

Like any love triangle, discussing the various lovers and partners can be confusing, so let's clarify the terminology I'll use when discussing this trope.

The **main character** is what I'll call the person who falls in love with the love interest and tries to break up the existing romantic relationship. While you may ultimately choose to tell your story primarily or completely from the point of view of the love interest—or even the partner about to get dumped—we need to label the three people in this love triangle in a way that won't drive us all crazy, so go with me, here. The main character is the interloper who will break up the existing relationship.

The main character's inner journey is often characterized by self-doubt or even guilt as he or she sets out to make the person they love miserable and force, coerce, or convince the love interest to break up with the partner. The main character may experience guilt over causing the partner pain and loss. The main character may question if his or her own happiness is worth the pain he or she will cause both the love interest and partner.

The **love interest** is the person who's already in love—or believes himself or herself to be in love—with the wrong person. This character's journey is often the most fraught emotionally as he or she loses (or destroys) one relationship while simultaneously falling in love and trying to build a new and high-risk relationship. Also, this is the character who's typically torn apart on the horns of the dilemma of who to choose.

The **partner** is the third corner of our love triangle. This is the "wrong" person with whom your love interest will start the story in love with. This is the person who ultimately must move aside, be dumped, or be eliminated altogether for the main character and love interest to end up together.

I'll reiterate, you can tell your story from the point of view of any of these characters or from some combination of them all. Also, you can choose to have the main character already be in love with the love interest before your story starts and have never acted upon those feelings or having been rejected in the past by the love interest. Or you can structure your story so the main character and love interest meet in the beginning of your story and commence challenging the relationship between the love interest and partner.

With me so far?

Your main character may be the one who clearly sees the flaws in the partner and that the partner will never make the love interest happy in the long run. He or she may spend much of the story trying to convince the love interest of this or scheming to show the love interest that the partner is not the one for them.

Your main character ultimately has two goals. First, he or she must effectively break up the love interest and partner. Second, he or she must convince the love interest to fall in love with him or her. These two goals contrast sharply with each other: one is destructive in nature, and one is constructive. There's a certain darkness in setting out to break up a long-term relationship, even if the main character is absolutely certain it's the best thing for the love interest.

This trope is frequently paired with another trope that explains why the main character and love interest aren't already together. If your main character and love interest already know each other and the main character already has feelings for the love interest, tropes like Commitment Phobia, a Bad Boy/Girl, Oblivious to Love, Feuding Families, Forbidden Love, may explain why the main character and love interest missed getting love right the first time around.

Tropes like Damaged Hero/Heroine, Plain Jane/John, or Only One Not Married may explain why your love interest has settled for love with someone who's not exactly right for him or her.

Tropes like Lone Wolf Tamed, Dangerous Past, False Identity, or even Back from the Dead may explain why your main character is just coming onto the scene of your story now and why he or she hasn't crossed the path of the love interest before now.

Before we move on in our analysis of this trope, I should also point out that the nature of the relationship between the love interest and partner at the beginning of your story isn't limited to the two of them just being in love. **They can already be engaged or even married in this trope.**

But for the sake of fitting on the page, I didn't name this, In Love/In a Committed or Long-Term Relationship/Engaged/Married to the Wrong Person Trope.

ADJACENT TROPES

- Love Triangle
- Right Under Your Nose
- Stop the Wedding
- Unrequited Love

WHY READERS/VIEWERS LOVE THIS TROPE

- sadly, this trope may speak to people who have settled for less-than-ideal love. Your audience may fantasize about a perfect mate coming along to rescue them from their less than perfect current partner
- having two awesome people both in love with you and determined to have you
- instead of having to pick between bad and less bad, your romantic choices range from good to great
- choosing right this time around in matters of love
- he or she loves you enough to fight for you

OBLIGATORY SCENES
THE BEGINNING:
The whole purpose of the beginning of this story type is to estab-

lish the love triangle. You'll show the main character meeting—or reuniting with—his or her future love interest. We'll see love interest interacting with the partner and you'll establish what their relationship is like.

You'll establish the attraction by the main character toward the love interest, who may or may not experience or acknowledge a reciprocal spark of attraction initially.

You may want to show a fly in the ointment of the love interest-partner relationship right away and establish that their relationship has some deep and fatal flaw. The audience will probably recognize it to be a fatal flaw right away, but your love interest may not...yet.

You may choose to let the new relationship between main character and love interest develop in secret throughout the beginning of your story. They may fight its development. The love interest is probably not going to want to reveal it to the existing partner or to anyone else, yet. This may be one of the earliest sources of conflict between the main character and love interest, in fact (other than the obvious conflict of the love interest fighting against getting into a relationship at all with the main character).

The love interest, who's approaching being in love with two people, is going to be thrown into enormous personal, emotional turmoil.

It's possible to end your first act with a declaration of attraction or even love from the main character and possibly a declaration of his or her intention to break up the existing couple.

OR

Your first act may end with a declaration by the love interest that he or she is NOT breaking up with the partner to be with the main character.

OR

Your first act may end with the partner chastising the love interest, declaring intent to fight to keep the existing relationship, or declaring that he or she is NOT going to step aside gracefully so the main character can move in on the love interest.

OR

Someone outside the love triangle may declare that the love interest MUST go through with or stay with the existing relationship with the partner regardless of the love interest's feelings for the main character.

What all of these possible endings of Act One have in common is the love triangle has been revealed to at least two of the three parties, and a crisis has been initiated in the existing relationship or in the newly developing relationship.

The trope is complex enough that it's not always necessary to build an intricate external plot to go along with the love triangle and all its complications. However, whatever external story you construct will undoubtedly have a major element that causes the love interest to want or need to remain with the partner and that may have serious negative consequences for the love interest and/or the main character if the love interest breaks up with the partner. Any potential stakes arising from your external plot are probably made clear by the end of Act One.

THE MIDDLE:

Simply put, in the middle of your story, complications ensue.

If you haven't revealed the new relationship to the existing partner yet, it will certainly happen in Act Two. As soon as this happens, a fight for the love of and possession of the love interest will ensue. This fight may play out in private interactions between the love interest and each of his or her suitors individually, or it may play out in a very public way.

The plot of your story builds, making the love interest's choice of who to be with MUCH harder. Friends, family, coworkers, and other outside characters will try to push the love interest to stay with the original partner or to choose the new lover, depending on each of their agendas and motivations within the story.

The entire middle of this story is the push-pull of all the involved individuals upon the love triangle. The main character must start to deal with the internal and external fallout of his or her decision to pursue having the love interest for himself or herself. The love interest dithers about his or her decision of which lover to choose. He or she may be drowning in guilt, doubt, uncertainty, fear, and a host of other emotions. The partner may be wrestling with rage, insecurity, betrayal and more, as well.

Act Two typically ends with the love triangle breaking under the accumulated pressures and stresses placed upon it.

The love interest may break up with the partner. Or the love interest may break up with the new lover (the main character). The love interest may break up with both of them. The love interest may try to find a way to have both lovers or at least keep both lovers happy.

The partner may get fed up and walk away from the existing relationship—taking his or her toys, money, protection, power, resources with him or her. Likewise, the new lover may have his or her arm twisted, be threatened, or get fed up with the love interest's inability/refusal to choose him or her and may walk away.

Lastly, external characters or the external plot itself may break up one or both relationships.

BLACK MOMENT:

Interestingly enough, the black moment in this trope isn't always the failure of the relationship between the main character and the love interest. It's also possible that the love interest loses BOTH relationships and is left completely alone, or that the love interest is going to have to stay with the partner.

Depending on whose point of view and emotional journey you choose to focus on in writing your story, that will likely determine what your black moment looks like. If you've told your tale primarily from the main character's point of view, the black moment will probably revolve around the love interest choosing to stay with the partner.

If you tell your story primarily from the point of view of the partner, the love interest probably chooses the main character as the partner's black moment.

If you tell your story from the point of view of the love interest, he or she probably loses the main character who is ultimately his or her true love/best choice. The love interest may or may not end up staying with the partner. If the love interest doesn't love the partner by this point in the story, being forced to stay with him or her could actually be a worse outcome than losing both the main character and losing the partner and being left alone.

THE END:

Your main character may be the prime mover in doing what it takes to be with the love interest, or it may be the love interest who has to take drastic action to end up with the main character. Or the two of them may have to work in parallel or together to get the love interest away from the partner so the two of them can be together.

In some cases, the love interest may have already left the partner, but the external plot of your story may be the thing keeping the main character and love interest apart, now. This external force or event keeping the main character and love interest apart may be what the two characters must work individually or together to overcome.

You'll want to think about the order in which you solve the lovers' various obstacles to being together. The general rule is you want to solve the easier problems first and save the biggest, most emotional obstacle—the one your audience is the most worried about—to solve last.

If you've done your job as a writer, your audience is by far the most engaged with the personal, emotional obstacles to love (as opposed to some political treaty, marriage bargain, terms of a will, or whatever external obstacle has helped tear your lovers apart).

So, your ending will probably be structured to solve any external obstacles first, and only then for the love interest to finally break away from the partner or finally resolve his or her guilt, doubts, or other issues that prevent him or her from being with the main character forever and without reservations.

The main character may have to make a grand apology or some sort of grand plea to the love interest to get him or her to finally see his or her true feelings or to get the love interest to forgive self or forgive the main character.

Both of these characters may have things to apologize for: the main character for breaking up an existing relationship and upending the love interest's life and the love interest for choosing wrong in the first place or for choosing to stay with the partner long after he or she should've walked away from the partner.

Both of these characters have been through an emotional wringer in this trope (and your audience along with them), and your audience is definitely going to want at least a glimpse of your long-suffering couple getting a passionate kiss, a moment of true joy, or even a quick look at this couple's life a few weeks or months down the road as they're getting or settling into their happily ever after.

KEY SCENES

- the love interest tells the main character about the partner and his or her existing relationship with the partner

- the main character puts the love interest in a position that would be compromising if they were caught
- the love interest initially rejects the advances of the main character
- the partner almost catches the main character and love interest together
- the partner does catch the main character and love interest together
- the partner confronts the love interest about the main character or at least about his or her flagging affection, attention, or loyalty
- the love interest renews his or her commitment to the partner (possibly in the presence of the main character)
- a stolen kiss
- a stolen love scene (or whatever the maximum level of heat in your story is)
- the love interest has to go back to the partner (possibly romantically) after being romantic with the main character
- the partner confronts the main character or vice versa
- the big fight between the partner and main character
- the big breakup scene
- the big makeup scene

THINGS TO THINK ABOUT WHEN WRITING THIS TROPE

What is the nature of the relationship between the love interest and partner when your story begins? Are they dating? Living together? Engaged? Contracted in some business, political, or personal way? Married? Are there children?

Why did the love interest agree to be with the partner? What does he or she see in the partner that made the love interest choose to be with this person? Is this thing still true?

Does the main character already know and love the love interest or will the main character first meet and fall for the love interest within the current action of your story?

If the main character walks into your story already loving the love interest, why didn't he or she make a declaration of love in the past? Or did the declaration happen and get rejected? Why?

What about the relationship between the love interest and partner is fatally flawed? How does the main character first see this fatal flaw(s)? Does the love interest already see the flaw(s)? If so, why is the love interest staying with the partner?

Does the partner have some non-love hold over the love interest that compels him or her to stay in the relationship whether or not they have any feelings at all for the partner? If so, what is it?

If the love interest doesn't already know the relationship with the partner is terribly flawed, how will the main character show this to the love interest? Will he or she point it out to the love interest? Will the main character manipulate the partner into revealing a fatal flaw about himself or herself in front of the love interest? Something else?

What positive or loving feelings does the love interest have for the partner now? What negative feelings and dislikes does the love interest have for the partner now?

How does the main character measure up to the partner? In what ways is the main character a better person? In what ways is the main character a worse person? When and how does the love interest see both of these?

How will the main character woo the love interest? Will he or she flirt openly? Secretly steal intimate moments together?

Who around the main character and love interest is aware of their budding relationship and/or stolen moments together? What do these people think of the new relationship?

How does your external plot put pressure on the love interest to stay with the partner? How can you increase that pressure? How can you make it all but impossible for the love interest to leave the partner? How can you make it truly impossible?

At what point does the love interest realize he or she loves the main character? How does he or she feel about that? How does he or she react?

How does the main character feel about the partner? How does he or she feel about breaking up the love interest and partner?

Why isn't the main character a bad guy for moving in on an existing relationship and blowing it up?

Why isn't the love interest a bad guy for dumping the partner with whom he or she is in a committed, serious relationship in which promises may already have been made?

How does the partner find out about the affair or near affair the love interest is involved in with the main character? How does the partner react? What does the partner do in response?

When and how does the relationship between the main character and love interest go public? How do people around them react?

What consequences are triggered by the relationship going public? (These may come from your external plot, from the partner, or from someone else with power, money, or influence over the love interest or main character or both.

What arguments occur and conflicts build between the main character and love interest as their relationship develops?

What arguments occur and conflicts build between the partner and love interest as their relationship crumbles?

Who chooses wrong in your black moment?

Who breaks up with or walks away from whom?

Who will solve the big external plot problem keeping the main character and love interest apart and how?

What happens to the partner to remove him or her as an obstacle?

Who will apologize to whom and for what in the end?

Who forgives whom for what?

How will your audience be dead sure the love interest is all in on this relationship and won't abandon the main character when someone better comes along down the road?

What does happily ever after look like for this couple?

TROPE TRAPS

Your love interest can't make up his or her mind and drives your audience crazy with his or her inability to make the obvious right choice.

Your main character is unlikable for moving in on an otherwise fine relationship and breaking it up so he or she can selfishly have the person he or she wants.

Your partner is so decent, honorable and nice (or hot) that your audience roots for the love interest to stay with him or her instead of the main character.

The partner is so awful the audience doesn't buy the love interest having stayed with this terrible person until now (in the absence of some non-love-based hold the partner has over the love interest).

The main character is seen as wimpy or indecisive for never telling the love interest that he or she has been in love with him or her for all this time.

The main character is seen as a jerk for waiting until the love interest is finally happy with someone else to move in on the love interest and try to win the love interest for himself or herself.

The main character and love interest are both perceived as jerks (and being horribly selfish) for not honoring the promises already made between the love interest and partner.

The external plot doesn't create any consequences for the love interest walking away from the partner.

The love interest is mean or even cruel in dumping (and devastating) the partner to be with the person he or she wants to be with.

The love interest is unlikable for not knowing what he or she wants and needs from love and getting into a relationship with a flawed partner or for settling for a flawed partner

The main character and partner get so wrapped up in fighting over the love interest that it becomes more about winning their fight than about true love.

Both the main character and love interest don't suffer enough emotionally for having engaged in infidelity.

Unless you're planning a sequel to deal with him or her, the partner doesn't leave the picture in a way that assures your audience he or she won't be back to cause trouble down the road.

The main character and/or love interest don't offer a sincere apology for putting the other one through hell, and thus don't deserve or earn the other person in the eyes of your audience.

You don't sufficiently convince your audience that this couple will stick together forever. They came together in infidelity...either one of them could go there again unless you make it very clear they're truly in love and are truly soul mates.

IN LOVE WITH THE WRONG PERSON TROPE IN ACTION
Movies:

- Anna Karenina
- The Devil Wears Prada
- Dr. Zhivago
- The Wedding Planner
- Call Me By Your Name
- Grease
- Pretty in Pink
- The Wedding Singer

Books:

- Anna Karenina by Leo Tolstoy
- Texas Destiny by Lorraine Heath
- Lit by Mary Karr
- Loving the Wrong Man by Mia Black
- What Price Paradise by Katherine Allred
- Suddenly Forbidden by Ella Fields
- Melt For You by J.T. Geissinger

15

INSTANT FAMILY

DEFINITION

We could debate whether this trope belongs in a volume of hook tropes or even external plot tropes, but for the sake of keeping the four volumes of universal romance tropes relatively similar in length, I opted to put this trope into the backstory volume. My thought process was that the main character in this trope has no family in his or her past. The appearance of an instant family in his or her life now is life-changing event to which he or she must adapt. At any rate...

In this trope one or both of the main characters, who have until now been without family or without this type of family, inherit or come into possession of a family all of a sudden. Then, he or she must adapt to having, typically, an instant child that thrusts the main character into a parental role completely without warning.

For the sake of readability in this write-up, I'll talk only in terms of a single child, but it's entirely possible the main character's instant family includes multiple children.

Even parents who have planned for, waited for, and prepared thoroughly for their first child will tell you that the transition from being not-parent to parent is enormous and causes tectonic shifts in your life. It's this shift that forms the backbone of the instant family trope.

In this story, the adjustment from non-family person to family person is a source of stress, conflict, and challenge to both the main character individually and to the budding romantic relationship between the main character and the love interest.

In this trope, the love interest may be one of the instant family members in the form of a surprise co-parent and may be the source of the child that transforms the main character into an instant parent.

OR

The main character may come into instant (surprise) responsibility for a child, and the love interest may enter the picture as someone who steps in to help the main character deal with his or her instant family and to help care for the child who's unexpectedly dropped into the main character's life.

In this trope, the instant family is usually a surprise. While the main character may be aware that he or she is a designated guardian for a child, in the case of both parents' deaths for example, the main character doesn't expect to ever become an instant parent.

It's possible the main character chooses to take on an instant family. For example, the main character may abruptly choose to foster or adopt a child. It's worth noting that the process of becoming a legal foster parent or adoptive parent is generally long and arduous and would negate the whole element of instant-ness.

Government entities in some places might, in an unusual case, plausibly designate your main character as an emergency caregiver. You'll need to research the legalities and circumstances in which that might happen in the specific location you've chosen for your story.

This story is always filled with the ups and downs of adjusting to family life and with the stresses and strains parenthood has upon the budding relationship that forms the core of your romance.

While this trope is a strong candidate for humor and romantic comedy, it can also revolve around the aftermath of a terrible tragedy that forced the formation of a new, instant family. It can also revolve around danger, typically to the child and/or instant co-parent or "spouse" for whom the main character has taken respon-sibility.

While this trope is most known for a carefree, single adult inher-iting a child, it's also possible that the main character is surprised with assuming responsibility for an adult—for example, a soldier, whose best friend has died, is asked to protect and look after the friend's endangered widow.

In the case of inheriting an adult as instant family, you'll need to create compelling reasons for:

- why the main character and this future love interest MUST stay together over the course of your story
- why they must imitate or approximate a (married) couple
- why the adult love interest cannot take care of himself or herself right now
- why the main character must assume responsibility for this adult
- in what way the main character must take care of the inherited adult who's going to grow into the love interest.

It's not uncommon in this trope to have a pre-existing boyfriend or girlfriend to the main character who acts as a foil to the instant family and to the romance with the love interest attached to the instant family.

This pre-existing boyfriend or girlfriend acts as a reminder of the family-less life the main character has lost, pushes the main character to get rid of the instant family, constantly reminds the main character that this instant family is only temporary, and ultimately forces the main character to choose between his or her old life without family or a new life with the instant family.

At its core, this story is about sacrifice—that is, putting the wellbeing of others above your own (or at least putting their needs before yours).

ADJACENT TROPES

- Baby On the Doorstep
- Lone Wolf Tamed
- Single Parent
- Secret Baby
- Is the Baby Mine

WHY READERS/VIEWERS LOVE THIS TROPE

- we'd all like to get the messy, impossible transition to parenthood right
- who doesn't get a kick out of watching a big, strong macho man or a confident, badass female brought to their knees by an adorable toddler or moody teen
- if something happened to us, we would want someone to care enough to step in and raise our kids and give it their all
- if my kids and I were in terrible trouble, I would want someone just like the main character to step in and rescue us
- for the parents in your audience, relishing the fantasy of dumping our kids on someone else to deal with for a little while
- the fantasy of having someone we love realize and acknowledge just how hard what we've been doing as parents day in and day out really is

. . .

OBLIGATORY SCENES
THE BEGINNING:

We may see the family-less main character going about a slice of his or her daily life and liking it just the way it is before an instant family is dumped on him or her...or you may choose to start your story with the moment in which an instant family is sprung on your main character. In almost all cases, the instant family is a total surprise to the main character. Even if the possibility of inheriting an instant family was known to the main character, the actuality of a child, children, and/or spouse showing up comes as a shock.

It's one thing to imagine having an instant family. It's another thing entirely to experience it for real.

The main character may initially resist accepting responsibility for his or her instant family. But the circumstances ultimately make it impossible for the main character to walk away from this family in need.

If the love interest is part of the instant family—a parent or care-giver of the child(ren)—the main character and love interest are immediately thrown into a role of co-parenting that may look and feel a lot like an instant marriage. Romantic sparks may fly right away, or friction and stress may be the order of the day in the beginning for this couple.

If the love interest is NOT a member of the instant family, the love interest arrives on scene or is recruited by the main character very early in your story to assist him or her in dealing with this instant family crisis. The main character may intend to foist off care of the instant family entirely upon the love interest...but the love interest won't put up with that for long. The love interest and main character find themselves functioning as co-parents of the child or children, and very quickly, their relationship starts to feel like a marriage part-nership.

. . .

THE MIDDLE:

The middle of this story is always punctuated by the struggles, successes and failures of being a parent. There's plenty of room for humor as the main character has to go overnight from zero to full-throttle parent. The child upends the main character's adult life in unexpected ways, both good and bad. If the main character had a dating life, that's imploded by the arrival of a child.

If the main character already had a romantic relationship, it may also implode. If this pre-existing boyfriend or girlfriend is going to end up being the love interest, he or she will also struggle with the transition to parent. The insertion of children into the relationship will certainly threaten to destroy it completely.

Typically, however, a pre-existing boyfriend or girlfriend will ultimately abandon the main character. The love interest will usually come as part of the instant family or as part of caring for the instant family.

If there is a pre-existing boyfriend or girlfriend in your story, he or she causes increasing problems as the story progresses. The instant family, be it a child or an adult or both, may overtly or covertly attempt to sabotage the main character's relationship with a pre-existing boyfriend or girlfriend.

The main character and love interest gradually find a rhythm of being together. They may learn how to be parents together. They may learn how to spend time together with the child and develop a romantic relationship. A child may throw the main character and love interest together intentionally.

In the middle of the story, the small daily issues of dealing with an instant family start to smooth out, often after a series of hilarious catastrophes. However, the larger problems of assuming a permanent parental or spousal role are continuing to grow in the background. A custody battle may be brewing. A danger to the instant family may be drawing nearer. The main character may be facing pressure at work or from a pre-existing boyfriend or girlfriend to get rid of the instant family that's distracting the main character from other responsibilities or commitments.

If the love interest is not part of the instant family but is, instead, a caregiver the main character has brought in to help deal with the family, the love interest will typically be completely accepted by the instant family and become an integral part of it before the black moment tears the main character away from the family.

As the costs and sacrifices of being an instant family man or woman mount, the main character approaches a crisis wherein he or she will have to choose to commit to his or her instant family forever or abandon them.

The external plot of your story also builds toward a crisis that probably exacerbates the difficulty of the main character's dilemma. Does he or she return to his or her old life or stay with this new and challenging life with the instant family?

All the frictions, conflicts, misunderstandings, and problems that the instant family brought with it finally boil over into a major confrontation or crisis.

BLACK MOMENT:

The main character chooses to walk away from his or her instant family.

OR

The instant family chooses to walk away from the main character.

OR

The main character loses the instant family because of outside events that he or she has failed to avert.

If the love interest was an outside caregiver who has been integrated into the family through the middle of the story, he or she definitely chooses to stay with the family the main character has abandoned. Thus, in the act of walking away from his or her instant family, the main character has also walked away from the love interest and destroyed that relationship, too.

In every case, the main character is devastated by the loss of his or her new family and realizes too late that he or she has well and truly fallen in love with the instant family. Moreover, in the act of walking away from the family, the main character has also abandoned and betrayed the person he or she loves.

The main character is well and truly alone once more. Except now, he or she knows what life *not* alone is like, and returning to his or her lonely existence is not only unsatisfying now, but devastatingly awful.

The black moment may result from some sort of ultimatum being delivered to the main character. Dump the kid or the boyfriend/girlfriend will break up and walk away. Dump the family or lose your job. Stop taking time off work to pick up the kid from school or spend time with the kid or lose the big promotion at work.

The black moment may come when the main character fails to protect the instant family from some threat. The instant "spouse" or child may be kidnapped. The state takes away the child that the main character has been trying to prove he or she is capable of parenting. A distant relative or absent parent shows up to claim the child.

The main character, having lost the instant family (and possibly having regained his or her old life), realizes that the one thing he or she wants above all else is the family back.

THE END:

The main character makes one last, Herculean effort to get back his or her family. This typically involves not only solving the external plot problem that has threatened the family's ability to stay together but also involves the main character having to win back his or her instant—and now lost—family. The main character usually makes a grand gesture to the family itself to prove just how much he or she loves the child and/or adult instant family member(s).

The main character may need to rescue the family before he or she can be with them again. In this case, the rescue itself may serve as the grand gesture that proves his or her love and commitment to the family. Even in this scenario, though, you'll probably need to have your main character make a grand declaration of love and devotion to the family.

The family member(s) need to forgive the main character for abandoning the family, and the family needs to fully and finally accept the main character as a permanent part of the family unit.

If the love interest is separate from the family members, the love interest must also forgive the main character and accept him or her into the family.

The story ends with the family finally together for good and the main character and love interest happily together.

KEY SCENES

- the moment the main character meets the child or adult he or she has inherited
- a moment when the family catastrophically messes up something in the main character's previous, family-less world. This can be a disaster at work, a ruined date, a destroyed house, and so forth
- the first time the main character has a tender moment with the child or adult—a hug, a thank you, a bedtime story and tuck-in, a sweet moment that first pierces the main character's emotional armor. And you may build in more than one of these moments

- a friend or family member of the beleaguered main character commiserates and/or gives the main character advice about parenting or marital relationships
- the main character and love interest finally get a quiet moment to themselves to discover or explore the romantic spark between them
- the main character almost but not quite admits to self or to an instant family member that he or she is learning to like or even love having a family
- the main character gets something disastrously wrong and narrowly avoids a disaster to the child or adult he or she is responsible for
- the big romantic moment between the main character and love interest that seriously tempts the main character to permanently embrace this instant family
- a big fight that nearly breaks up the main character and love interest

THINGS TO THINK ABOUT WHEN WRITING THIS TROPE

What are the circumstances around the main character suddenly inheriting or acquiring an instant family?

What is the makeup of the instant family? Just an adult? One child? More than one child? What age(s) of child?

What does the main character's family-less life look like? How would a family disrupt this life?

Why does the main character not have a family already? Is there an event or trauma in his or her past that makes the main character afraid of having a family?

What scares the main character to death about being a parent?

Who is the love interest? Is he or she part of the instant family that shows up in the main character's life, or is the love interest someone else?

If the main character recruits the eventual love interest to help care for the instant family, who is the love interest? What's his or her role in helping out?

Does the main character already know the love interest? If so, how did the main character and love interest meet? What's their relationship before the story starts?

What external plot problem is going to threaten to tear the instant family apart?

Based on the age of the child, what parenting catastrophes will the main character experience? Will any of them be dangerous to the child? How will the main character react to his or her mistake(s)?

How does the child or adult instant family member feel about the main character when they first meet? How about as they get to know each other?

Will the instant family resist falling in love with the main character or not? Why? How?

Is there a pre-existing boyfriend of girlfriend to the main character? How does he or she react to the arrival of the instant family? How will he or she interfere with, sabotage, or threaten the instant family? Will the instant family try to sabotage him or her in return? If so, how?

What will ultimately break up the main character and the pre-existing boyfriend or girlfriend?

What external event(s) breaks apart the main character and the instant family?

What personal problems, conflicts, traumas, or issues break apart the main character and the instant family? Who walks away from whom?

What does the main character's life look like after he or she abandons the instant family? Does it go back to exactly the way it was before, or is his or her life different now?

What moment, object, or event makes the main character realize just how terribly he or she misses the instant family?

What lessons does the main character have to learn about family and about himself or herself before he or she can earn back their lost family? What do these lessons teach the main character about his or her life? Do these lessons resolve some past trauma in the main character's life?

What does the main character have to do to get the instant family back? Is there an external plot problem to solve first? If so, what, and how will he or she overcome it?

What does the main character have to do to earn the forgiveness of the instant family?

What does the main character have to do to earn the forgiveness of the love interest?

What does the main character's new life look like with the family firmly ensconced in it?

What does happily ever after look like for this newly formed family?

TROPE TRAPS

Failing to create a compelling reason why the main character has to completely disrupt his or her life by taking on an instant family.

Not creating a strong reason why the instant family must stay with the main character specifically and not seek shelter or care elsewhere.

Creating a main character who's initially so unlikable or selfish that the audience won't stick around long enough to see this person become worthy of having a family.

Creating a child who's so consistently awful that no reasonable adult would tolerate the child's behavior and would take action to discipline the child or seek counseling for the child.

Creating a child who's so consistently adorable that no real child would act that way ALL the time. Every kid has bad moments now and then.

The behaviors of the children in the story are wildly inappropriate for their age. That said, most little kids tend to act MUCH wiser than their years in these types of stories. Your audience will forgive you to some degree...but be careful not to push the boundaries of believability too much with your children's dialogue and observations.

Failing to address the trauma of loss and grief the instant family members are going through.

Ignoring the legalities of custody and of when state agencies would intervene to take custody of a child and provide care.

In the case of an adult instant family member, having that adult fall in love WAY too quickly with the main character. This adult has just experienced a major trauma or loss that has thrust him or her into the protection, care, or responsibility of the main character. He or she is in no headspace to fall head over heels in love with anyone...at least not in a healthy way.

The main character doesn't have to work hard enough or risk enough or sacrifice enough to get back his or her family, and the audience doesn't think he or she deserves to get back the family.

The instant family forgives the main character way too easily for walking away and abandoning it in the black moment.

The main character doesn't have to sacrifice enough to earn back the instant family.

The main character doesn't do enough to plausibly regain the trust of the instant family members in the end.

INSTANT-FAMILY TROPE IN ACTION
Movies:

- Three Men and a Baby
- Instant Family

- We're the Millers
- Big Daddy
- Life As We Know It
- Blended
- Daddy's Home

Books:

- Sustained by Emma Chase
- Sunrise Point by Robyn Carr
- Things We Never Got Over by Lucy Score
- Heartless by Elsie Silver
- Tattered by Devney Perry
- Prickly Romance by Nia Arthurs
- Noxx by Tasha Black
- Securing Piper by Susan Stoker
- Finding Home by Emilia Finn
- Private Property by Skye Warren
- The Governess of Penwythe Hall by Sarah E. Ladd
- Hold You Close by Corinne Michaels and Melanie Harlow

16

IS THE BABY MINE

DEFINITION

Because a baby is conceived before this trope begins, this trope pretty inevitably involves a man and a woman...unless you're writing some sort of paranormal or alternate reality where conception doesn't require a male and female participant. In which case, ignore the pronouns in this write-up and insert whatever ones work for your story.

At any rate, the heroine in this trope is either pregnant or has a baby/child when the story begins whom the hero has reason to suspect may be his child.

This trope differs from the Secret Baby trope in that the Secret Baby has been intentionally kept secret from the father of the child. In this trope, the mother may not have gone out of her way to hide the child, but for some reason, the father left the picture before the pregnancy was discovered or before the child was born and simply hasn't been around to find out the mother had a child.

This trope often follows a casual relationship or one-night-stand where a baby resulted, but the mother has no reason to believe the birth father will be interested in the child or willing to participate in the child's care.

That said, the heroine may approach the hero in this trope with the news that he's going to be a father, and he may doubt that he's the father.

OR

The heroine may have had a baby she didn't tell the hero about either because she wasn't in contact with him or he physically left. The hero discovers by accident or someone other means that a woman he slept with has a child...and when he counts back, they were together about nine months before her child was born.

The father may then approach the mother to demand to know the parentage of her child. SIDE NOTE: It's deeply cliché in this version of the trope for the child to look *just like* the father. The mother may admit that the father indeed is the father, or she may deny it.

Regardless of how the father finds out about a baby and asks, "Is the baby mine?", fallout ensues:

- A fight may follow over DNA testing to determine parentage.
- There may be a custody battle.
- There may a fight over child support.
- The father may or may not want to or be readily able to step into a parental role for some reason.
- The father may be very wealthy and suspect the mother is trying to trap him into marriage, or at least into hefty child support.
- The mother may not want to share the child with the father.
- The father may have an important reason he needs or wants to acknowledge the child as his...that the mother may or may not want to go along with.

- The parents may or may not like or even really know each other.
- The parents may or may not want to form any long-term relationship (romantic or otherwise) for the sake of the child.
- The parents may or may not have any interest in pursuing or renewing a romantic relationship initially.

Whatever obstacles you choose to put in the way of the mother and father of the child, the end result is that they fall in love to form a nuclear family by the end of the story.

ADJACENT TROPES

- Instant Family
- Baby On the Doorstep
- Accidental Pregnancy
- Secret Baby
- Dangerous Secret

WHY READERS/VIEWERS LOVE THIS TROPE

- my choice in romantic partners was a good one after all… the absent parent is a good person after all, and he/she came back to help me raise our child
- how sexy is a man who steps up to parent a child he may not even know is his for sure? Likewise, how sexy is a woman who steps in to be a mom to a child she may not even know for sure is he
- getting help with being a (single) parent, and possibly getting a financial rescue

- being taken care of and swept away from the exhaustion and drudgery of my current life
- not only I, but also my child, is finally safe
- a miracle intervening to provide a better life for me and my family

OBLIGATORY SCENES
THE BEGINNING:

We may meet the mother or mother-to-be first, where we establish that the father is not in the picture. At all. And she doesn't expect him to show up down the road, either.

We definitely meet the father, who starts the story with no inkling that he is a parent or is about to be a parent.

The meet cute may be a chance meeting between the hero, heroine, and baby (or baby bump). Or the open may be the hero finding out somehow that a woman he used to know is a parent now.

You may be tempted to start your story with the original, inciting event—which is to say the conception of the baby in question—but unless your story moves forward from that moment and never takes a jump forward in time, I urge you to consider whether you can show that moment as backstory somewhere else in your story.

The problem with prologues that open with *six months ago* or *two years ago* is they kill the immediacy and forward movement of what's happening to your characters now. The past is all well and good, but your audience is much more interested in the right now. This translates to your audience being much more interested in the current consequences, crises, and questions that swirl around your main characters and not how they got to this point.

Remember: humans are curious by nature. We want to solve the puzzle and understand the thing that's confusing us. We hate leaving unanswered questions. We want to know what happens next. The worst possible thing you can do in the opening of any story you write is to tell your audience everything they need to know right up front.

In this trope, you want your audience's internal mental monologue to sound something like this. "Wait. The father of that cute baby left before the kid was born? Why? Didn't he know the mom was pregnant, or is he just a big jerk? Why didn't she track him down and tell him about the kid? Why's she not angry with him now? I'd sure be angry if my baby-daddy split. Who is the father, anyway? Surely, it's not that hunky guy she just bumped into in a coffee shop. But it would be cute if it was. Nah...maybe it's the hunk's best friend. Oooh. I wonder if the hunky guy will tell the real father he just saw the father's ex, and she's got a kid about a year old..."Do the math, already, dude. That kid's yours!"

Questions and more questions. That's your goal in the opening of your story. Just dive into the middle of the action just when the action gets interesting (or dangerous or exciting) and take off telling the story. Your audience will stay glued to its seat, inhaling your story to find the answers to all the questions they have as they get to know your characters, their problems, and the world they inhabit.

Backstory should always be served up to your audience in the smallest possible pieces necessary for your audience to understand the significance of the current action. And you should do your best not to let backstory kill the forward momentum and pacing of your story. Hence, you must get your story really barreling forward, having built up a lot of steam, before you can afford to risk dropping in a bit of backstory that yanks your audience out of the forward motion of events to share some side details with them about the past.

And yes, those details can be incredibly important and change everything we think we know about the current action. In fact, any backstory you include in your story must rise to that level of importance to be worth inserting into your story.

At any rate, Act One often ends with the father confronting the mother with the key question, "Is the baby mine?" or with the mother finally answering the question, which has been asked earlier.

. . .

THE MIDDLE:

This is where the fight over the child and/or the mother's failure to let father know about the child before now gathers steam. Regardless of how committed, casual, or completely unknown to each other the mother and father were at the time the child was conceived, their relationship probably has to start over at square one. But now there's a child in the mix, as well.

Either parent may deeply resent being forced into trying to build a relationship with the other parent. They may have old conflicts that broke them up the last time that resurface now. One or both parents may need to explain where they went when they separated before the pregnancy was discovered or the child was born.

The insertion of a child into anyone's life changes absolutely everything, and for the father, these changes hit all at once. It's hard enough to prepare for a child when you know it's coming and have months to get ready. But going from zero to full parent in the blink of an eye is a huge adjustment.

The external plot of your story probably serves to makes the question of "Is the baby mine?" more difficult to ask, more difficult to answer, or introduces huge complications once asked and answered. Act Two is where these difficulties present themselves and cause problems for mom and dad.

In fact, as Act Two draws to a close, these difficulties may build toward some sort of crisis that threatens one or both parents, possibly threatens the future of the child, and threatens to separate our little family again...possibly permanently this time.

At the same time external problems are tearing the family apart, internal conflicts are also building to a crisis that threatens to tear apart mom and dad for good. There may be trust issues to work out, there may be issues of secrecy, abandonment, anger, and forgiveness to navigate. The end of Act Two is where these conflicts come to a head.

. . .

BLACK MOMENT:

All the building pressures and crises take their toll and the family breaks apart. The father may choose wrong and walk away from mother and child. The mother may choose wrong and walk away, either taking the child with her or leaving the baby with daddy. A third party may step in and snatch the baby away from both parents.

In this moment all is lost to everyone. The father has lost his chance to be a father. The mother has lost her chance to have a partner in raising their child. The baby has lost a chance at having both parents present in his or her life.

THE END:

Regrets, grief, loneliness, and loss follow in the wake of the black moment. Perhaps the single most devastating loss any person can experience is losing their family, and this slams into your hero and heroine. In the wake of this wave of emotion, the mother and father must individually or together decide to make one last try at getting things right. They have to overcome the external plot obstacle to being together, which may involve having to physically do something to restore their family.

Then, the hero and heroine probably need to exchange apologies and forgiveness and commit to a forever family together. They don't necessarily have to get married by the end of your story, but you do need to demonstrate some tangible evidence that both parents will be present for each other and their child permanently. This might involve a contract, changing a birth certificate to reflect the father's name, changing a will, naming the child one's heir, publicly acknowledging the child, or the like.

Last but not least, your audience will want a glimpse of this family together as a happy family. Your reader or viewer will want to know without a shadow of a doubt that the child is okay and has two loving parents and a safe, loving home.

KEY SCENES

- mother first sees father and vice versa
- the moment when the father first sees the child without knowing if it's his or not
- mother rejects father's initial offer to become part of her and the child's life
- first time the father is left alone with the child
- father protects mother and baby from some potential danger or harm
- first romantic moment between mother and father
- father realizes he loves the baby
- mother realizes she loves the father
- a threat or danger to the baby pulls mom and dad together to protect the child

THINGS TO THINK ABOUT WHEN WRITING THIS TROPE

What kind of relationship did the mother and father have before the baby was conceived? What are the circumstances around the actual event that resulted in the conception of the baby?

Who left back then? Why?

How soon after the conception of the baby did the father exit the picture? Why? Where did he go? What did he do?

How quickly did the mother find out she was pregnant?

Did the mother have the means to contact the father and let him know about the child? If so, why didn't she? If not, why not?

At what point in the pregnancy, birth, or raising of the child will the father find out about the child's existence?

How will he find out?

How old is the child now?

How does mom feel about dad showing up in her and baby's life?

Does the mother initially lie about the child and or the child's parentage? If so, what does she tell the father? Why does she lie about it? How is the lie revealed as a lie?

What complications arise in the father's life from the existence of a child? How can you make those worse? How can you make them much worse?

How does the external plot of your story put pressure on the mother or father or both around the question of who the father of the child is?

Does the mother suffer negative consequences from not having told the father about the baby? If so, what?

What conflict from their past resurfaces between the mother and father?

What new conflicts arise between the mother and father that cause problems?

What things do the hero and heroine really like and admire about each other?

How quickly and completely will the father move into the child's life? How about into the mother's life?

What complications arise in mom's life because of the reappearance of her baby's father? How can you make these worse? How can you make them much worse?

What do the friends, family, and coworkers of the mother and father think about this couple getting back together? Do they try to help along the relationship or sabotage it?

What is the baby doing throughout all the drama and relationship building? How does he or she help along the romance? How does he or she hinder the romance?

Is there some sort of danger or threat to the baby's safety that draws mom and dad together? If so, what?

Is there some threat to custody of the child? If so, what?

Does the father insist on proof that he's the child's father before he'll step up to parent the child...or does he fall in love with the kid and declare himself ready to parent the child regardless of who genetically fathered the child?

What breaks apart the family? How will mom and dad fix it?

Does one of the parents have to make some sort of grand sacrifice to have his or her family? If so, what?

Who has to apologize to whom and for what so the family can reconcile and be together again in the end?

What does happily ever look like for this family?

TROPE TRAPS

The father is initially such a jerk we don't want him to be anywhere near mom or the baby.

The mother is unlikable for having withheld the information about the child's existence from the father.

The child acts as little more than an object in your story and contributes nothing and has no effect on it.

The child acts WAY older and wiser than his or her age. While it's fine to have precocious kids, the child probably shouldn't be the one giving pithy relationship advice to either parent unless we're talking about a teenaged child.

There's no external threat to the little family. If the only conflict to overcome is him being mad she didn't tell him and her being mad he left before she could tell him, you don't have a whole story's worth of conflict or threat to your family unit.

Spending too much time on backstory.

Failing to use current events to parallel past events.

The father accepts too easily that the baby is his or doesn't accept readily enough that the baby is his. In either case, his reaction isn't plausible for him and the story you're telling.

Nobody in your story is working to keep the family apart. Which is to say, you have no conflict in your story.

The child looks just like the father, and furthermore, interrupts multiple love scenes by needing to be fed, diaper changed, or wanting to be picked up. Which is to say, you dive headfirst into the clichés associated with this trope.

You force together a hero and heroine who don't belong together forever and your audience sniffs that they only got together for the sake of the kid and are going to be miserable together and make the child's life miserable going forward.

If the mother or father has to actually change in order to step up to his or her responsibilities, failing to show the ongoing and hard work of making a real and lasting change in oneself or one's life.

IS THE BABY MINE TROPE IN ACTION
Movies:

- Knocked Up
- Juno
- Fools Rush In
- Saved!
- Nine Months
- Tully

Books:

- Pieces of Us by A. L. Jackson
- Condemned to Love by Siobahn Davis
- Unrivaled by Jerrica MacMillan

- Hendrix by Kelsey Clayton
- Best Laid Plans by L.K. Farlow
- The Goal by Elle Kennedy
- Dr. Stanton by T.L. Swan
- Wait For Me by Tia Louise

17

LEFT AT THE ALTAR/JILTED

DEFINITION

In this trope, one of the main characters either is left at the altar or has been left at the altar recently when your story begins. Then, the story unfolds from there.

Will the bride or groom who fled reconcile with the almost spouse who got left behind? Will the jilted bride or groom run straight into the arms of another person who turns out to be his or her true love after all? Will the jilter come after the jilted bride/groom and threaten his or her in some way while the future spouse protects the jilted bride/groom?

There are lots of possibilities in how you unfold your story after one of your main characters is jilted. But the core of this story is probably going to revolve around learning to trust again. Not only is it a huge shock to think everything is hunky dory, only to have your future spouse dump you without warning, but it's also one of the most embarrassing and possibly humiliating moments in a person's life, depending on how the jilter goes about doing the jilting or leaving at the altar.

The jilted bride or groom has every reason to be suspicious of the next person who comes along, vowing eternal love and loyalty, and is likely to put the new love interest through the ringer before actually letting the new love earn his or her trust.

While it is possible that the "new" love is actually the old love who once jilted the bride or groom, it's going to be very difficult for the jilted bride/groom ever to trust that person again. In this scenario, the love interest is going to have some very heavy lifting to do to prove that he or she can really be trusted this time. And heaven help that love interest if he or she jilts the bride/groom a second time. (Is it just me, or did little plot bunnies start scampering around in your head at the prospect of a second jilting?)

This story typically ends with a wedding...and this goes much better than the first one. Nobody runs, fails to show up, or says no at the last moment. While it is possible to end this story with a couple in love and committed to each other without marriage, because the main character's goal was marriage the first time around, odds are good he or she is looking for marriage the second time around as well.

That said, it's possible the jilted bride/groom has sworn off marriage for good after being left at the altar or jilted the first time. But this is definitely a trope that ends in happily ever after as opposed to happily for now.

There's one last possibility for this trope, and that's telling the story from the point of view of the person who did the jilting, the bride or groom who, at the last moment, backed out of the deal, didn't show up at the church, or showed up at the site of the wedding but fled, or actually made it down the aisle before chickening out or summoning enough courage to call it off.

In this case, the story will probably revolve around why the jilter waited so long to do the jilting and what prevented him or her from doing it much sooner. There may be a suspense element to this version of the trope...otherwise, your main character is probably a big ole' coward and has some growing to do before he or she is ready to enter into another relationship and get it right next time.

. . .

ADJACENT TROPES

- Commitment Phobia
- Stop the Wedding
- Only One Not Married
- In Love With the Wrong Person
- Fear of Intimacy
- Reconciliation/Second Chance

WHY READERS/VIEWERS LOVE THIS TROPE

- who doesn't love a delicious scandal
- the fantasy of wishing we'd fled our own wedding
- the fantasy of my secret crush fleeing his or her own wedding to be with me
- being saved from a disastrous mistake in the nick of time

OBLIGATORY SCENES
THE BEGINNING:

Whether or not you choose to open your story with the jilting event is up to you. But I can say, you may be wasting a wonderfully fascinating train wreck of a scene if you don't open with the moment of jilting.

There are not too many more events with which your audience will sympathize more strongly than being in what your main character believes to be the happiest moment of his or her life and then having the rug yanked out from underneath him or her in the most embarrassing and humiliating way.

Talk about utter devastation. Your audience will be desperate for your main character to find happiness after watching him or her suffer through such a disaster.

The eventual love interest is introduced. This trope almost always includes a meet-cute. Cue the distraught bride in a disheveled wedding dress, or the groom with his bow tie hanging around his neck, untied. Enter the handsome or beautiful love interest-to be to give the jilted bride/groom a ride, fix their flat tire, buy them a drink, or in some other cute, original way, rescue the devastated bride/groom.

Initially, the jilted bride/groom is going to be upset—perhaps angry, perhaps grieving, perhaps refusing to go home, perhaps hiding from family and friends. This is going to be an emotional crisis in which we'll see the jilted main character let all their emotions hang out for the world to see.

The love interest, who is probably more rational and calmer at the beginning of this new relationship with the jilted main character may notice the attraction and see a possible good romantic fit for the two of them long before the distraught jilted bride/groom clocks it.

The jilted bride/groom is going to be skeptical of love in general, suspicious of any feelings of attraction he or she might feel toward anyone else at the moment and is likely to test the trustworthiness of any new person he or she meets.

It's not uncommon for the beginning of this story to end with the jilted bride/groom putting the future love interest through some entirely unreasonable test to see if he or she will take off when the going gets tough, too.

If the person doing the jilting is your main character, you'll still likely show the moment of jilting to open your story and then will follow the jilter on his or her initial departure from the scene. You'll need to show why he or she jilted their intended spouse at the last moment before the wedding.

No matter who jilted whom, in the beginning the fallout from that event will start to happen and cause complications for your main character, be that person the jilter or jilted one.

. . .

THE MIDDLE:

The complications resulting from the wedding not happening and being called off in such a dramatic fashion continues to unfold, but that fallout gets more complicated as your story progresses. The person who did the jilting may come back into the picture. He or she may regret having left the main character at the altar and now wants the main character back.

If the love interest is a third party who entered the story after the main character was jilted or jilted the almost spouse, a love triangle may ensue.

Or the jilted bride groom may not want a thing to do with their ex. So, rather than a love triangle, you may merely have two people competing for the love of the jilted bride/groom. The jilted bride/groom despises the almost spouse who's back and groveling (or threatening), and the jilted bride/groom may not trust the other competitor for his or her affections.

If there was a compelling non-love-based reason for the original wedding to happen, that reason probably rears its ugly head in the middle of the story to cause problems. The consequences of the wedding not taking place start to happen.

Meanwhile, the jilted bride/groom and new love interest are growing closer and falling in love...despite the grave mistrust the jilted bride/groom is wrestling with. The new love interest may be interested in moving full speed ahead with this new relationship, but the jilted bride/groom may be standing on the brakes.

As conflicts mount between the jilted main character and new love interest, each new conflict proves to the jilted bride/groom that his or her suspicion of love, loyalty, and promises is fully justified.

As the plot consequences of the failed wedding build toward a crisis, so do the conflicts between the main character and love interest (and possibly the almost spouse from the failed wedding).

. . .

BLACK MOMENT:

The jilted bride/groom cannot bring himself or herself to take another chance on another wedding. He or she, when faced with a choice of committing to the new love interest and getting married or losing the new love, chooses wrong. The jilted bride/groom cannot overcome his or her embarrassment, humiliation, and/or distrust to give marriage another chance.

All is lost. In the absence of trust, there's no way the love interest can prove his or her love to the main character's satisfaction. Their relationship is doomed.

The worst possible consequence of the original wedding not taking place happens, devastating the jilted bride/groom or at least ruining his or her life.

THE END:

The new love interest may decide to give it one last try to convince the jilted bride/groom to give marriage a try. The new love may make some sort of grand gesture to prove that he or she would never, ever, leave the main character in the lurch the way the last almost spouse did.

The jilted main character may finally realize, in his or her devastation and grief over losing a second person he or she loves with all their heart, that it's worth taking one more chance on love.

If the main character was the jilter originally, he or she may make some sort of grand gesture to the love interest to prove that he or she is not going to run this time...or run ever again.

If there's an external plot problem that must be solved before the lovers can finally marry/be together forever in a committed relationship, that problem is solved by one last Herculean effort. The main character, the love interest, or the pair together may solve the big plot problem, clearing the way for the two of them to be together.

The jilted main character may need to apologize for his or her lack of trust. The love interest may need to apologize for pushing the main character so far out of his or her comfort zone. Once these apologies are made, the way is cleared for a post-black-moment reconciliation.

This story usually ends with a wedding in which neither person flees, refuses to say I do, or in any way ruins the wedding. Regardless of whether or not there's a wedding, the lovers are shown to be happy...and it's going to last forever.

KEY SCENES

- the moment when the jilted bride/groom or jilting bride/groom stops running to catch his or her breath
- the jilted main character sees his or her almost spouse for the first time since the failed wedding. They may or may not interact
- we see what happens to the honeymoon. Does someone go on it alone or are tickets refunded and reservations canceled
- the aftermath among the family, friends, and other wedding guests. (Possibly the jilted main character is part of this scene, but not necessarily)
- the main character almost flees (again) or starts to flee and stops himself or herself
- meeting between the new love interest and the jilting almost spouse
- the second proposal between main character and new love interest
- history almost repeats itself and the jilted bride/groom freaks out

THINGS TO THINK ABOUT WHEN WRITING THIS TROPE

Who jilts whom in your story? Why?

How did the original couple (jilted bride/groom and almost spouse) meet? How did their relationship develop? What did they see in each other?

Why did the original couple fall in love? Get engaged?

Why did the jilter go almost all the way through with the wedding before calling things off? Why didn't he or she do it sooner?

Is there a non-love reason the first wedding needed to happen? If so, what?

What are the consequences of Wedding #1 not happening? Can you make them worse? Can you make them much worse?

Where does the jilter go after the failed wedding? Where does the jilted party go immediately afterward?

How do the main character and love interest meet (assuming the original couple isn't your eventual lovers)?

What emotions does the jilted bride/groom experience after the jilting? In what order? How will he or she act out these emotions?

What will the love interest do to overcome the main character's distrust of love in general and of declarations of everlasting love?

What attracts the main character and love interest to each other?

What conflicts threaten to tear apart the main character and love interest? How will these manifest?

How does the external plot of your story push your main character and love interest together? How does it pull them apart? What threat does it cause to the two of them ending up together?

Will the person who did the jilting try to win back the jilted bride/groom? If so, why? If so, how? If not, why not?

What do the friends and family of the original couple and the new couple think of everything that's happened? How will they interfere, sabotage, or help along events and the various relationships?

What does a confrontation between the new love interest and the almost spouse look like? Can you work this into your story?

How will the love interest prove his or her complete trustworthiness and steadfastness to the main character?

Why does the main character walk away from the new love interest?

How does the external plot help break up the lovers?

What do the main character and love interest have to do to solve the main plot problem? What do they have to do to repair their relationship?

Who apologizes to whom for what?

What finally gets the main character past his or her distrust to be able and willing to marry again?

Will your story end with another wedding or not? If not, how will you set up a happily ever after for your audience?

TROPE TRAPS

Creating a main character who's so flighty or flaky that your audience thinks the almost spouse did the right thing by bailing out.

The main character is so willing to settle for an inferior spouse that he or she comes across as deeply insecure and ultimately unheroic or unlikable.

Creating a main character and almost spouse who were so obviously and wildly unsuited for each other that the audience doesn't buy the two of them ever agreeing to marry each other in the first place.

There are no negative consequences for whoever fled the wedding—no bills to pay, no apologies to make, no penalties or problems with vendors or honeymoons or rent deposits together.

The jilted bride/groom should have seen the warning signs and comes across as stupid to the audience.

The jilted bride/groom comes across as shallow for being so fixated on the idea of getting married that he or she didn't stop to think about who he or she was marrying.

The new love interest comes across as taking advantage of the jilted bride/groom, who's in no rational emotional state or condition to be making big decisions about love or new relationships.

The external plot doesn't complicate the romantic plotline at all.

The main character is unrealistically trusting of the new love interest when he or she comes along.

There's altogether too much screaming in your story. While this is a fraught situation, and some screaming may certainly be in order, people don't have to remain wildly upset throughout the entire story. At some point, the main players should probably calm down and start to sort out the aftermath of the failed wedding in a somewhat reasonable—if not particularly friendly—fashion.

The jilted bride/groom is so mistrusting that he or she makes the love interest suffer far too much before earning his or her trust.

The new love interest is so perfect and perfect for the jilted main character as to be implausible.

LEFT AT THE ALTAR/JILTED TROPE IN ACTION
Movies:

- Sweet Home Alabama
- Runaway Bride
- They Came Together
- The Last Fling
- My Best Friend's Wedding
- Serendipity

Books:

- Getaway Girl by Tessa Bailey
- The Worst Best Man by Mia Sosa
- Stone Princess by Devney Perry

- Reckless Miles by Claire Kingsley
- Trust Me by Jayne Ann Krentz
- Honeymoon for One by Chris Keniston
- In a Jam by Kate Canterbary
- Runaway Love by Melanie Harlow

18

LONE WOLF TAMED

DEFINITION

This is the modern version of an ancient trope—a lone warrior wandering the world in search of noble deeds to do. Ancient Asian mythologies are rich with these archetypal noble warriors. The knight errant of Medieval Europe was the same, riding his white charger to the rescue of damsels in distress and righting wrongs with his lance and sword. North America had the gunslinger cowboy who rode the Wild West, shooting bad guys, saving widows in distress, and bringing law-and order wherever he went.

The contemporary version is the (ex-) soldier, (ex-) cop, (ex-) FBI agent, or private investigator who rights wrongs for those who have been wronged and may work outside the law to see justice done upon those who've, until now, avoided paying for their crimes.

In this trope, the main character in your love story is a "lone wolf", which is to say, he or she doesn't form or have many or any social connections and prefers to be alone. This person may be a wanderer who doesn't stay in any one place for long. He or she comes to town, stays until people start trying to get too familiar with him or her or the itch to wander strikes, and then the lone wolf moves on.

Worth noting: most lone wolves (and actual wolves) possess some kind of special skill, usually lethal in nature. They're excellent problem solvers, trackers, hunters, and will kill when necessary.

Ironically, wolves are incredibly social animals that would never voluntarily be alone. The one possible exception is wolves are known to leave their pack if they sense they're dying and they will almost always choose to die alone. So, if we're going to follow the wolf analogy in this trope, we can think in terms of the lone wolf hero or heroine isolating himself or herself in a metaphorical death.

This might be a death of the soul (meaning a death of hope, a death of faith, a death of belief in self, in something, or in someone else), a death of the heart (meaning death of his or her ability to love or a death of love in his or her past), or a death of the mind (meaning he or she has made a decision to isolate self, perhaps as punishment for some perceived failure, to focus on some goal, or to recover from some wound).

The lone wolf may be isolating himself or herself intentionally in response to some terrible recent past event, or the lone wolf may isolate himself or herself habitually—meaning it's a learned behavior from someone or that started in his or her distant past.

At any rate, the love interest to this lone wolf must find a way to break through the wolf's self-imposed isolation, convince the wolf to take a chance on a relationship with another person, and to settle down and stop wandering.

The love interest, in taming this wolf, will probably need to proceed as if taming an actual wild animal, moving cautiously, trying not to spook the wolf into fleeing, pushing the wolf's boundaries of comfort a little bit at a time, and slowly earning this very anti-social wolf's trust.

The theme of this trope is typically that beneath the lone wolf's prickly, isolated, unfriendly exterior, lies a terrific person, a perfect mate who is worth all the time, patience, and effort of taming.

The lone wolf differs from the recluse in that the recluse hides from the world and chooses to be alone out of fear, insecurity, pain, or some other trauma, whereas the wolf is fearless and moves through the world freely, merely choosing to be alone while doing so.

This trope is often paired with another trope that may explain why the lone wolf is, well, alone. A few of many possible examples include Dangerous Secret, Hero/Heroine in Hiding, Bad Boy/Bad Girl Reformed, On the Run/Chase, Damaged Hero/Heroine, and Burned By Love.

ADJACENT TROPES

- Reclusive Hero/Heroine
- Socially Awkward Hero/Heroine
- Newcomer/Outsider/Stranger
- Oblivious to Love
- Cold/Uptight/Serious Hero/Heroine

WHY READERS/VIEWERS LOVE THIS TROPE

- the fantasy of the knight errant, the lone cowboy, the noble cowboy sweeping into town and rescuing me from the problem, trouble, or danger I can't handle on my own. I mean, who doesn't want to be rescued by a handsome, dangerous, silent stranger who appears out of nowhere and protects or saves us
- being swept away from my mundane life into the lone wolf's special world
- being the center of someone's universe
- I'm the only one who could get through his or her emotional defenses to find the wonderful person beneath
- we'd love to believe the cold, distant, or rather unfriendly person we're involved with (or perhaps have to work

with) actually has a warm, protective, loving side somewhere under that gruff exterior

- he or she loves me enough to stop wandering and open up to me emotionally

OBLIGATORY SCENES
THE BEGINNING:

The lone wolf comes to town or is first spotted in town by the love interest. Someone, often the love interest, approaches the lone wolf, who rebuffs him or her. The "lone-ness" of the lone wolf is firmly established.

The love interest's problem is established. It may already be in place before the lone wolf arrives, or it may develop soon after the lone wolf arrives in town. This external plot problem will serve to bring together the lone wolf and the love interest initially since in the absence of it, the lone wolf isn't likely to get involved with anyone voluntarily and would leave town rather than engage in a voluntary social interaction.

The lone wolf is drawn into helping the love interest with his or her problem. This may happen accidentally or the lone wolf may decide to involve himself or herself without the love interest asking for help. Or, of course, the love interest may turn to the lone wolf and ask outright for help. The noble lone wolf can't very well turn down an innocent person in trouble and who needs exactly the lethal skills the lone wolf possesses to handle that trouble.

THE MIDDLE:

The lone wolf prepares for battle. He or she studies the foe, tracks the foe, and develops a plan for defeating the foe. Lone wolves are nothing if not patient and tend to be single-minded in their focus.

The love interest commences wolf taming. He or she starts

getting to know the lone wolf, getting the wolf to talk about himself or herself, and gaining the lone wolf's trust. The love interest will try to learn all he or she can about the lone wolf—his or her past, how he or she became a loner, what brought him or her to this place at this moment.

A game of advance and retreat, pushing the lone wolf's boundaries bit by bit, breaking down the lone wolf's emotional walls one stone at a time, waiting out the lone wolf's inevitable shutdowns, happens in the middle of your story.

This is a time of emotional struggle for the lone wolf as he or she wrestles with his or her own demons, unwillingly falls in love, and tries not to hurt the love interest, knowing that he or she is going to leave town and move on as soon as the love interest's problem is solved.

The external plot problem builds toward a crisis. The romantic relationship also heads toward a crisis as the love interest falls fully in love and the lone wolf remains committed to not getting into a committed relationship.

BLACK MOMENT:

The external plot problem goes terribly wrong. The lone wolf fails in his or her quest to take care of the problem. Not only has he or she failed the love interest externally, but this is also the moment when the lone wolf drops the bomb that he or she cannot or will not enter into a long-term romantic relationship with the love interest.

The love interest has gambled and lost *everything*. Whatever was at stake in the external plot problem is lost, and the ideal mate for life has also slipped through his or her fingers.

As devastated as the love interest is, the lone wolf may be even more devastated. Not only has he or she failed to live up to his or her own ideals, but wrong has triumphed over right, and he or she has had a taste of perfect love and now must walk away from it, knowing now just how sweet it is.

The devastation is complete.

THE END:

The lone wolf, after wallowing in the dark night of his or her soul, gathers himself or herself for one last, heroic effort to right the wrong. The wolf may or may not get help from the love interest, but one or both of them finally triumph over the evil that threatens the love interest.

Typically, the lone wolf has some sort of emotional breakdown or breakthrough that the love interest may or may not provoke. Regardless, the love interest is the beneficiary of the lone wolf's emotional shell cracking wide open. The lone wolf may make a grand gesture of love or may make a grand apology or both.

The love interest forgives the lone wolf for his or her earlier rejection, and the lovers can finally be together forever. The love interest has been completely admitted to the lone wolf's fortress of solitude, or the fortress may have been completely destroyed by the end of your story, allowing the lone wolf to finally re-enter and rejoin the world.

There's usually a dramatic, and swoon-worthy embrace between the lovers who have overcome every obstacle between them to be together. The knight errant has found his lady/lord love. The damsel/dude in distress is rescued, safe, and protected. Evil has been vanquished. All is right with the world. The wolf will remain on guard against new evils but with his or her true love at his or her side. And the lovers will live happily ever after.

KEY SCENES

- the first time the lone wolf rebuffs the love interest's overture of friendship

- the first time the love interest gets right in the lone wolf's face and confronts him or her about being anti-social
- the first time the lone wolf confesses something personal about himself or herself to the love interest
- the first kiss
- the lone wolf's panic/retreat after the first kiss
- the love interest retreats from the lone wolf after a romantic encounter
- the love interest tries to declare his or her love and the lone wolf stops him or her from saying it
- the lone wolf humbles himself or herself before the love interest in an act of contrition

THINGS TO THINK ABOUT WHEN WRITING THIS TROPE

Why is the lone wolf a lone wolf? What event(s) in his or her past have set him or her on this solitary path?

Is the lone wolf comfortable being alone? Is he or she happy? At ease?

Does the lone wolf have any sense of humor or joy, or is he/she serious, dour, sad, angry, or unable to experience happiness? Why is he or she this way?

If the lone wolf is shut down emotionally, why is that?

How do the lone wolf and love interest meet?

What is the love interest's external plot problem? Why can't he or she take care of it by himself or herself? What about this problem will require the special skills of the lone wolf to resolve it?

How dangerous is the external plot problem to the love interest? How can you make the problem worse? How can you make it much worse? How can you make it (nearly) impossible for anyone to fix?

How and at what point in your story does the lone wolf get involved with the love interest's problem?

What attracts the love interest to the lone wolf?

What gives the love interest an inkling that there's a lovable person beneath the lone wolf's gruff or unfriendly exterior?

What about the love interest does the lone wolf find attractive? What does the lone wolf find irresistible about the love interest?

What in the lone wolf's past or personality makes him or her reluctant to get into a romantic relationship with anyone and/or with the love interest specifically?

How will the external plot of your story force the lone wolf and love interest into repeated and frequent proximity so they can develop a relationship and fall in love?

What things will the love interest do in his or her efforts to get to know the lone wolf?

What do retreats by the lone wolf look like when he or she gets spooked or overwhelmed by the love interest's attention?

When does the love interest let the lone wolf retreat and be alone, and when does the love interest follow the lone wolf and not let him or her pull away?

What do they argue over? How does that go?

What flaw(s) does your lone wolf have that make him or her human and not a perfect, cardboard cut-out of a character?

Does the love interest struggle to live up to the lone wolf's noble ideals or not? What's a moment when the love interest fails to live up to the lone wolf's extreme standard(s) of honor?

How and why does the lone wolf fail to solve the plot problem in the black moment?

When does the lone wolf reject the love interest? How does the lone wolf do it?

What will the lone wolf and/or love interest ultimately do to resolve the big plot problem? Why couldn't they do it before now?

Who apologizes to whom for what?

Who makes a grand gesture of love to whom, and what does that look like?

Will the love interest leave with the lone wolf and wander beside him or her, or will the lone wolf stop wandering and stay beside the love interest in his or her home?

TROPE TRAPS

The lone wolf is too perfect for someone not to have seen his or her perfection before now and found a way to get the lone wolf to love him or her.

The love interest is a limp-wristed hand-wringer unable to care for himself or herself, and who has no spunk, which makes him or her unlikable to your audience.

The lone wolf must break a vow of some kind to love anyone and comes across as less than noble for giving in and breaking that vow too easily or for falling in love with the love interest without enough angsting over it.

The love interest has a gray enough set of moral that, in the eyes of your audience, he or she doesn't deserve the lone wolf.

Failing to give the lone wolf the redemption arc he or she needs to forgive himself or herself for a past failure that made them a lone wolf.

Failing to explain plausibly why the lone wolf became a loner.

The lone wolf falls in love too easily and is too ready to settle down too quickly.

The lone wolf is so rigid in his or her values and beliefs that he or she would never plausibly fall in love with anyone or stop wandering for anyone.

The love interest doesn't have to work hard enough to earn the love of the lone wolf...anyone could've done it and the love interest isn't special enough to deserve the lone wolf.

The solution to the external plot problem is too obvious or should've been the first thing the lone wolf tried heading into the black moment, which makes the lone wolf look stupid or self-destructive, and/or makes the love interest look weak, helpless, or too stupid to live for not having done it himself or herself.

Failing to embrace the mythic aspects of this trope.

Failing to deliver a dramatic love story worthy of these epic characters.

LONE WOLF TAMED TROPE IN ACTION
Movies:

- Shrek
- Jack Reacher (TV show)
- Desperado
- Lone Wolf McQuade
- Kingdom of Heaven
- Lone Wolf and Cub
- Solo: A Star Wars Story (actually, the entire Han Solo arc across the Star Wars movies)

Books:

- Darling Beast by Elizabeth Hoyt
- Hold by Claire Kent and Zannie Adams
- For Love of the Duke by Christi Caldwell
- How to Flirt With a Naked Werewolf by Molly Harper
- Reasonable Doubt by Whitney G.
- Return of the Rogue by Donna Fletcher
- Darkness by Laurann Dohner

19

MAFIA ROMANCE

DEFINITION

One of the most enduringly popular tropes in romantic stories of any kind is the alpha male with lethal skills who protects (and loves) a woman in jeopardy. Many of the most popular tropes in romance are a variation of this, and the mafia romance trope is one of them.

The lone wolf hero/heroine is a noble wanderer who does good deeds. The soldier or cop protects the public (protects Man, as it were) with his or her lethal skills. The lone cowboy uses his lethal skills to metaphorically tame Nature. Billionaires use wealth, power, and lethal financial skills to protect the woman in jeopardy, but it's all the same principle.

Other variations include the knight errant, ninja, monster- or dragon-slayer, Scottish chieftain, biker with a heart of gold, bodyguard, professional athlete, fire fighter...you get the idea. The variations on this theme are endless.

The mafia hero or heroine is unique in that he or she has learned their lethal skills doing bad deeds...but transforms into a hero/heroine who uses those ill-gotten skills for good, typically to protect his or her true love from jeopardy.

Worth noting: the Ex-Convict Hero/Heroine has already transformed his or her bad past into commitment to do good going forward. The mafioso character undergoes that transformation in real time over the course of this story.

In this trope, the mafia hero or heroine may or may not remain within a criminal organization at the end of the story. In general, the mafia member undergoes an epiphany and repents of his or her criminal ways. The mafioso may leave the mafia, may turn informant, work undercover for law enforcement, help take a mob group down, or testify against his or her former employers, for example.

In the anti-hero version of this trope, the mafia member remains an unrepentant member of a criminal organization. However, he or she might direct the group's activities away from particularly heinous crimes like murder or human trafficking as a demonstration of growth, redemption, or becoming a heroic character.

Or, this unreformed criminal might become a Robin Hood, doing bad deeds in the name of good or for a greater good outcome.

The love interest in this trope may be part of the criminal enterprise, or perhaps peripherally related to it (the child or sister of a mobster), or the love interest may be a target or victim of the criminal group.

If the mafia hero/heroine does something bad to the love interest, it typically happens very early in the story, and the mafioso repents of it very quickly—perhaps by not following through with an attack on the love interest or immediately trying to make amends for it in some way.

This reversal of bad intent toward the love interest typically happens as a result of seeing or meeting the love interest and feeling an immediate and overpowering attraction, admiration, respect, or need to protect the love interest.

It's also possible that the jeopardy the love interest faces has little or nothing to do with the mafioso's criminal group. However, the skills and knowledge the mafioso possesses are specifically necessary to and critical to solving the love interest's terrible problem.

Once these two characters meet and enter into a relationship, the story pretty much follows the archetypal knight-protector pattern.

They fall in love and deal with various disagreements, moral clashes, and conflicts of values and behavior as the crisis facing the character(s) in jeopardy builds to a crisis. The mafioso must sacrifice everything he or she values to save the person he or she loves, and the love interest in jeopardy must choose between the person they love and solving their own problem or between love and personal safety.

Much drama ensues, the hero and heroine save each other (in this case both metaphorically and literally), and then they can settle down to their happily ever after.

Where the mafia romance differs from a typical "hero rescues damsel/dude in distress" story is that the mafioso in this trope also undergoes a transformation from unheroic into heroic over the course of heroically rescuing the love interest.

I should mention that in some mafia romances, the story ends with the mafioso remaining inside the criminal organization and the love interest joining him or her inside the criminal enterprise and becoming part of it.

I would call this a tragic ending at best and ethically dubious at worst. Destroying the ethical and moral foundations of a character and devolving them from good to bad, lawful to unlawful, non-violent to violent, non-exploitative of others to exploitative of others, isn't a recipe for safety, healthy emotional development, or a peaceful, supportive, open, honest, and stress-free relationship that, for most people, constitutes happily-ever-after.

ADJACENT TROPES

- Bad Boy/Girl Reformed
- Redemption
- Dangerous Past
- Ex-Convict Hero/Heroine
- Lone Wolf Tamed

- Billionaire Romance
- Bully Turned Nice
- Stockholm Syndrome/Slavery
- Anti-Hero/Heroine

WHY READERS/VIEWERS LOVE THIS TROPE

- a powerful hero arrives to protect me, keep me safe, or fix my unfixable problem
- being swept out of my mundane, boring, scary life and taken into the protection of a strong, aggressive, alpha hero/heroine able and willing to snarl off all potential threats
- becoming part of a secret world or secret organization, being an insider to a community closed to outsiders
- never having to be scared again, feeling totally safe
- he or she loves me enough to change—and the transformation from criminal to hero is a HUGE one
- he or she loves me enough to choose me over the criminal group to which he or she has been utterly loyal

OBLIGATORY SCENES
THE BEGINNING:

The mafioso and love interest meet. Because this is typically a suspenseful story of danger and need for the mafioso to use his or her lethal skills and knowledge, meet cutes are not the norm. Rather, a big action opening that establishes the danger to the love interest is more typical.

The mafioso's criminal ties are established. You may choose to let your audience know about these before you let the love interest know, but by the end of the beginning, both your audience and your love interest are undoubtedly aware of just who the main character actually is.

The mafioso's attraction to and fascination with the love interest must be established quickly. Otherwise, why would he or she stick around to help the love interest who is probably not part of the mafioso's inner circle of trust and criminal activities.

The external plot problem that threatens the safety of the love interest is established and we probably see the first crisis as this problem ramps up in danger and intensity.

THE MIDDLE:

As the mafioso and love interest start to build a personal relationship, get close, and fall in love, the complications increase considerably. The love interest may be forbidden to the mafioso in some way. The love interest may challenge the mafioso to leave behind his or her criminal activities and associations.

The mafioso may challenge the naïveté of the love interest and try to educate him or her into the ways of the criminal world. The mafioso gathers information, plans, and prepares for battle. The couple has near misses with harm or death and may nearly get caught by the bad guy(s), the mafia organization, or both.

The consequences of the mafioso and love interest continuing to pursue a romantic relationship are spelled out. Ultimatums may be given as to what will happen if the love interest isn't handed over to the bad guys. Law enforcement types or the mafia group may issue threats if the mafioso and love interest don't stop seeing/being with each other.

The mafioso's unheroic beliefs start to fall apart, and he or she fights transforming into the thing he or she has been taught to despise. The love interest may make an ultimatum of his or her own— change your bad ways and become a good person or I'm out of here.

. . .

BLACK MOMENT:

The external plot threat to the love interest explodes and goes terribly wrong. The mafioso has reverted to his or her old ways of thinking and acting, has broken a promise not to do criminal things, or has failed to make a heroic sacrifice. The love interest may be destroyed by the mafioso's rejection of the heroic values or change the love interest has been asking for.

The mafioso fails to keep the love interest safe. Not only is the mafioso devastated by this failure, but so is the love interest who was counting on the mafioso to protect him or her. The consequences to the couple for staying together happen and may be part of what tears them apart. The lovers are not only physically wrenched apart by events but emotionally as well.

In effect, both parts of this trope fail. The mafioso fails to protect the damsel/dude in distress, and the mafioso fails to stick by or to complete his or her transformation into a heroic, good-guy character.

The love interest's gamble to love this bad guy has failed completely and not only is the love interest not saved, but now he or she has a broken heart, too.

THE END:

The devastated mafioso must collect himself or herself and finally commit to a heroic decision to sacrifice everything, do the right thing, and save the love interest even if it means the mafioso will be kicked out of his or her crime family, go to jail, or die in the process.

The love interest may decide to try one last time to get through to the mafioso and appeal to the mafioso's better nature, which the love interest hopes is under all that criminal badness (but isn't sure of anymore after the black moment). This is potentially a huge, even suicidal, risk to take. But the love interest may not care if he or she lives or dies if he or she turns out to be wrong about the mafioso's desire to do and be good.

The external problem is finally solved in dramatic fashion. This is often a big action scene and may involve violence and death or may involve the mafioso and love interest individually trying to sacrifice themselves to save the person they love.

Having finally proved through major action and grand sacrifice that he or she has transformed from a bad guy at heart to a good guy at heart, the mafioso apologizes to the love interest and/or asks the love interest to take him or her back.

The love interest accepts the apology and accepts that the mafioso has, in fact, turned into a hero (at least in the love interest's eyes).

If the mafioso is going to redeem himself or herself with regard to the law and being part of the mafia, this action comes to fruition. The mafioso turns over information to law enforcement, or testifies, or maybe enters witness protection with the love interest.

We get a glimpse of happily ever after for the mafioso and love interest in whatever world they've settled into after the events of the story conclude.

KEY SCENES

- the mafioso rescues the love interest willingly or unwillingly to set the story in motion
- the love interest first realizes the mafioso is a criminal
- the love interest does something criminal or morally gray to protect the mafioso, and the mafioso is appalled
- the mafioso does a good guy thing that's unexpected and surprises both the love interest and your audience
- the love interest is nearly harmed, killed, or caught and it scares the mafioso
- the mafioso is nearly harmed, killed, or caught and it scares the love interest
- the lovers argue and when one of them storms away, something very bad happens

- the love interest confronts the mafioso about being a bad guy
- the mafioso is given an ultimatum by the criminal organization
- the love interest is given an ultimatum by law enforcement, the criminal organization, or both

THINGS TO THINK ABOUT WHEN WRITING THIS TROPE

Who is your mafioso? What kind of criminal organization is he or she part of? How did he or she come to be part of it? How long has he or she been part of it?

Where is your mafioso in the hierarchy of his or her criminal organization?

How bad is your mafioso? What's the worst thing he or she has ever done? How does he or she feel about it? What's the worst thing he or she routinely does? How does he or she feel about that?

Who is your love interest? Is he or she part of, aware of, or attached in some way to a criminal organization or the same criminal organization as the mafioso, or is he or she an outsider, a civilian?

Is the love interest criminal in any way?

Is the love interest a target or intended victim of a crime? If so, by whom? Why?

What is the jeopardy the love interest faces over the course of your story? Can you make that worse? Much worse? Even worse than that?

What about the problem the love interest faces requires the special knowledge and/or skills of a mafia member/criminal to fix it?

Why can't the love interest go to law enforcement for help? Or has he/she done so already? Did the police/FBI/and so forth help or not? Why or why not? How much or how little?

How will you demonstrate an inkling of goodness in the mafioso very early in your story so the audience can identify with him or her as a potential heroic character?

What story device will you use to throw the mafioso and love interest together frequently and repeatedly (or continuously) so they can build a relationship and fall in love?

What attracts the mafioso to the love interest and vice versa?

How do their morals, beliefs, and values clash, and how will you demonstrate those clashes?

What will happen to the mafioso that's so significant and life-changing that it actually gets him or her to change one of his or her fundamental, core beliefs permanently?

What causes the mafioso to fall back into old habit patterns before the shock that makes his or her transformation permanent?

How does the mafioso betray the love interest and vice versa?

How does the crisis/confrontation/event of the black moment go completely, horribly wrong? How can this event not only fail to fix the external plot problem but also act to break up the mafioso and love interest romantically?

What must the mafioso sacrifice to prove his or her love and change to the love interest?

How will the external plot problem finally be solved? Who fixes it—the mafioso, the love interest, or both of them?

Who apologizes to whom and for what so the relationship can be restored?

How transformed is the mafioso? Does he or she stay in the criminal organization and bring the love interest into it? Transform it in some way? Leave it? Tear it apart? Turn on it? Flee it?

What makes the love interest believe the mafioso's change is permanent by the end of the story?

Where will they establish a life together? Is there still any danger to them? If so, how will they avoid it?

TROPE TRAPS

The mafioso is portrayed as not really being a bad person, and yet, he or she is doing solidly criminal and bad things. The audience will judge the mafioso on his or her behavior, not on what he or she says or thinks of self.

The love interest is so naïve and unaware of the possibility that the mafioso is a bad person that your audience hates him or her.

The love interest completely ignores the bad things the mafioso does and makes excuses for his or her bad behavior, thereby alienating the audience. In the words of the brilliant and wise Maya Angelou, "When someone shows you who they are, believe them the first time."

Creating such a violent and angry mafioso that nobody believes this person could do a complete personality turn around just because he or she falls in love.

Creating an external plot problem for the love interest that any sane person would have gone straight to law enforcement for help with...but your love interest for some reason didn't.

Creating law enforcement characters in your book who are too corrupt, too stupid, too blind, or too uncaring to be the least bit plausible.

Creating a dumb bad guy. The goodness of your good guy is defined by the badness of your bad guy. If you paint a dumb bad guy, your mafioso doesn't have to be very smart or skilled to defeat the bad guy. And who wants a dumb good guy?

Expecting the audience to buy that a single realization or rather mundane event will be enough to permanently and fundamentally change your mafioso's bad morals, values, and beliefs into heroic ones. Peoples' characters are set in stone by about age seven. After that it takes a significant shock, a life-changing event, usually a traumatic one, for most people to make any change. Even then, it may not stick permanently. We all tend to revert to old habits and ways of thinking and acting.

Failing to show the mafioso's commitment to change and plan to continue working to maintain this new, heroic attitude and behavior transformation.

The love interest devolves into a bad guy to stay with the mafioso forever...unless you were planning all along for the love interest to be an anti-hero or for yours to be a tragic story. Criminal together ever after is not the same as happily ever after.

Normalizing violence as okay or heroic.

Failing to show the serious legal and psychological consequences of engaging in violence or crime, which are particularly pronounced when violence or crime is repeated and habitual.

Normalizing abusive behavior, be it verbal, emotional, physical, or sexual abuse.

Rough sex without the love interest's full and enthusiastic consent, complete with safe words that are scrupulously obeyed. (Dubious consent, BDSM, and exploring taboos are their own tropes and fraught with potentially serious ethical problems that must be navigated thoughtfully and carefully.) For a discussion of the ethics of consent, take a look at the Stockholm Syndrome/Slavery trope write-up in this volume.

MAFIA ROMANCE TROPE IN ACTION
Movies:

- Carlito's Way
- In the Arms of an Assassin
- China Girl
- I'm In Love With a Church Girl
- The Mexican
- On the Waterfront
- Mickey Blue Eyes
- Bugsy
- A Bronx Tale

. . .

Books:

- The Sweetest Oblivion by Danielle Lori
- The Professional by Kresley Cole
- Beautifully Cruel by J.T. Geissinger
- Bound by Honor by Cora Reilly
- Nero by Sarah Brianne
- Monster In His Eyes by J. M. Darhower
- Carter Reed by Tijan
- Elite by Rachel Van Dyken
- Crow by A Zavarelli

20

NOT GOOD ENOUGH FOR HIM/HER

DEFINITION

In this trope the main character believes himself or herself not to be worthy of being the permanent romantic partner of the love interest. The main character has past baggage of some kind—past acts, past trauma, past mistakes, deep-seated insecurities—or some other flaw, perceived or real, that makes him or her not good enough for the love interest.

This trope can go one of two directions from this initial perception or misperception: either the main character embarks on a journey of self-improvement to become worthy of the love interest, or the love interest embarks on a journey of convincing the main character that he or she is fine just the way he/she is.

I've said it before and I'll say it again. Making any significant and permanent personal change in a core value, belief, or ethic is incredibly difficult. It takes real commitment and long-term effort to turn change into a permanent behavior pattern.

There are a few caveats to this trope. 1) If the love interest at any point in your story tells the main character that he or she is not good enough for him or her (and it's a true statement that the love interest can back up with facts or examples of behaviors), this is an unequivocal rejection and should END the relationship right then and there. 2) It's never the responsibility of your romantic partner to fix you. All adults are ultimately responsible for themselves. 3) Nobody is EVER perfect. We all have flaws, traumas, wounds, scars, and imperfections that could use work. That being the case, we will all grow, change, and improve throughout our lives but never achieve perfection.

The main character who steps away from love may do so out of insecurity, or the main character may do this out of a sense of noble sacrifice—it will break my heart to leave the person I love, but if I love the love interest, I'll leave him or her and let this person I love find someone who will make them truly happy.

To which a worthy love interest will snort in disgust or irritation and call B.S. This love interest's challenge will be to convince the main character to stop trying to martyr himself or herself, to remind the main character that the love interest has the intelligence, wisdom, and self-knowledge to choose for himself or herself who is worthy of their love, and to convince the main character that he or she is, in fact, worthy and deserving of love.

At its core, this is a trope about insecurity or lack of self-esteem on the part of the main character. The message this trope generally conveys is something along the lines of I had a low self-opinion or didn't believe in myself. But then you came along and loved me, and that convinced me I'm able to do the thing I couldn't do before or that I was afraid to try doing before or that I must be pretty special if someone as awesome as you loves me, and now I'm all better because you loved me.

Indeed, when we choose a partner for life, we're making an agreement to grow together, to help each other heal from past wounds and traumas, and to stand by each other no matter what. The act of someone loving us that unconditionally can go a long way toward healing wounds and insecurities, and it may give the main character a safe space in which to do the work of healing and growing.

But here's the problem with this whole message. Love—in and of itself—doesn't fix a thing. Not. One. Thing.

Improving one's self-esteem or experiencing personal growth must ultimately come from within oneself. Nobody can give either to you. The mere fact that someone loves you may or may not be enough to motivate a person to engage in the difficult work of self-improvement, self-healing, or self-love.

Of course, the loving support of a life partner can make the work easier, and that partner can encourage you and bolster your resolve when it waivers. But the person making the change must do the work.

I propose that it's more likely the act of loving someone else that prompts a person to engage in such work.

What's the difference, you ask?

If your story's message is that the love interest "loves the main character into being a better person," you're creating a PASSIVE main character who is acted upon by the love interest.

If your story's message is that the main character loves the love interest enough to launch into a project of healing self, personal growth, or learning to love self, this main character is ACTIVELY moving his or her own story forward.

Active characters are heroic. Passive characters are not.

Moreover, we root for active characters (for my non-native English-speaking colleagues, to root for someone is **to express or show support for a person, a team, and so forth: to hope for the success of someone or something).** We find active characters interesting and we want to be like them. These are characters we want to learn life lessons from.

If your main character suddenly decides to believe in himself or herself because someone came along who loves them, your main character could just as easily have made that decision to believe in himself or herself at any time. Instead, your main character passively waited until someone else came along to do the heavy lifting of convincing him or her to get off his or her butt and do the work. Passive characters do not initiate action or change, and instead rely on someone else to act or to force change.

Now, if your story is purely about the love interest, you might get away with a passive partner for him or her. However, I do wonder how much your audience will approve of a love interest's choice to fall for someone who shows so little initiative.

Another pitfall of the insecure main character is forming an image of yourself solely through the eyes of someone else is a recipe for even more self-image issues in the long run.

At the end of the day, self-esteem must come from within you. You must find the things about yourself that you love. You must learn to be yourself and be true to yourself despite what others might think.

As the old saying goes, you must love yourself before you can love others...and before you can accept the love of others.

My last problem with this trope (and then I swear I'll quit picking on it) is the notion of the main character in effect telling the love interest he or she is wrong for falling in love with them. What does it say about the main character's lack of faith in the love interest's judgment to tell the love interest, "you shouldn't love me"?

In reality, this is perhaps one of the most relatable tropes of all the universal romance tropes. We all have insecurities and doubts about our lovability (well, those of us who don't have serious, diagnosable personality disorders, at any rate).

We ALL can relate to a character who worries about being good enough for the amazing person we're attracted to or falling in love with. We all worry about being rejected by the person we bare our soul to and to whom we dare to show our traumas, wounds, scars, flaws, and idiosyncrasies.

Showing another human being *everything* about you is perhaps the most vulnerable thing any human does...apart from daring to love another person.

It takes huge courage to love, and it takes huge courage to tackle one's weaknesses, flaws, and insecurities. It's vital when writing this trope to display that journey of courage to your audience. So, while at its core this is a trope of insecurity, this is also at its core a trope of great personal courage.

.   .   .

ADJACENT TROPES

- Reclusive Hero/Heroine
- Lone Wolf Tamed
- Makeover
- Fear of Intimacy
- Clumsy/Thoughtless/Bumbling Hero/Heroine
- Unrequited Love

WHY READERS/VIEWERS LOVE THIS TROPE

- this is the MOST RELATABLE main character ever. We ARE this person
- if someone that flawed or insecure can find love, then I have a chance, too
- fixing the fixer upper (with the caveat that this is a fantasy. Ultimately, nobody can fix anyone else
- he or she loves me enough to do the hard work of changing, growing, or healing
- loves heals our loved ones, and love heals us

OBLIGATORY SCENES
THE BEGINNING:

All that's required in the beginning of this story is that the main character and love interest meet. Since the main character's journey is to love a person whom they don't feel good enough for, he or she is required to be attracted to the love interest and start to fall in love.

The realization by the main character that he or she isn't good enough may or may not happen in the beginning of the story. However, in this first act you do need to signal to your audience where this story trope is heading...so you probably need to hint at the main character's insecurity or perhaps that there's a terrible wound/trauma/scar/flaw lurking beneath the surface of this character.

You may want to establish the nobility and self-sacrificing nature of the main character if you want to signal that this character is going to do the noble-walking-away thing later in your story.

The love interest doesn't have any inherent journey to take as part of this trope other than talking the main character into sticking around, standing beside and supporting the main character, and standing up for his or her agency to decide whom they think is worthy of their love.

None of these acts involve change or personal growth for the love interest, thus it's typical to pair this trope with another one that forces the love interest on a journey of growth and change of his or her own. Barring that, the love interest will need, at a minimum, a compelling external plot to deal with in the story. Otherwise, the love interest threatens to become a secondary character or mere prop for the main character.

The beginning of the story ends with a mini-crisis—this can be the moment the main character first declares himself or herself unworthy of the love interest. The love interest may or may not take the main character seriously. It can be the first resurfacing of the main character's terrible wound or insecurity. It can be someone or something from the main character's past making a surprise appearance. Whatever you choose, it's the first big challenge to the relationship.

And, of course, we reach the first mini-crisis in the external plot problem your story revolves around.

THE MIDDLE:

The main character's doubts, insecurity, fears, trauma, wound, scar, or flaw becomes clear to all involved. The budding romance between the lovers is a push-pull of what the main character wants to do and what he or she allows self to do. The main character's heart wants to be fully engaged, but his or her head is fighting the romance every step of the way.

We may see the main character actually attempt to break up or walk away in the middle of the story, but for some reason, he or she fails to leave or is foiled in his or her attempt to leave.

The love interest may be engaged in battle with the main character's insecurities, doubts, fears, shame, guilt, and/or a myriad of other emotions. The love interest may be trying to argue that the perceptions aren't true, or that the love interest doesn't care about the wounds/trauma/flaws or may be trying to encourage the main character to work on healing himself or herself.

The love interest may also be engaged in battle with the main character's sense of honor, duty, or self-sacrifice as the main character tries to disengage from the relationship, nobly sacrifice his or her own happiness to allow the love interest to find someone more worthy, or to walk away altogether.

The love interest will likely fight to be seen in the main character's mind as a real, flawed person and not some perfect being on a pedestal.

Secondary characters may interfere, reinforcing the worst the main character thinks of himself or herself.

The external problem of the plot gets worse and builds toward a crisis.

BLACK MOMENT:

The main character breaks off the relationship in such a dramatic or final way that it seems there will be no way to repair the now-broken relationship between him/her and the love interest.

The love interest is devastated. All of his or her efforts to convince the main character that he or she is enough have failed. The main character has insisted on following through with his or her self-destruction, which the main character believes to be some sort of noble sacrifice.

The main character may also do something self-sacrificing in an effort to solve the external plot problem for the love interest, but his or her grand sacrifice to solve the big problem also fails.

The plot problem has gone as terribly wrong as it's possible for this problem to go wrong. No matter what direction the main character or love interest looks, everything has gone as badly as possible. All is well and truly lost.

THE END:

If it's possible to solve both the plot problem and force the lovers to confront their issues simultaneously, that's your optimal ending.

If they need to be solved separately, start by solving the plot problem. This may be the event that brings the lovers back into proximity after their tragic and devastating breakup.

Once they've put aside their individual pain to solve the big external problem, now it's time for one last effort by the love interest to drag the main character out of his or her fortress of solitude.

The main character, having experienced that pain of heartbroken loss may finally be willing to concede that his or her noble sacrifice was ridiculous, or excessive, or not the only possible solution to his or her trauma/wound/insecurity.

The main character also finally concedes that the love interest truly does love him or her, that the love interest is actually willing to be a partner for life through good and bad times, accepting the main character exactly as he or she is.

The main character is now willing to go forward with a partner who will stand beside him or her through the long process of healing, making the changes he or she has already made permanent, and supported by the love interest's steadfast love.

· · ·

KEY SCENES

- the first hint to the audience (and maybe to the love interest) that the main character has a terrible wound
- the love interest tries and fails to convince the main character that the insecurity/trauma/wound/scar is not a deal breaker
- the main character tries to leave but doesn't succeed
- the love interest blows his or her stack at the main character over a declaration of not being good enough
- the love interest worries (or expresses) that he or she is not good enough for the main character
- the main character doesn't believe the love interest's declaration of love
- they finally have a romantic scene and the main character walks away afterward, devastating the love interest

THINGS TO THINK ABOUT WHEN WRITING THIS TROPE

What in the main character's past makes him or her believe now that he or she is not worthy of love?

What about the love interest makes the main character think he or she isn't worthy of the love interest?

How do these two meet?

What about your story will force them together repeatedly or continuously?

What about the value system, upbringing, or past of the main character makes him or her have a rigid set of values?

What makes the main character self-sacrificing?

What flaw(s) does the main character actually have?

What flaw(s) does the love interest have? Does the main character have the flaw(s)? If not, why not? If so, what does he or she think about them?

How aware is the love interest of his or her flaw(s)? How healthy or unhealthy is his or her sense of self-esteem?

When and how will the main character reveal to the love interest what his or her big insecurity/trauma/wound/scar is?

How will you hint to your audience that this wound exists before the main character reveals it to the love interest?

What will the love interest do to seduce the main character?

How will the love interest try to show his or her flaws to the main character?

How do secondary characters feel about this relationship and how will they try to sabotage it or advance it?

Is there a third party in the picture whom the main character thinks is worthy of the love interest? If so, who is it? What does the love interest think of this person? In what ways is this person actually flawed and not at all right for the love interest romantically? How will you show that flaw to the audience? How will the love interest try to convince the main character this person is fatally flawed?

What's the plot problem that throws these two together? How will it get worse? How will it get much worse? How will it get so bad that the main character thinks he or she may have to sacrifice everything (maybe even die) to solve it?

What setbacks will the main character have in his or her efforts to grow/heal/change for the better? How will the love interest react to these? How does the main character react?

In what ways does the love interest help the main character in his or her journey of change? In what ways does the love interest hinder that change? Is it intentional or unintentional, conscious or unconscious?

What does negotiation between the love interest and main character for the main character to stay look like?

Why and how does the main character finally walk away from the love interest?

How does the love interest find out the main character has left? How does the love interest react?

Does the main character find out how the love interest reacted? If so, who lets him/her know?

How will the main plot problem actually be solved? Does it take both the main character and love interest working together to fix it? If not, who fixes it? Also if not, how will the lovers be forced into the same room to confront their relationship issues?

Does solving the big plot problem require the lovers to face their relationship problem simultaneously or not?

What does the love interest say or do that finally gets through to the stubborn main character?

What grand apology does the main character make? How? Where? When?

What does happily ever after look like for this couple?

TROPE TRAPS

Creating a main character so stubborn that he or she can't hear reason from the love interest or from the audience, who is yelling at him in their head.

Creating a main character who doesn't ever recognize the love interest is smart enough to choose correctly for themselves who to love.

Creating a main character who doesn't respect the love interest's choices or decisions.

Creating a love interest who's actually so perfect that the main character has good reason to be intimidated by him or her...which is also off-putting to your audience (NOTE: readers or viewers of this trope are drawn to an imperfect character, so it's a good bet they may not be enamored of a totally perfect character. The reason audiences liked Edward in Twilight was because he was jealous and overprotective and got himself into trouble with both.)

Creating a main character whose values, morals, beliefs, rules of behavior are so rigid that he or she wouldn't ever plausibly be talked out of walking away in a noble self-sacrifice once he or she decides he or she is not good enough for the love interest.

Having a main character with a very rigid set of values being talked out of them too easily by the love interest

Creating a love interest who your audience doesn't think deserves the main character because he or she isn't good enough or doesn't appreciate the main character enough.

Dragging out the angst, self-doubt, and suffering so much that your audience loses interest or starts to want the main character (or love interest) to just walk away.

Creating a whiny main character.

Creating a passive main character.

Crafting a story where the love interest has to do all the work of "fixing" the main character.

Creating a love interest who's no more than a prop as the main character takes up the entire story angsting over his or her personal issues.

Having love magically fix everything and not making the characters actually work to change/grow/heal themselves.

Not showing the long-term commitment to change, the long-term hard work of growing/changing/healing.

Not showing what the couple is going to do to sustain the main character's changes.

Using a lame plot problem that doesn't plausibly throw the main character into a huge dilemma that requires him or her to sacrifice everything.

Creating a solution to the plot problem that allows the main character to fix it completely on his or her own without any help or input from the love interest.

The main character gives in too easily in the end. The love interest forgives too easily in the end.

Not giving your audience a really satisfactory moment of true love expressed (the big, romantic embrace) after all the suffering these two characters have been through.

NOT GOOD ENOUGH FOR HIM/HER TROPE IN ACTION
Movies:

- Titanic
- Me Before You
- She's Out Of My League
- Sideways
- Swept Away
- King of Staten Island
- The Graduate

Books:

- Melt For You by J.T. Geissinger
- Bound by Honor by Cora Reilly
- The Hook Up by Kristen Callihan
- Eye of the Beholder by Ruth Ann Nordin
- Surviving Raine by Shay Savage
- Boss Man by Vi Keeland
- Confess by Colleen Hoover
- The Sweet Gum Tree by Katherine Allred
- Dear Aaron by Mariana Zapata

21

REBOUND ROMANCE

DEFINITION

After going through a (usually) bad, but always painful, break-up, your main character jumps into another romantic relationship before being fully recovered from the last one.

Typically, the main character is not ready for a new relationship or gets into a relationship that's supposed to be no more than a palate cleanser and nothing serious.

It's worth noting that if a character has had a breakup, the next relationship isn't automatically a rebound. It's only a rebound when the main character isn't fully recovered from the previous breakup and takes emotional baggage into a new relationship. It's this baggage that causes the bulk of the problems in this trope.

Your main character may have tried to avoid getting into this new relationship out of concern that he/she isn't ready to be in another relationship, in which case, the love interest may have to work to convince the main character that this is the real deal.

The main character will have to overcome his or her doubts, fears, and wounds from the last relationship before this one can work.

OR

Your main character may dive headlong into a new relationship to distract himself or herself from the last relationship and the lingering pain of the bad breakup.

In this case, he or she may not be ready for the love that comes barreling his or her way. The main character may still be feeling hurt, vulnerable, or grief stricken from the failure of the previous relationship.

Again, the main character must work out his or her feelings before being entirely ready to step into happily ever after with this new love interest.

ADJACENT TROPES

- Burned By Love
- Only One Not Married
- Fresh Start
- Home for the Holiday/Vacation Fling
- Nobody Thinks It Will Work
- Love Triangle

WHY READERS/VIEWERS LOVE THIS TROPE

- someone comes along to sweep away all my pain, heartbreak, loss, or grief
- the sweet revenge of finding true love after the ex dumped me
- finding love when and where I least expect it
- the perfect person is out there and will find me, no matter what
- finally getting love right

- tossing the not quite right one, the fixer upper, the one I was going to settle for or did settle for, and replacing him or her with Mr. or Ms. Perfect-for-me

OBLIGATORY SCENES
THE BEGINNING:

We may see the main character's ugly breakup, or we may see the miserable aftermath of his or her bad breakup. You may also choose to open with the rebounding main character meeting the new love interest. Regardless, the one thing you must establish early on is the rebounding nature of the main character's entrance into a new romantic relationship.

What distinguishes a rebound romance from a plain, old boy-meets-girl romance (fill in the correct pronouns for your story) is the emotional pain the main character is still mired in after his or her last romance failed. Hence, this emotional pain, imbalance, vulnerability, fear, insecurity MUST be established in Act One.

A romantic flirtation and getting to know you ensues.

The beginning typically starts with the first mini-crisis the main character faces as his or her new feelings collide with old feelings...or worse, the ex collides with the new romantic partner.

This story isn't a love triangle in the traditional sense. After all, the main character and ex are completely broken up and stay broken up in this story. But the ex certainly poses a threat to the new relationship and knows enough about the main character and his or her past to throw some serious monkey wrenches into the new relationship. The ex can play head games with both the main character and the new love interest.

If you do choose to structure your story as a metaphorical love triangle, you can think of the third person coming between your main character and love interest to be the ghost of the past relationship.

This ghost may take the form of the actual ex showing up in your story or may take the form of memories, regrets, or lingering, unresolved feelings.

If you plan to introduce a metaphorical love triangle, you probably will want to establish the presence and interference of the ghost of relationships past by the end of Act One.

THE MIDDLE:

Complications ensue. Your rebounding character is in full rebound mode, bouncing back and forth between his or her past feelings and new feelings. This is the source of crossed wires, ups and downs, misunderstandings, and conflict between the main character and love interest.

The main character begins to suspect this could be the real deal in love but is afraid to believe it's true. The love interest may be ready and willing to charge full speed ahead into happily ever after, but the main character is beset by doubts, grief, unresolved feelings for the ex, and questions his or her motives in getting into this new relationship.

Secondary characters (friends, family, coworkers) of both the main character and love interest may have big opinions about the old relationship and the wisdom or stupidity of leaving the ex, about the new love interest, and about the wisdom or stupidity of diving into this rebound romance at all. They're likely to assist or sabotage the new relationship according to their opinions.

There may or may not be much of an external plot to this trope. The machinations of the ex, the love interest, and the secondary characters toward the main character may be plenty to sustain the majority of your story and may provide enough action to carry your plot.

It's also not unheard of for the main character to go through several rebound relationships in quick succession, perhaps passing up the "right" person and having to circle back at some point to reconnect with the person he or she should have identified sooner as the perfect fit.

The attention of the main character wandering to someone else is a fear the love interest may have to grapple with. What's to say the main character won't do to this new love interest what was done to the main character (or that the main character did to the previous love interest) and dump them abruptly?

Sometimes the main character has to go through a bad relationship (or several) to figure out what kind of person is actually right for him or her. This learning process probably happens in the middle of your story, as well.

The middle of your story typically builds toward some conflict or crisis in the rebound romance that threatens to destroy it. We end the first part of the middle (Act Two A) with a crisis that's not quite the black moment but comes close to being that bad and probably triggers the actual black moment.

BLACK MOMENT:

In this story, the main character breaks up with the love interest. It's usually the main character, full of doubts and buyer's remorse at having rebounded in the first place, who calls off the romance.

It is possible the love interest has had it with the main character's waffling, pining for the departed ex, and questioning the authenticity of the new romance and the love interest is the one to walk away.

In either case, the rebound romance has gone fully as badly as everyone said it would. It was fully as big a mistake as everyone warned the main character it was. Not only has the main character hurt himself or herself, but now the main character has also hurt the love interest while trying to get over his or her own issues.

If there's an external plot problem in your story, it falls apart as well. It may be precipitated by the breakup, or it may be the thing that triggers the rebounding main character and love interest to split.

. . .

THE END:

If there's a plot problem to resolve, it probably resolves before the couple gets back together, or the big resolution of the story problem may be the thing that triggers the love interest to speak to the main character and finally let the main character apologize.

The main character finally realizes the error of his or her decision to break up with the love interest. This is the love of the main character's life, after all, and the main character resolves to do whatever it takes to win the love interest back. This trope almost always includes a grand gesture or grand apology by the main character to the love interest...who richly deserves it.

The love interest, who has already been a long-suffering good guy/gal throughout this story, is magnanimous one last time and accepts the main character's dramatic and heartfelt apology.

Happily ever after may be a bit tricky for this couple. There may be an ex to appease or to make clear to him or her the main character is off the market once and for all. The couple may have to convince others that they're making the right decision to be with each other forever.

But the main character may be in a big hurry to lock in this relationship and your story could plausibly end with a fast wedding. For that matter, the love interest may also be in a hurry to lock down the main character before his or her attention wanders again.

KEY SCENES

- the love interest finds out he or she is a rebound for the main character
- the ex makes his or her first appearance in the story— either physically or in a conversation between the main character and love interest
- the main character tries to back out of the rebound romance and break up but fails

- some event or moment causes the love interest to nearly walk away from the main character, but the love interest changes his or her mind at the very last second
- the main character compares the ex and the new love interest (this may be to himself or herself, it may be a conversation with a trusted friend, or it may be a conversation with the love interest)
- people who've previously accused the main character of rebounding change their tune and support the new relationship
- after the first major romantic encounter, the main character says or does something boneheaded to ruin the moment
- the love interest demands that the main character choose —stay or break up, but quit waffling
- the love interest refuses the main character's first attempt to apologize. It may not be a big enough or sincere enough apology, or the love interest may simply refuse to listen or even let the main character speak to him or her

THINGS TO THINK ABOUT WHEN WRITING THIS TROPE

Who was the main character involved with before the rebound romance? What was that relationship like? What were its strengths and flaws? Why did the main character and that person break up? Who initiated the breakup?

What emotional state is the main character in just before commencing the rebound relationship? What feelings is he or she experiencing primarily? What secondary feelings is he or she experiencing?

How will you let your audience know the main character is not fully recovered from the last relationship?

Does the main character go out in search of a new relationship or does someone else encourage him or her to go forth and date again?

How do the main character and love interest meet? Meet cutes are the norm in rebound romances. Where do they meet?

What is the main character's intention initially in this relationship? Does he or she want no relationship at all? Friendship with benefits? A fling? A distraction? Does he or she secretly hope this new relationship will be the One?

Does the main character have a friend or wingman present with him or her when the main character meets the love interest? If so, who? What part does the friend play in the meet cute?

How soon after meeting the main character does the love interest find out this is a rebound relationship for the main character? What does he or she think and feel about that?

Does the love interest try to break off contact with the main character after finding out he or she is a rebound?

What attracts the main character and love interest to each other the most? What flaws do they each bring to the relationship?

If there's an external plot problem, how will it act to throw the lovers together and/or ultimately pull them apart?

Will the main character's ex show up at any point in the story? What happens then?

If the ex doesn't show up in person, how does the specter of the ex make his or her presence known and felt?

What breaks up the main character and love interest?

Does the love interest reject an attempt at an apology from the main character?

How will the main character convince the love interest that he or she won't break up with the love interest abruptly?

How does the main character finally make peace with all the emotions he or she brought into the rebound relationship in the first place?

What physically draws the lovers back together after they've broken up?

Who apologizes to whom? How?

How grand a gesture does the main character have to make to win back the love interest?

What does happily ever after look like for this couple?

TROPE TRAPS

The main character is SO unready for a new relationship that it's wildly implausible that he or she would enter into one or that the love interest would engage romantically with this person.

The love interest is so patient with the main character as to approach martyrdom and becomes implausible and/or unlikable.

The main character isn't really rebounding...he or she is already over the last relationship as much as he or she is ever going to be...but you, the writer, force him or her into acting insecure, emotional, or upset in an implausible way.

Having no plot at all to hand all the relationship ups and downs on.

Failing to create a strong conflict between the main character and love interest above and beyond (or in addition to) the rebound-ness of their relationship.

The love interest never has any doubts about going forward with the relationship once he or she finds out it's a rebound.

The main character never tries to (do the right thing and) back out of the new relationship. At all.

The main character never faces his or her baggage from the previous relationship and deals with it.

The main character throws himself or herself too hard into the new relationship in an unlikable attempt to ignore or bury the emotions and vulnerability from the previous breakup.

Nobody (no friend, family member, or coworker) keeps it real with the main character and tells him or her not get their act together or perhaps to stop taking advantage of the love interest.

There IS no baggage from the previous relationship.

Just how shallow is your main character if they're not feeling anything after a recent, painful breakup?

The main character's epiphany that he or she has made the biggest mistake of his or her life by breaking up with the love interest happens out of thin air. It isn't prompted by plausible events or a learning curve that open the main character's eyes.

The love interest puts up with way too much crap from the main character and comes across as weak, too self-effacing, too low in self-esteem, and too willing to let the main character walk all over him or her.

The main character's grand gesture or grand apology doesn't convince your audience that the love interest should forgive the main character and take back him or her.

REBOUND ROMANCE TROPE IN ACTION
Movies:

- The Company You Keep
- Save the Date
- The Rebound
- The Resident
- Table 19
- Rebound Sex

Books:

- Best Man by Lily Morton
- Honeymoon for One by Kiera Andrews
- Tangle of Need by Nalini Singh
- Jilted by Sawyer Bennett

- Virgin River by Robyn Carr
- Christmas Eve at Friday Harbor by Lisa Kleypas
- Heaven and Hell by Kristen Ashley
- While It Lasts by Abby Glines

22

RECONCILIATION/SECOND CHANCE

DEFINITION

In this perennially popular trope, the main character and love interest have had a romantic relationship with each other in the past that has failed. They broke up, went their separate ways, and now they're going to give a romantic relationship another try.

This is a wildly popular trope because lots of people do this in real life. Studies vary somewhat, but between 30% and 44% of all people surveyed do get back with an ex at some point in their lives. About half of those who get back together stay together and about half break up again.

Your job, then, is to get these ex'es back into physical proximity with each other and cause enough interaction, friction, and attraction to force them to consider rekindling their old relationship.

The word reconciliation suggests this couple retains at least a little connection or some remnant of a connection that is going to be repaired. This is possible. It's also possible they complete severing their relationship in the past and are going to have to rebuild a new one from scratch.

In either case, there are unresolved issues from the previous attempt at love between them that will have to be resolved before they can get it right this time around and get to happily ever after.

If the couple's issues from the past are complicated and dramatic enough, the work of solving them may be enough to sustain your entire story. However, you should probably consider introducing a new set of problems or conflicts on top of the original set for the couple to have to solve. People do not remain the same over time, and they fix some of their issues at the same time they're accumulating new traumas, wounds, scars, insecurities, and other problems that form an obstacle to a healthy relationship.

At its core this is a trope of forgiveness...however, it's reductive to suggest that all these people have to do to be happy forever is forgive each other. They're going to have to resolve their old and new conflicts, fix their traumas/wounds/scars, rebuild trust, build a new framework for their relationship, and only then forgive each other and move forward.

ADJACENT TROPES

- Couple's Therapy
- Forgiveness
- Bad Boy/Girl Reformed
- Redemption
- Coming Home

WHY READERS/VIEWERS LOVE THIS TROPE

- who doesn't wonder what would have happened if we got back together with a past love
- getting a do-over on past mistakes and answering the question of "what if I had only..."

- being forgiven for past mistakes, transgressions, and harms I inflicted on someone
- he or she loves me enough to come back and try again
- I'm lovable enough that he or she never got over me
- finally catching the one who got away

OBLIGATORY SCENES
THE BEGINNING:

The main characters are thrust back together, and the mood of their meeting will set the tone for the rest of your story. A re-meet cute is normal if this is going to be a comedic or light-hearted story, and a tense opening is typical for a more suspenseful story.

It's a good bet at least one of these two people who've broken up once before isn't going to be thrilled to see their ex—at least not overtly. The degree of friction you establish in the opening will signal to your audience just how difficult this couple's past issues are going to be to overcome.

Of course, it's possible to paint two people who loved each other deeply, were broken up by circumstances beyond their control, one or both of their situations has changed, and now they have a chance to finish what they started long ago. However, beware of failing to create a real possibility that this couple won't find their way back to love lest your story have no tension at all, no stakes, nothing to keep your reader turning the pages to find out what happens next.

It's important, in a story where the characters already know each other very well and have already found a love connection together before, to throw a new complication or two into the mix that they haven't dealt with before. Otherwise, your story threatens to become no more than an extending telling of a backstory as this couple recreates their past relationship and moves through the same issues they did before in search of a solution to whatever problem(s) they face.

The beginning typically ends with a mini-crisis where the couple encounters some unpleasant reminder of what broke them up before or runs into a conflict that threatens to estrange them from each other again.

It's a common device to create some sort of external plot problem that forces these two people back into the same place at the same time. Otherwise, they'd not likely choose to see each other or interact ever again. After all, if these two are, in fact, destined to be together, their first breakup must have been painful indeed.

THE MIDDLE:

It's in the middle of your story where you're likely to show your audience what happened in the past that ultimately broke up the couple. As always, be stingy with flashbacks whenever possible and try to keep the present action moving forward at a brisk pace.

You'll want to take the old problem and make it even worse this time around. Ideally, you'll make it much, much worse to deal with this time around. New complications, consequences, or ramifications have come along to make a solution to the old problem even more intractable.

Whatever external problem brought the main character and love interest back together has to build toward a crisis in this part of your story. This problem can either pull the couple together as they have to work together to solve it, or it can push them apart as they disagree over how to solve it, or it can do both at the same time.

Whatever new complications you've thrown at the couple also build toward some sort of crisis. This complication may interact negatively with their old deal breaker problem, or it may be an entirely separate complication that also has to be dealt with.

BLACK MOMENT:

All of the pressures on this relationship overwhelm the couple and break them up...again. It's even more painful the second time around after they dared to hope they might find a way back to each other. In addition to the pain of losing love, they also have the recriminations of knowing it was never going to work...it was doomed to end the same way it did the first time.

Failing once at love is bad. Failing a second time with the same person—when one should have known better—is exponentially worse.

The external plot problem explodes and whatever negative consequences of not successfully solving that problem happen. These consequences probably contribute to breaking up the couple or at least yank them apart even further.

If one of the lovers has physically come back to a place where the other one lives, the visiting lover is likely to leave and have no desire or plan to ever return. The implosion of the problem and rekindled love is complete.

THE END:

It's often the external plot problem that forces the lovers together one last time. The need to solve the problem is so great, the consequences of not succeeding so dire, that the couple has to put aside their breakup and give it one last try to fix the problem.

For people who've been twice burned at love, now, odds are that nothing short of a huge consequence will force them to face the other one again.

It's not uncommon that the second breakup is so traumatic it actually provokes some significant life lessons that lead to fundamental character, value-based, ethical, or moral changes in each of the lovers. It's possibly these changes arising from the ashes of devastation that allow the couple to finally overcome all their issues, old and new.

It may take a significant confrontation or conversation to sort out everything this couple needs to sort out. Given that this can turn into a massive talking heads scene, it's not uncommon to break up their big airing out of everything with action sequences or to interweave their big reconciliation talk with some sort of action.

At any rate, the external plot problem is finally solved and its negative repercussions avoided or fixed. The couple finally solves all their deal breaker issues, forgives each other, and can finally be together happily and healthily.

KEY SCENES

- the first rehashing of old grievances between the lovers
- the first time they go out in public together again as a couple
- the first romantic scene where they rekindle the old flame between them
- the first time they each remember why this person drove them crazy
- the new conflict and old conflict overlap or amplify each other into an even bigger conflict than ever
- they nearly split up again but don't quite manage to go through with it
- the big epiphanies that cause each of them to grow enough to be able to forgive past wrongs and move forward

THINGS TO THINK ABOUT WHEN WRITING THIS TROPE

How did they meet the first time around? How did they fall in love?

What broke them up the last time? How bad a breakup was it?

How hard did they try to save the relationship the first time? What did they try? Why did they fail?

How did they each feel about the first breakup? Did they feel the same way or differently? Why?

What brings them back together now? How do they each feel about that—how do they really feel in their heart of hearts, and is that different or the same than the reaction they show the world and show the other lover?

Do they fight having to come back together to solve a problem or not?

Has either of them thought about trying to get back together with the other person before they come back into proximity?

Has either of them had regrets about how it ended before?

Did either of them wish for a different outcome the first time?

Has either of them considered finding the other one before now? It's worth noting that in studies, up to 88% of single people and 65% of married people check out their ex on social media to find out what they're up to.

How do the people around them feel about this other person coming back into their lives? What do friends, family, and coworkers do about it?

What old problems between them will resurface now? How will you introduce them? How can you make them worse than before? How can you make them *much* worse now?

How have the main character and love interest changed since they last saw each other? How have they become better people? How have they become worse?

What new conflicts will you introduce between the lovers? Do these new conflicts interact with the conflict(s) that broke them up or not? If so, how? If not, how do the two conflicts tug each lover in opposite directions?

What's going to break them up the second time? What about this is going to be even more devastating than their first breakup?

How will the external plot problem have awful consequences for them if they don't solve it?

Is the external problem the mechanism by which you'll force the couple back together one last time? If so, how?

What do they each feel and learn after their second breakup? How does this allow them to do what's necessary to get back together in the end?

How will the external plot problem be solved?

What do the lovers need to confess, apologize for, and forgive to be able to move forward together?

Does either of them need to make some sort of grand gesture to demonstrate their apology? If so, what's the gesture?

How will you show your audience that both of these people have truly made the changes necessary to sustain a healthy relationship for the long term?

TROPE TRAPS

Creating two people who hate each other so bitterly after their first breakup that they would never plausibly get back together...ever.

Casting one of the lovers as the sole villain in the previous breakup. It's rare that only one person makes any mistakes that cause a relationship to fail.

These exes say things to each other when they first come back into proximity that are so mean or hurtful there's no way they would ever rekindle a relationship with each other

The attraction is purely physical. Great sex is not enough to sustain any relationship forever.

One or both of the main characters is so unlikable your audience roots for them not to reconcile.

The behavior by one or both main characters that broke them up the first time is a big enough red flag that no sane or smart person would go back to that person.

Failing to show the long, hard work of making changes to improve self that one or both characters has undertaken in the interim before the last relationship and now.

Failing to up the consequences of not solving the old problem between the lovers.

Failing to give the lovers a new problem to wrestle with and crafting your entire story around rehashing old grudges and arguments.

Using too much backstory to tell what happened in the past and killing the pacing of your current story.

Failing to have your characters change or grow since the last time around.

The external problem that brings the lovers together is lame, could have been handled from afar, or isn't interesting to your audience. Yes, this problem is a MacGuffin and not central to this trope. But don't be lazy about creating it.

The external problem has no serious consequences to the lovers of failing to solve it.

If the lover's relationship problems were solvable by just sitting down and having an honest, adult conversation, why didn't they do that long before the end of your story?

Failing to create personal problems between the lovers that take actual effort to resolve.

Failing to put the characters in situations or emotional pain suffi- –cient to provoke major epiphanies—epiphanies your audience will need to see if they're to believe the couple can actually fix their problems.

The lovers forgive each other too easily for past wrongs.

The lovers don't earn the forgiveness the other ultimately grants.

Your audience doesn't believe the changes one or both characters have made are going to stick and this couple is going to end up breaking up again.

RECONCILIATION/SECOND CHANCE TROPE IN ACTION
Movies:

- Die Hard
- Fatal Attraction
- Sweet Home Alabama
- Cat On A Hot Tin Roof
- The Notebook
- Something's Gotta Give
- Mamma Mia
- Ticket to Paradise

Books:

- Love and Other Words by Christina Lauren
- People We Meet On Vacation by Emily Henry
- Final Offer by Lauren Asher
- Every Summer After by Carley Fortune
- Before We Were Strangers by Renée Carino
- It Starts With Us by Colleen Hoover
- The Mistake by Elle Kennedy
- Seven Days In June by Tia Williams
- Persuasion by Jane Austen

23
REDEMPTION

DEFINITION

Redemption stories all have three parts: 1) the main character makes a terrible mistake or has a disastrous failure; 2) the main character realizes he or she has done a bad thing or failed in a big way; 3) he or she sets out to make amends.

In the redemption trope, you can start your story at any one of these three points. But, if you don't start at the beginning, which is fine, you will have to show or tell your audience and the other characters in your story the terrible mistake/disastrous failure in backstory, flashback, or narrative.

Likewise, if you start your story with the main character having already realized he or she has done a bad thing or failed in a big way, you'll undoubtedly have to recount that moment of epiphany in backstory, flashback, or narrative within your story.

Don't let having to drop into backstory or flashback put you off of starting your story at or after the point where your main character has decided to make amends if that's where you'd prefer to start. Just beware of inserting this background information too early in your story where it interrupts the forward movement of the story, where it slows the packing, or where it pulls your audience out of a story to which they're not fully committed, yet.

At any rate, your main character may have wronged the love interest in the past and seeks in your story to make amends, or the thing for which he or she is seeking redemption may have nothing at all to do with the love interest.

Your story will mainly revolve around your main character's quest to make amends and redeem himself or herself—either in someone else's eyes or in his/her own eyes.

The love interest is instrumental in helping or hindering the main character's quest to make amends and is probably instrumental in granting absolution for the past mistake or failure. Which is to say, the love interest's opinion of the main character and his or her quest to make amends will be of key importance to the main character.

Typically in this trope, the main character has ONE chance to make amends. It may be an only chance, or it may be a last chance, but either way, this is it. The main character succeeds or fails on this attempt and that's what he or she will have to live with for the rest of his or her life.

(If this character has all the chances in the world to make amends, then there will be no tension whatsoever to your story, no stakes as it were. If he or she messes it up this time, the main character will just try again.)

The nature of the mistake or failure you choose for your main character will set the entire tone of your story's quest for redemption. Is it a life-or-death quest? Is it a public humiliation or public redemption quest? Is personal happiness or a personal relationship at stake?

Not only is this a quest for forgiveness for the mistake, but it's also a quest to make things right or to get it right this time. It's a do-over, but this time the stakes are even bigger than ever—all or nothing, win or lose *everything*. For that reason, you must force your main character to put everything on the line in his or her pursuit of redemption.

. . .

ADJACENT TROPES

- Forgiveness
- Bad Boy/Girl Reformed
- Reconciliation/Second Chance Romance

WHY READERS/VIEWERS LOVE THIS TROPE

- we all have mistakes or failures in our pasts we'd love to make amends for
- he or she loves me enough to do the hard work of making amends/making it right to me
- we all have had people do things to us we wish they'd apologize for and make amends for
- seeing someone arrogant or who thinks he/she is better than us brought low and having to grovel and work hard for redemption
- any mistake or failure can be fixed if one is but willing to do the work

OBLIGATORY SCENES
THE BEGINNING:

The hero and heroine meet or meet again. If they meet for the first time, this meeting will set the tone for their future relationship, be it cute, fraught with danger, or filled with sparks of attraction or angry friction. If they're meeting again, this reunion will likely be tinged with the tone of their last parting, be it acrimonious, hurt, sad, outraged, or something else.

The external plot problem of the story may be the main character's quest that must be completed to gain redemption.

OR

The external plot problem may be something that interferes with the main character achieving redemption. In this case, the plot problem must be solved so the main character can move ahead with his or her quest for redemption.

OR

The external plot problem can be completely unrelated to the main character's quest for redemption. It can be a problem pertaining mainly to the love interest or it can be a problem that distracts the main character from his or her primary quest of making amends.

By the end of the beginning, the first big problem with the external plot has happened and is causing problems. Also, the first big challenge to the relationship between the main character and love interest has reared its ugly head and is causing a threat to the nascent romance.

THE MIDDLE:
This is where the main character's quest really gets rolling, with successes and failures, ups and downs.

At the same time, the relationship between the main character and love interest faces challenges—possibly rehashing past grievances, remembering past reasons for attraction and anger.

Or, if this is a new relationship, the main character's drive to make amends begins to conflict with the love interest's desire for attention and time with the main character. As the middle draws to an end, the conflict between the needs of the relationship and the needs of the main character's quest draws to a head and forces a crisis.

. . .

BLACK MOMENT:

The main character, forced to choose between love and his or her quest, chooses the quest...and destroys the relationship. The main character may walk out on the love interest to go pursue making amends, or the love interest may give an ultimatum, after which the main character walks away. In either case, the relationship falls apart as the main character's obsession with redemption wins out.

In the meantime, the quest itself falls apart. The main character's big effort to achieve the objective fails spectacularly and completely. He or she has lost everything. Not only has he or she failed to attain redemption, but he or she has also lost the love of his or her life. All is lost.

THE END:

The main character must gather himself or herself and make one last, Herculean effort to achieve the goal that will give him or her redemption. If the redemption has nothing to do with the love interest, the main character may or may not do this with the help/support of the love interest. If the redemption requires gaining forgiveness from the love interest or making amends to the love interest, obviously the love interest will be involved in the final effort.

After having finally achieved redemption, the main character can finally turn his or her attention to matters of love. Then and only then can he or she apologize to the love interest, declare his or her love, and ask the love interest to be with him or her forever.

While it's a given in most adventure stories that the love interest will enthusiastically embrace the triumphant main character, all excited at the main character's victory over evil or some difficult challenge, you should feel free to make the main character grovel a bit before the love interest takes him or her back. It's not necessarily a pleasant experience to play second fiddle to the main character's obsessive quest, and the love interest can demand an apology and a promise that he or she will never be put second to anything in the main character's heart or mind.

KEY SCENES

- the aftermath to the main character of the mistake or failure from the past is revealed
- the main character declares his or her intent to make amends
- if the thing the main character is making amends for has to do with the love interest, the first confrontation between the pair when the love interest declares having no interest in amends being made to him or her
- the main character has to choose between the quest and love interest early on, and chooses the quest...a harbinger of things to come
- the love interest helps the main character with his or her quest in some meaningful way
- after a failure by the main character in the course of the quest for redemption, the love interest comforts the main character and offers encouragement

THINGS TO THINK ABOUT WHEN WRITING THIS TROPE

What is the event, mistake, or failure from which the main character feels a need to redeem himself or herself?

Why does the main character feel compelled to make amends for this past thing?

To whom does the main character owe amends? If it's the love interest, what did he or she do to the love interest?

Does the main character know initially what form the amends

must take? If so, what is it? If not, when and how will the main character figure out how to make amends?

How do the main character and love interest meet in your story? If they've never met, what brings them together not only to meet but to stay together through your story?

If the main character and love interest have a past, how is the love interest involved with the main character's quest to make amends? Is the love interest pleased or displeased to be involved in this quest? Is the love interest willing or unwilling to be involved?

What steps does the main character have to take to make amends and achieve redemption? What successes will he/she have along the way? What failures?

What's the external plot problem if it isn't solely the thing the main character has to do or achieve to make amends?

What is the love interest trying to do in this story that gives him or her something to do besides act as a prop to hinder or help the main character's quest?

What attracts your lovers to each other? What drives them crazy in a good way and bad way about each other?

What do the people around these two think of their new or renewed relationship? Will these people try to support or sabotage the relationship? How?

What in the relationship is going to become a crisis that threatens to break them up?

What in the quest to make amends threatens to break up the couple *besides* the main character's obsession with it?

What will make the plot problem worse? Much worse? Nigh impossible to resolve?

What will make the main character's quest for amends harder? Ever harder? Nearly impossible to succeed at?

What will happen if the main character fails in this one, last effort to achieve redemption? (Or what won't happen?) How can you make this outcome worse? Much worse? Absolutely terrible?

Why does the main character choose the quest over the love

interest to cause the romantic black moment? Why does he or she think it was the right decision? What does the love interest think of both the decision and the reasoning for it?

How does the main character fail in his or her quest, fail to make amends, and fail to achieve redemption as part of the black moment? NOTE: This is the penultimate effort as opposed to the final effort in which he or she finally succeeds.

What will the main character do differently to succeed when he or she gives it one last try to succeed in his/her quest for redemption? Does the love interest help or make the difference in this final attempt?

Does the main character's success in his or her final attempt to make amends resolve the romantic conflict, or is that going to take a separate action/conversation/apology/gesture? If so, what is that separate thing?

Who has to forgive whom for what between the main character and love interest?

Who makes a grand gesture of devotion to whom? What is the gesture?

What is said or happens that makes the main character know he or she has finally, irrevocably achieved redemption?

Does the main character have any other redemption quests to complete, or is he or she done with such pursuits?

What does happily ever after look like for this couple?

TROPE TRAPS

The main character is so obsessed with his/her quest for redemption that he/she has no time or attention to give to a potential love interest.

The love interest is little more than a prop to support the main character's quest.

The love interest—if the target of the main character's amends—

too readily forgives the main character or too obstinately is unwilling to accept the amends.

The love interest is so unimpressed with the main character's efforts to do better, to be better, and to make amends that the audience finds him/her completely unlikable and undeserving of the main character.

The main character is too perfect from the very beginning. Yes, the person's quest is noble at its core and admirable, but he or she needs to actually have some lesson left to learn or some mistake/failure to be corrected.

The quest or thing to be achieved to earn redemption is too easy.

The main character doesn't fail badly enough along the way to put the successful outcome of his/her quest in any doubt.

The main character fails to feel legitimate remorse for past mistakes and relies instead on some big action or gesture to make it all better instead of sincere remorse and apology.

The main character never makes a serious apology at all.

The main character's apology doesn't include all the elements of a good apology:

- Expression of regret
- Explanation of what went wrong
- Acknowledgment of responsibility
- Declaration of repentance
- Offer of repair
- Request for forgiveness

The moment the main character achieves the huge quest, the love interest forgives

him or her for all past transgressions or mistakes without ever requiring the main character to own up to his or her failings and offer an apology.

. . .

REDEMPTION TROPE IN ACTION
   Movies:

- Everything Everywhere All At Once
- Starbuck
- Amélie
- The Butterfly Effect
- What Dreams May Come
- Lost Christmas
- It's A Wonderful Life

Books:

- The Third Baseman by Lulu Moore
- Renata Vitali by Parker S. Huntington
- Until My Last Breath by Tiffany Patterson
- For the Love of Whiskey by Melissa Foster
- Promise Me Always by A.L. Jackson
- Beautifully Broken Control by Catherine Cowles
- Forget Me Not by Q.B. Tyler
- The Happy Ever After Playlist by Abby Jimenez
- The Secret of Ella and Micha by Jessica Sorensen

24

REHABILITATION/ RECOVERY

DEFINITION

In this trope the main character has undergone or is undergoing some sort of rehabilitation or recovery process.

To differentiate this trope from the Disabled Hero/Heroine who has a physical disability, I'm going to limit this trope to characters undergoing therapy for addiction or a psychological issue, or recovering from some sort of choice, action, or event that they've done or that has happened to them.

While it's possible for both main characters to simultaneously be on a journey of rehabilitation or recovery, you're biting off a lot of big emotional issues and problems to deal with if both of your main characters are completely dismantling their old lives and trying to build new, healthier lives, all while falling in love and trying to form a long-lasting relationship. By all means, feel free to tackle this sort of story. Just expect it to be complicated and messy.

For what it's worth, most therapists do not recommend that anyone currently undergoing intensive rehab or recovery try to build a new relationship with anyone else at the same time.

The work this person must do on himself or herself is typically all-consuming and as difficult as one person can reasonably handle.

This kind of work does not usually benefit from the added complication of falling in love with all its emotional ups and downs.

At any rate, you've probably got a main character who is currently in rehab/recovery, or has relatively recently completed it, and is now moving forward with his or her life. Into this new life comes the love interest and a new romantic relationship.

The lingering issues the main character is still wrestling with, learning to live with, or establishing new behavior patterns to combat are a primary source of challenge to this new relationship.

Exactly what your main character is recovering from or completing rehabilitation from can vary widely. Most obvious: a drug or alcohol addict who has recently gotten clean and is going straight.

But there are lots of other possibilities:

- You might choose to write about a criminal who has recently completed his or her sentence (rehabilitation programs are common inside prisons and many transitional programs upon departure from incarceration include rehabilitation support).
- Perhaps your main character has had some sort of mental or emotional breakdown.
- Perhaps he or she has been the victim of a serious crime and had to undergo intensive therapy to deal with it.

Recovery and rehabilitation after a physical injury, for example, a major accident or surgery, can also contain a heavy psychological element. For the person who killed someone else in an accident or tragedy, the person whose spouse or child died in an accident or tragedy, or the person who lost a limb or major organ in a surgery, there's definitely a psychological component to recovery.

Regardless of what type of recovery or rehabilitation you choose to write about, your main character is dealing with some big emotions and likely a serious reboot of his or her life. In the timeframe of your story, he or she is probably stepping out into their new life for the first time. This is also probably the first romantic relationship he or she has attempted after rehab or recovery.

Sadly, stigma is often attached to rehabilitation or recovery. Your main character may be reluctant to talk about it or may not admit to having done it right away, which can be a source of conflict or trust issues for the love interest.

Depending on how recently completed or ongoing the rehab/recovery is, your main character may have backslides, recurrences of problems, or fall off the recovery wagon altogether, creating sources of trouble for this budding romance.

Also, rehab and recovery aren't easy. The difficulty of knowing oneself more deeply, facing one's traumas, and healing deep emotional wounds is hard work that requires facing the exact things a person least wants to face. If these aspects of one's life were easy to face and deal with in the first place, this character would probably have done it long ago and have already moved on with his or her life.

There are any number of possible sources for conflict that threaten to break up your lovers in this trope. For example:

- Old problems may not be fully solved and cause new problems.
- People from the main character's past may try to suck him or her back into an old, self-destructive lifestyle.
- The main character may not have adapted to new ways of acting and feeling.
- The main character may not have forgiven himself or herself for past mistakes or transgressions.
- The love interest may not trust the permanence of changes the main character has made.
- The love interest may not believe the main character will choose their relationship over self-destruction.

It is these sorts of conflicts that drive this trope forward and give it movement and shape its archetypal structure.

. . .

ADJACENT TROPES

- Bad Boy/Girl Reformed
- Damaged Hero/Heroine
- Disabled Hero/Heroine
- Fresh Start

WHY READERS/VIEWERS LOVE THIS TROPE

- I can fix the person I love
- what would fixing my flawed romantic partner look like
- my romantic partner loves me enough to do the hard work to become better or perfect for me
- real and lasting recovery is possible from my own traumas and for those of the people I love
- the fantasy of a dark, dangerous lover who's right on the edge of taboo

OBLIGATORY SCENES
THE BEGINNING:

The hero and heroine meet. The way they meet will set the tone for the rest of your story. Rehab and recovery stories historically tend to deal with heavy, dark issues. Regardless of what kind of recovery your main character is undergoing, the fact is it's going to be hard. Hence the typical choice to lean toward a dark story. That doesn't mean you can't inject humor and lightness into this type of story, and a meet cute is a good way to do that.

The main character may or may not tell the love interest right away about his or her rehab/recovery process, particularly if the main character has completed the in-patient or most intensive portion of the journey. After all, recovery is often a lifelong process that never really ends.

The love interest finds some aspect of the main character attractive, and which aspect(s) you pick will likely point at the path your story goes down. If the love interest is attracted to new behaviors, newly forged pieces of the main character's personality, the romance will probably reinforce these character qualities.

But, if the love interest is attracted to one of the self-destructive elements of the main character's psyche, this is likely to cause big problems for the main character in stepping away from that side of self.

Huh, I hear you asking? How about an example...

Let's say a main character recently released from prison intervenes to save the love interest from a mugging, has to violently fight off the attackers, and the love interest is attracted to that physical protectiveness. This has a lot of potential to cause trouble for the main character who must stay out of fights or who is now committed to finding non-violent solutions to all the problems in his or her life.

In the beginning of this trope, the external problem of your story is, of course, introduced. Often, writers reach for someone or something out of the main character's past that comes back to haunt him or her or tries to draw him or her back into their pre-rehab/pre-recovery patterns of behavior.

Side note: I personally like to make this problem involve the love interest heavily, since the main character already has tons of angst and drama surrounding him or her. The external problem is a way to give the love interest a balancing amount of angst and drama in the story.

The beginning of this trope usually ends with some sort of challenge to the main character's recovery or rehabilitation. It can be a major setback in recovery or a backslide that threatens to derail the whole recovery process. This may be the moment the main character reveals his or her rehab/recovery to the love interest. Someone may show up out of the main character's past and try to suck him or her back into a self-destructive behavior.

Whatever you choose, this moment is a shock to the main character and a shock to the new romantic relationship.

THE MIDDLE:

The complications of the main character's past really get messy in the middle of this story, which in turn cause problems in the budding romance.

The love interest may be trying to help the recovery process or may be kept outside of that process by the main character. The love interest may not understand the process or may hinder it in some way—intentionally or unintentionally. Although I have to say it's not the least bit heroic to hinder someone's recovery process. I might be careful of having your love interest interfere with the main character's hard work to build a new life unless your love interest has a really compelling and justified reason to interfere with it.

Regardless, in the middle of your story, the challenges to the main character's rehab/recovery get exponentially more difficult to deal with. The external plot problem(s), secondary characters, people from the main character's past, old patterns of behavior in the main character, or the love interest himself or herself are a few possible sources of these challenges.

It's easy for the love interest to get lost in this story. The main character's big issues, big struggles, and big journey tend to overshadow the love interest. So, it's important to find a way to make the love interest an integral part of the main character's journey toward recovery and not just a prop that acts as the external reason the main character keeps fighting to recover.

In this trope, you may find it useful to think of the middle of the story as a pressure cooker. More and more problems, push-pulls, and demands, temptations, and dilemmas pile onto the main character until he or she implodes...or explodes.

As the main character reaches a crisis, so does the relationship. Whatever the love interest has been dealing with personally also comes to a head and collides with the main character's issues and the conflicts within the relationship itself.

And last but not least, the external plot problem boils over in the middle of everything else coming to a head. This is one of those tropes that gets well and truly messy before it gets better.

BLACK MOMENT:

The main character, forced to choose between his or her rehab/recovery and something else—the romantic relationship, the love interest, going back to old ways, old friends and associates, old patterns of behavior—chooses wrong.

The love interest walks away if he or she hasn't already been pushed away by the main character.

The external plot problem goes terribly wrong and the consequences of the couple's failure to solve it come crashing down upon their heads. Now it's going to be even harder to fix the problem if it's even possible at all.

The main character's rehab/recovery evaporates and his or her life goes to hell. Again. But this time it's even worse because he or she has just thrown away all that hard work to get it right, do things better, be a better person. Now he or she knows how in the wrong he or she is for acting this way and making this choice.

THE END:

A whole bunch of problems have to be resolved in the end of your story. Perhaps least important of them will be sorting out the external plot problem. Even though fixing the plot problem might require big physical risk or danger, this scene may be completely overshadowed by the looming emotional confrontations necessary for the main character, the love interest, and the two of them as a couple to work out their issues.

Before the grand gesture(s), big apologies, and forgiveness can happen, the main character either has to learn a big new lesson or remember one he or she has already learned. This character has to drag himself or herself back onto the path of healing and growth through sheer stubborn determination...frequently fueled by love and his or her determination not to lose the love interest forever.

Whatever lessons the love interest has to learn so he or she can work out his or her own issues must happen before the big reconciliation can happen. It's easy to overlook the love interest's change/growth arc in this trope because of how much oxygen the main character tends to take up with his or her giant emotional arc.

Once the characters forgive each other, they have one more leap to take—trusting each other enough, and trusting the main character's recovery enough, to commit to a long-term relationship.

Then, you can finally give the pair of lovers their happily ever after moment. It's usually a hard-earned one for both your characters and your audience.

KEY SCENES

- the love interest finds out about the main character's difficult past. (the main character may or may not be the person who reveals it)
- the love interest confronts the main character about some aspect of his or her past that the main character has kept secret
- the love interest reveals or demonstrates some flaw of his or her own
- the love interest fails to trust the main character in a situation that the main character asks him or her to

- the main character gives in to a temptation or falls off the recovery wagon to the detriment of the love interest
- the love interest gives the main character an ultimatum

THINGS TO THINK ABOUT WHEN WRITING THIS TROPE

(Obviously) What is your main character rehabilitating or recovering from?

What's the backstory that led up to the event(s) that the main character now has to rehab or recover from?

How much rehab/recovery has the main character completed before the story begins?

Who is administering the rehab/recovery for the main character? Is this person a mentor? A friend? An antagonist? A pain in the main character's butt? What role will this character play in your story? What kind of relationship will this person have with the love interest? Will he or she encourage or warn off the love interest?

Who is your love interest?

How do the main character and love interest meet? What tone does it set for your story?

What about these two people attracts them to each other?

When does the main character reveal his or her rehab/recovery process to the love interest? How does the main character do it or avoid doing it?

If the main character doesn't tell the love interest everything, what does he or she leave out? Does someone else fill in the gaps for the love interest? If so, who, how, and when?

How little or much does the love interest trust the main character initially? Why?

What is the main external plot problem? Does it mainly cause problems for the love interest, the main character, or both of them? What tone does this problem set for your story?

How will the plot problem get worse? How will it get MUCH worse? How will it become impossible or unbearable?

How will the plot problem challenge the main character's rehab/recovery process? How will it REALLY challenge the process? How will it make it nearly impossible for the main character to stay on track?

What is something endearing the main character can do for the love interest, and vice versa?

What are some quiet moments of affection, peace, or happiness these two characters can experience in contrast to all the emotional baggage and drama they're grappling with?

How do the friends, family, and coworkers of the main character and love interest feel about this relationship and this new person in their loved one's life?

Which people around the couple will support the relationship and which ones will try to sabotage it?

What secret(s) have the main character and love interest been keeping from each other, if any? When and how do these get revealed? How does that go?

What conflicts develop between these two characters that are unrelated to the rehab/recovery journey?

What big issue threatens to break up this couple? Trust? Back-sliding? Temptations? Bad decisions? Lack of communication? Something else?

How does the plot problem help break up this couple?

What is the final straw that breaks this couple up? Does one character walk away from the other? If so, which one? Or is it a mutual break-up? If so, what reasons does each character have?

What lesson(s) do each of the characters need to learn or remember over the course of this story?

What epiphany does each character need to have to decide to give the relationship one last chance?

How will this couple solve the external plot problem? Will the main character have to do one last "bad" thing to solve the problem, or is there another way to solve it?

Who sacrifices what for the other person in this story?

What kind of reckoning do these two people need to have individually with themselves and with each other? Who owes whom an apology and for what?

Who will make a grand gesture to whom to prove his or her love? What's the gesture(s)?

What big emotional payoff moment will you give your characters and audience...who've definitely earned one by the end of this story?

How will the main character convince the love interest that he or she has permanently changed and can sustain his or her new life, new values/beliefs, new behaviors for the long term?

How will you convince the audience the main character can sustain his or her rehabilitation or recovery permanently?

What does happily ever after look like for this couple? Will you give your audience a glimpse forward in time to reassure them the couple is okay, or will you end your story on the promise of a future?

TROPE TRAPS

Describing the rehabilitation/recovery journey in an implausible or unrealistic way that ticks off people who've actually been through the process. Trust me: these audience members won't hesitate to leave scathing comments and reviews.

Creating too perfect a main character with few to no scars from his or her past and is unbelievable.

Creating too perfect a love interest to be plausible.

Creating too naïve a love interest to be plausible.

The love interest trusts the main character too easily or conversely, doesn't trust the main character enough after the main character proves himself or herself.

The love interest is too judgmental of the main character.

The love interest has no growth arc of his or her own and is a cardboard character with no purpose other than being a prop for the main character's journey.

The love interest fades into the background and is completely uninteresting...when in fact, that character should plausibly have a major story of his or her own. The classic example of this is Adrienne in the movie, "Rocky."

The main character has nobody who was involved in his or her rehab/recovery checking up on them, keeping tabs on them, or showing any interest in them.

The main character too easily falls back into old ways without internal emotional conflict or conversely too easily resists falling back into old ways without internal emotional turmoil.

The main character has to do all the growing, make all the concessions, do all the sacrificing to make the romance work, and the love interest does nothing.

Your audience doesn't believe the love interest appreciates or deserves the main character.

Your main character is so flawed, damaged, or traumatized that he or she can't plausibly achieve the degree of rehabilitation or recovery you portray in your story, particularly given the timeline you choose or the amount of rehab/recovery work you describe or portray.

You fail to show the ongoing nature of rehab and recovery.

You fail to acknowledge that nobody ever completely recovers from and moves on unscathed from any major trauma or tragedy; rather, we learn to live with them and with the scars they leave behind.

You fail to convince the audience that the main character is able to make the changes in his or her life permanent.

You fail to convince the audience this couple is going to be okay.

You don't give the couple or your audience the big emotional payoff at the end of the story that they've all worked so hard for and suffered so much for, leaving everyone dissatisfied with the ending of your story.

· · ·

RECOVERY/REHABILITATION TROPE IN ACTION

Movies: (NOTE: there are a LOT out outstanding movies about rehabilitation and recovery you won't see listed here. That's because the majority don't include love stories for reasons discussed in the trope description. Also, the preponderance of romantic movies dealing with this topic don't end well or have heavy tragic elements.)

- Rocky
- Notorious
- A Star is Born
- Days of Wine and Roses
- Krisha
- Smashed
- When A Man Loves A Woman

Books:

- Lover Enshrined by J.R. Ward
- Simply Irresistible by Rachel Gibson
- The Rake by Mary Jo Putney
- Come Unto These Yellow Sands by Josh Lanyon
- Unholy Ghosts by Stacia Kane
- Addicted by Charlotte Featherstone
- Heart Throb by Suzanne Brockmann
- Rachel's Holiday by Marian Keyes

25

REUNION

DEFINITION

This trope is about two characters coming back together after being separated for a long time. This time around, they work through their problems and get it right, at long last getting their happily ever after.

For what it's worth, psychologists cite nostalgia as the number one reason people look up love interests from their pasts. This may not be the world's best foundation for a solid, long-term relationship going forward into the future, particularly given that all of the problems in the now the lovers may be trying to forget by looking backward in time are still very real and still must be dealt with.

However, this classic trope within the romance industry remains very popular not only in romance stories but in romantic stories within other genres of fiction. Lest you think only women look back fondly on past loves, and this trope only applies to female characters, studies show that men are six times more likely to remember a past love fondly or warmly than women are.

Yes, you read that correctly. Male characters in your stories are factually much more likely than the female characters to consider reuniting with a past love.

. . .

Unlike the Childhood Sweethearts who were probably separated not by their own choice but by their parents' choices, this couple made the decisions leading to their separation, either physical or emotional.

Unlike the Reconciliation/Second Chance Romance, where the couple broke up of their own volition in the past and is deciding whether or not to give the relationship another try, the reunion romance does not involve a previous (ugly) breakup. Rather, the couple has been physically separated and now has an opportunity to come back into physical proximity to each other and decide if they're interested in picking up the relationship where it left off.

So, the reunion trope is more about picking up where a couple left off than it is about repairing a past failure in the relationship. The challenge to this couple is the passage of time, the inevitable changes they've both made in their lives and in themselves in the intervening time apart and whether or not the relationship fits into each of their lives as those lives currently are.

This by no means is to suggest that everything was perfect in this couple's past. They can still have serious, unresolved issues that threaten the survival of the relationship and must be sorted out. In this case, your couple will have to pick up more or less where they left off with the challenges to their relationship...potentially with each partner remembering the past quite differently from the other.

Typically these people are overjoyed to see each other when they first reunite, and their past relationship, while flawed, did not fail or implode. Hence, this tends to be a lighter romantic trope in tone than some.

Dr Nancy Kalish, professor emeritus at California State University in Sacramento, researched how many people reunite with a former love. Her findings suggest that most people have no interest in rekindling former romances because they ended for a good reason. But for those who cannot forget a lost love and seek to reunite, the result is often a long-lasting and meaningful relationship.

From 1993 to 1996, Kalish conducted a survey of 1001 people who had broken off a relationship and then rekindled the romance at least five years later. The longest wait to reunite was 75 years. She found that 72% were still with their 'lost love' at the time of the survey, 71% said the reunion was their most intense romance of all time and 61% said that, second time around, the romance started faster than any other relationship.

Kalish found the typical pattern was the couple had a strong relationship but an external factor—such as interfering parents—split them up the first time.

ADJACENT TROPES

- Coming Home
- Reconciliation/Second Chance Romance
- Childhood Sweethearts
- Home for the Holiday/Vacation Fling
- Long Distance Romance
- Online Love/Pen Pals

WHY READERS/VIEWERS LOVE THIS TROPE

- who doesn't wonder what would've happened had we stayed with a past love instead of moving on or moving away?
- a do-over on the "almost" love from our past, the one who got away
- fixing past mistakes or being forgiven for past mistakes
- finally finding the happily ever after that has eluded you for so long
- nostalgia for the past

. . .

OBLIGATORY SCENES
THE BEGINNING:

You can choose to have your couple reunite intentionally or by accident, but in either case, this story necessarily begins with former loves who've been apart coming back together in some way. They can reunite in person, or you may choose to have them simply get in contact with each other, perhaps online or by phone. Many, many people look up lost loves online, partially because it's so easy to do these days, and partially out of a sense of nostalgia.

It's worth noting that we don't always remember the past accurately and we tend to forget the worst aspects of past events. In some cases, people rewrite history in their own minds to remember it without their own mistakes or failings. So, although your characters may be delighted to see each other again, they may very well be going into this renewed relationship with unrealistic expectations or memories. If this is the case, you'll probably open by portraying the relationship through these rose-colored lenses.

The beginning of the story is usually taken up by the "catching up" phase of this reunion. Where did you go? What have you been doing all this time? Did you get married? Have kids? What happened to them? Why are you here now?

Psychologists who study these types of relationships find that reunited couples tend to have sex much more quickly than couples who are meeting for the first time. Even though it may have been a very long time since your characters have been together, they may still feel as though they know each other well enough to jump ahead to a sexual relationship very early in your story.

Beware of how you write your way out of an early romantic or sexual encounter. It's critical to introduce a new twist or problem very quickly afterward, lest your reader or viewer feel as if the tension between the couple has completely evaporated already and stop reading or watching right then.

Typically, the first warning sign of trouble marks the end of the beginning of this story. Some argument from the past crops up. Some unresolved issue from the past becomes a problem. Someone remembers something they really didn't like about the other one in the past... something they never resolved back then and perhaps that isn't resolved now.

It's also possible your beginning ends with some intrusion from the present into the couple's nostalgic fog to jar this pair out of their flush of remembered love.

THE MIDDLE:

This is where the past and present collide in a big way. Whatever current-day problems face each of these people come roaring into the middle of the relationship to cause new problems or perhaps to mirror or amplify old problems.

This is also when expectations and reality collide. The nostalgia that drove this pair to go looking for each other or to answer the call when one of them reached out to the other must give way in the middle of the story to the reality of now. This can be a pleasant and relatively easy process, punctuated by comic situations, or it can be a difficult and possibly disillusioning process as the good old days fail to materialize anew.

If one or both partners left an existing relationship to resume this old one, buyer's remorse might be an issue in the middle of the story. Responsibilities from the previous relationship may pop up to interfere with the new-old love. One or both characters may struggle with doubts, difficulty committing to one relationship or the other, and paralysis when faced with having to choose an existing relationship over the recently reunited relationship.

The middle is also when hazy memory and the past reality collide. All of the things we tend to forget over time may come back to this pair as they try to pick up where they left off so long ago. Each partner may remember past events differently and conflict may arise as to whose version is most accurate. Unresolved issues between the couple will undoubtedly come up again as will all the little things about each other that they disliked before.

The question of why the couple didn't find a way to stay together in the first place, if everything was so perfect back then, is bound to arise. Was the thing that tore them apart inevitable or could one or both of them have made a different choice way back then? Why didn't they fight for the relationship, sacrifice whatever was necessary, to be together? Is there blame to be assigned, apologies to be made, or regrets to be worked out about their past parting of the ways?

As all of the nostalgia and excitement of falling in love all over again give way to the necessity of building a long-term relationship, of working out past and present problems, and going forward into the future rather than looking back in time, the reunited couple's problems mount until they reach a crisis of choice. Do they stay together or do they walk away from each other again?

BLACK MOMENT:

One or both of the lovers, when forced to choose, chooses to walk away from the reunited relationship again. The reasons may have nothing to do with the relationship—the external plot problem may tear them apart. One of them may have a family responsibility to a child, spouse, or parent that supersedes his or her own happiness in this moment. Or the reality of getting back together with their past love simply may not be what he or she expected it to be.

Of course, it's likely to be a combination of factors that cause one or both of the lovers to walk away. But the reunion collapses completely.

This black moment is made all the more painful because this pair already knows how much it's going to hurt, how long they'll both think about this breakup, and how many years of regrets they may have waiting ahead of them. It's bad enough to fail at love once. It's even worse to do it a second time with the same person.

One or both characters may bitterly regret their decision to give love another go. They may also regret having destroyed the lovely memory of their past love long ago and replaced it with a new, recent, and raw ruination of that love.

THE END:

Out of their suffering, grief, and fresh loss, one or both characters decide to give saving their relationship one last try. If there's one last issue to resolve, one last confession to make, one last apology to offer, this is the moment to do so. Otherwise, all will be lost for this pair forever. This is their last shot at getting love right between them.

Whatever external story problems this couple has been dealing with also must be resolved. These may be the catalyst for throwing the couple together one last time to realize just how much they love each other, or the external plot problem may be the reason they're at least forced into the same room wherein they'll finally talk things out and clear the air between them.

The final act of your story is where the lovers must set aside their distorted and nostalgic memories of the past and fully embrace the relationship they've built since they reunited. For only this version of them is real.

This trope typically involves some sort of grand gesture or grand apology by one or both characters to rekindle the romance one last time. Often this moment is a nod to their past but brings it forward into the present.

Forgiveness is granted, problems solved, and this couple can—at last—have their long-delayed happily ever after.

KEY SCENES

- the first time the main characters see each other—having aged—since they last saw each other

- the first time people, problems, of events from the couple's lives during the interim between their last parting and their new reunion collides with the couple's reunion
- the first time an old argument or conflict resurfaces
- the aftermath of the first romantic encounter where a bomb drops into the relationship
- an almost breakup in the middle that they pull back from
- the couple is confronted with the reality that the good old days are gone and can't ever be fully recreated
- a moment of mutual reminiscence about some happy moment
- the couple discusses or confronts why they parted the first time

THINGS TO THINK ABOUT WHEN WRITING THIS TROPE

What is this couple's backstory? You'll probably need to develop a fully fleshed out story of how they met, fell in love, and parted ways so you can build the reunion on that foundation.

How does your couple find each other again?

How do they first get in touch again?

Do they meet by accident or is it an intentional meeting? If it's intentional, who arranged the meeting? Did the other person know about it, or was one of your lovers surprised by the encounter?

Why now? Why is NOW the moment they're reuniting? Why not years ago?

Why is this the couple's only shot at a reunion? What will happen if they blow it now to keep them apart forever?

How much time has passed since they parted ways before?

Why did they part ways before? What tone does that reason set for the reunion portion of this couple's story?

What has happened to each of these people since they parted ways and up to the moment they reunited? How will these events, people, and decisions affect both the reunion and the love story to follow?

How have each of your main characters changed since they parted ways the first time?

How have each of your main characters stayed the same since they parted ways the first time?

What first attracted these two people to each other?

What attracts them to each other now?

What drove them crazy in a bad way about each other in the past? How about now? Is that still a problem? If not, why not? If so, when and how will this problem surface?

What new problems will crop up between your lovers as they resume a relationship?

How quickly will these two jump into bed or have a romantic encounter commensurate with the heat level of your story?

What big twist, bombshell, or relationship-threatening problem will result from this couple having sex/a big romantic encounter or will hit immediately after the first big love scene to raise back up the tension, conflict, or stakes in your story? How will this big twist threaten the survival or success of the reunion?

How much of this couple's reunion was driven by nostalgia, and how much of it by enduring love they've each never gotten over?

When in the story will you drop in the backstory about their original romance?

What are the ABSOLUTELY NECESSARY things to know about this couple's previous romance? Make a list of these things, if necessary. Be ruthless about paring down this list. Backstory kills your forward pacing and should only be included when your audience must know some detail from the past to understand what's going on in the present moment.

How will present events mirror past events for this couple? Is this a good thing? A bad thing? Some of each?

What external plot problem will you throw at this couple? Does it mainly target one of your lovers, or does it target both of them?

What conflicts from their past were unresolved in the past? How will these come forward into the present relationship and cause trouble?

How do the people around this couple feel about them reuniting? Are there friends and family who were present the first time around who can give commentary now about that past relationship? Do friends and family remember the past relationship the same or differently from how the couple remembers it?

If one or both main characters married someone else in the interim, is/was that person exactly like the past love or diametrically different? What has happened to this spouse? Is he or she still in the picture? Why or why not?

How will the main characters get to know the people, places, or events of the other main character's life that happened after they originally parted ways? Will one of the lovers integrate smoothly into the other one's life? Will they both have to integrate into each other's lives? Will they have to blend families? Will one of them have to move geographically so they can be together? Does one of them have to give up a job so they can be together? In other words, what are the logistic problems of reuniting now?

What is an important moment or event from the couple's past relationship that each of the lovers recalls differently now? Why do they remember it differently? How is this a source of conflict between them? Are there other moments where this has happened?

When will the couple nearly break up but pull back from the brink...which serves as a harbinger of things to come later in the story when the black moment hits?

What will actually break up your reunited couple? HINT: It's probably a combination of multiple problems, conflicts, or decisions. Who walks away from whom, or is it mutual?

How long does it take each of your main characters to regret the big breakup?

Why is this breakup more devastating to each of them than their original parting of ways?

Why is this the couple's one and only shot at reuniting? Why, if they fail this time around, will they never try or never be able to get back together again?

How will the external plot problem resolve? Does one of your main characters have to deal with it, or does it require both of your main characters to resolve it?

How will you force your main characters back together to resolve their relationship issues...or will one of them approach the other and ask for a conversation?

What will it take for each of the lovers to forgive the other one?

Who makes a grand gesture to whom and what is the gesture? Who apologizes to whom? For what? How will he/she apologize sincerely enough for the other person to accept the apology?

What will be the logistics of their happily ever after? What does being together look like? How will their families react to blending into a new family?

How will you make your audience believe this couple is going to be together forever and not break up again?

TROPE TRAPS

Creating unlikable enough main characters that your audience either doesn't want them to reunite or doesn't care if they reunite.

The couple's desire to reunite is driven purely by longing for the good old days and your audience sees it as a flimsy and unstable foundation for a long-term relationship.

The couple spends much of (or the entirety of) the story reliving the past and not ever moving forward into the future.

One of both lovers cheats on an existing spouse to reunite with the past love, which triggers fears in your audience that their own spouse will leave them for a past love and upsets your audience enough that they walk away from your story.

One or both main characters have wildly unrealistic expectations of what a reunion will be like, and you, the writer, deliver those unrealistic expectations...which your audience doesn't buy for a minute.

No problems or irritations from the past come forward into the reunion story.

The reason the couple walked away from each other in the past is never addressed.

The reason the couple parted ways in the past was completely external—someone or something else broke them up completely against their will—and the couple let it happen.

> NOTE: The couple either looks weak to have let this outside person or force break them apart in spite of how much they loved each other, or the couple obviously didn't love each other enough to fight to stay together back then. In either case, the couple comes across as unworthy of getting their big reunion and happily ever after, now.

Both main characters remember everything from the past in exactly the same way. Nobody revised any history in their own mind at all, and they both remember every little detail perfectly.

The people around this couple have no good reason for opposing a reunion even though they do everything in their power to sabotage the reunion.

Vice versa, the people around this couple have every reason to be against a reunion and yet support the reunion unrealistically.

Why, if these two were so in love with each other that they couldn't get over each other, did they go off and get romantically involved with or marry other people? Which is to say, failing to address why and how they gave up on the past relationship and how they fell in love with someone else...if they did.

Failing to address why this couple hasn't reunited long before now.

Failing to create a good reason why this is the couple's one shot at a reunion, thereby failing to create high enough stakes for your audience to be nervous and worried about the success or failure of the reunion.

Blending the main character's families into one goes perfectly and seamlessly, with no hitches or glitches whatsoever, and your audience doesn't buy it. At all.

Failing to convince your audience that this couple can make it forever going forward and won't eventually break up again.

REUNION TROPE IN ACTION
Movies:

- The Princess Bride
- The Notebook
- The Far Pavilions
- Cold Mountain
- Moonlight
- Serendipity
- Casablanca
- Sweet Home Alabama
- Before Sunset
- The Lake House
- Dear John

Books:

- Happy Place by Emily Henry
- The Bromance Book Club by Lyssa Kay Adams
- Not the Witch You Wed by April Asher

- Back to You by Priscilla Glenn
- The Sweet Gum Tree by Katherine Allred
- Rock Hard by Olivia Cunning
- The Broken Vows by Catharina Maura
- The Buy-In by Emma St. Clair
- The Road Trip by Beth O'Leary

26

REVENGE

DEFINITION

In this trope one or both of the main characters is obviously out for revenge. But what makes this trope interesting is *who* the main character is targeting for revenge and *why*. Is it the love interest? Is it someone the love interest loves or cares about? Is it someone with the power to harm the love interest in retaliation for whatever the main character does to exact his or her revenge?

While it's not strictly required by this trope that the love interest somehow be tangled up in the main character's quest for revenge, it certainly adds an interesting twist to this type of story.

At any rate, something terrible has happened to the main character or to someone he or she cared about deeply, and now the main character is out to get back at the perpetrator of this terrible deed. It's an angry head space to be in when one meets the love of his or her life.

So, at a minimum, the main character in this trope is going to feel conflicted or pulled in opposite directions by the euphoric feelings of falling in love in contrast to the rage and calculation of seeking vengeance.

It's possible someone has put your main character up to taking this revenge, for example, a promise extracted on a deathbed, a contract of some kind, a familial expectation of defending the family honor. In this case, reluctance and doubt may color the main character's quest to extract revenge.

Regardless, this trope is defined by the conflict between love and whatever emotions motivate the main character's quest for revenge.

The common wisdom is that vengeance is a self-destructive behavior that tends to harm the person seeking it as much or more than the person targeted by it. Hence, your main character is also going to be pulled in opposite directions by his or her pursuit of self-destruction in contrast to his or her pursuit of happiness.

As for the love interest in this story, if he or she is the target of the revenge or cares deeply about the target, the love interest, too, is going to be pulled in opposite directions by his or her attraction to the vengeful main character and his or her repulsion by the vengeful behaviors of the main character.

The love interest is being asked to stand by and watch the person he or she loves self-destruct, and perhaps he or she is being asked to help the main character self-destruct (either by someone else or by the main character himself or herself).

The core of this trope boils down to the dichotomy between love and hate.

ADJACENT TROPES

- Anti-Hero/Heroine
- Divided Loyalties
- Feuding Families
- Love-Hate Relationship
- Mafia Romance

WHY READERS/VIEWERS LOVE THIS TROPE

- who doesn't have someone in his or her life, past or present, with whom they'd like to get even for the wrong they committed against them
- having your cake and eating it too...getting both revenge and true love
- someone will fight your battle for you and give you vigilante justice
- seeing bad people get their comeuppance...which gives us hope that the bad people in our lives will get what's coming to them one day, too
- he or she loves me enough to self-destruct on my behalf and give me justice
- he or she loves me enough to set aside his or her anger and need for vengeance
- (when the system fails) somebody will step up and punish the bad guy who otherwise would get away with it

OBLIGATORY SCENES
THE BEGINNING:

The main character and love interest meet. This can be an accidental meeting, which usually happens in the case where the love interest has nothing to do with the revenge the main character seeks. Or it can be an intentional meeting, typically engineered by the main character in his or her quest for revenge.

The main character and love interest may already know each other, particularly if their paths crossed as part of the event for which the main character is now seeking revenge.

You may or may not choose to reveal the main character's plan to get revenge right away. It's fine to unfold that slowly. However, you'll probably want to drop in hints that something it up with your main character in the beginning of the story—hints that make your reader or viewer question the main character's motivations and ask what he or she is really up to.

Typically by the end of Act One, you've revealed to the audience (if not to the love interest) what revenge the main character is seeking and why. It would be odd not to have the love interest at least suspect something is up by the end of Act One and be asking some pointed questions of his or her own about what the main character is really up to.

Act One usually ends with some sort of mini-crisis between the main character's budding feelings of love and his or her quest for revenge.

In this story, the external plot almost always revolves around the person or entity against whom the main character is seeking revenge. It could be that the main character is setting out to sabotage some aspect of the target of revenge's life. The main character could be plotting to harm or kill the target as the main external plot.

For that matter, the main character could be plotting to harm or kill the love interest and may set events in motion in Act One that become difficult or nearly impossible to stop by the end of the story.

THE MIDDLE:

The conflict between both of your main character's feelings of love and hate, love and fear, love and self-destruction all come into high relief during the middle of your story.

This is where you main character is going to put into motion his or her plan for revenge. The plan will have successes and failures, triumphs and setbacks as the main character sets out to destroy some or all of the target of revenge's life.

Both the love interest and your audience may experience emotional whiplash as the main character bounces back and forth between seeking revenge and falling in love.

As the revenge plot draws toward a climactic confrontation or climactic event that will ruin, harm, or even kill the target of revenge, the love interest may become increasingly frantic to interfere, mitigate, or stop the plan altogether. The main character might even think better of his or her plan and try to stop it, but the plan has taken on a life of its own and cannot be stopped by the end of the middle.

As this plan races toward exploding, so does the relationship between the vengeful main character and the love interest. The conflict between love and whatever negative emotions the main character is acting out rises to the level of a crisis and spirals completely out of control.

BLACK MOMENT:

It's into the middle of this mess that your main character, when faced with an ultimatum by the love interest or by an impossible choice between love and revenge, chooses revenge.

The love interest may walk away from the main character, or the main character, faced with an either-or choice between revenge and the love interest, walks away from love.

Of course, the revenge plan goes terribly wrong in some way. Either it's much more successful than the main character intended or it misfires and hits someone else (perhaps the love interest, for example), it can backfire and hit the main character, or the entire plan can fail catastrophically and cause a cascade of unintended consequences.

In Western culture, revenge is generally seen to be a very bad thing, hence the expectation among audience members is that it will ultimately fail or there will be some terrible price for the main character to pay after pursuing revenge so relentlessly.

THE END:

The main character, devastated by the success or failure of his or her revenge plot now must also reckon with having lost the love interest.

The main character's plan is finished one way or the other, and he or she is left with nothing. The emptiness of having fulfilled or failed at the plan for revenge cannot be filled by the love interest, whom the main character has successfully driven away, lost, or walked away from.

It's into this void that the main character has an epiphany about what's more important—love or hate, love or revenge, love or rage... whatever you've decided upon as the theme of your story.

The main character must make a grand apology to the love interest, may need to make a grand gesture, and may need to make amends. The amends may be owed not only to the love interest but also to whomever the main character damaged in his or her quest for revenge. The main character may even need to go so far as apologizing to whomever he or she took revenge against.

The end of the revenge plot typically involves a complete reversal from the vengeful main character into contrition, forgiveness, amends, and rejecting revenge in the future.

Once this epiphany and reversal are complete, only then can the love interest forgive the main character and take him or her back. Only then has the main character earned true love and happily ever after.

That said, I'm not here to tell you the main character has to reject revenge, walk away from seeking justice for the wronged, or forgive whomever he or she took revenge against.

It's entirely possible this story ends with the main character continuing to feel fully justified in having taken revenge for some past wrong. Having completed that revenge, or vigilante justice if you will, he or she can now move on with his or her life in peace, confident that the scales of justice have been balanced and the wrong righted...or at least paid for in full.

· · ·

KEY SCENES

- the love interest realizes why the main character has appeared in his or her life
- the love interest has to play second fiddle to the main character's quest to seek revenge
- the love interest gives the main character an ultimatum—him or her versus vengeance—prior to the final ultimatum. This acts as a harbinger of things to come. The main character may choose correctly in this earlier scene but waivers in the choice
- the main character sets aside his or her quest for vengeance for a little while and feels overwhelming relief, which makes him or her question the path of vengeance
- the love interest stages an intervention with the main character to stop him or her from self-destructing
- the plan for revenge takes a major, unexpected turn or there's a big twist introduced
- the plan for revenge spins out of the main character's control in some way

THINGS TO THINK ABOUT WHEN WRITING THIS TROPE

What has happened in the main character's past to set him or her on the path of seeking revenge?

Is the main character seeking revenge of his or her own accord or has someone else put him or her up to it? If so, who, why, when, and how?

Who is the main character seeking revenge against? Why that target? How does he or she plan to exact revenge upon this person(s)?

Is the love interest involved in some way with the target(s) of the revenge? (Or is the love interest the actual target?)

How do the main character and love interest meet? Is it accidental or intentionally arranged by one of them? If so, which one, how, why, when, and where?

What attracts them to each other right away?

What aspect of your story will throw these two people together again and again so they can fall in love?

When does the main character reveal his or her revenge plot, or does someone else reveal it to the love interest?

How does the love interest feel when he or she finds out about the main character's plan to take revenge and when he or she finds out who the target is?

When do the main character's feelings of love and need for revenge start to come into conflict? How will you show this conflict in the character and in the story?

Is the main character's journey of vengeance destructive to him or her? How will you show that? How can you make this journey more destructive? How can you make it even more devastating than that?

How will the love interest try to intervene to stop the plan for revenge...or will he or she support it and try to help?

Is the target of the main character's revenge a good guy or a bad guy? Does he or she deserve the revenge that's racing toward him or her?

What ups and downs will the main character's plan for revenge experience?

What conflict will the lovers experience besides their disagreement over the main character's plan to exact vengeance on someone?

What about each other is so irresistible that the lovers keep coming back to each other even though they disagree about something so important and fundamental as whether or not it's good or right to seek revenge? If they agree on that topic, what other value, belief, or moral do they fundamentally disagree over that threatens to break them up?

How do the people around the couple feel about their relationship? Do other people around them know about the main character's plan for revenge?

If the main character's plan for revenge is secret, who besides him or her knows about it? When does the love interest find out about it? What does the love interest do when he or she finds out about it, and will he or she keep the secret? Why or why not?

What goes terribly amiss with the revenge plan? It can go much better or much worse than planned or the main character can lose control of it.

Why does the love interest deliver an ultimatum—me or revenge —to the main character? When does he or she deliver it? How does the main character respond?

What finally forces the main character to choose revenge over the love interest?

Who walks away from whom in the black moment?

How does the revenge plan help break up the lovers?

What triggers the main character's epiphany about revenge and love? (And there are many possible epiphanies, depending on the degree of righteousness of the vengeance the main character has sought.)

Who does the main character need to apologize to by the end of the story? For what? To whom does he or she owe amends of some kind?

What must the main character do to regain the trust and love of the love interest or vice versa?

Who makes a grand gesture or grand apology to whom? What is it?

Who was ultimately right about love and vengeance...or does it matter in your story?

What will this couple do now that the quest for revenge is finished? Will the main character settle down peacefully, or will they go forth as a couple looking for other wrongs to right? Will they leave the local area or will the main character stay there with the love interest?

TROPE TRAPS

Creating a main character so focused on revenge that he or she wouldn't plausibly be distracted by love.

The main character comes across as a bully and mean and is unlikable to your audience.

Failing to give the main character a really noble reason for seeking vengeance.

The love interest comes across as weak, or worse, as aiding and abetting (or at least encouraging) the main character's bullying, mean, or violent behavior.

Creating a love interest who's so naïve about the realities of the world that he or she cannot understand the main character's need for revenge.

Creating a love interest who's so judgmental of the main character's plan for revenge that he or she would never plausibly fall in love with the main character.

There's no justice in the revenge the main character is seeking. It's revenge for revenge's sake, and the perceived wrong being righted isn't big enough to justify the size of the main character's reaction.

The main character is so hyper fixated on wrong(s) done to him or her that he or she comes across as violent, psychotic, hair-triggered, or fixated on rage—and the veracity of the perceived wrongs comes into serious question in your audience's mind.

The revenge plan is out of proportion to the wrong done in the first place.

The act of revenge in your story is part of a larger cycle of violence and revenge that will inevitably be answered by more violence and revenge. There's no end in sight to the cycle of fighting and revenge.

The love interest never questions the main character's quest for vengeance, thereby encouraging an ongoing cycle of violence and harm to others...and acting totally unheroic in the process.

The main character (and possibly love interest if he or she helps) gets away with a criminal act that the audience thinks he or she should be punished for.

Love doesn't win out over hate, rage, violence, or whatever else you choose to juxtapose it against.

REVENGE TROPE IN ACTION
Movies:

- Fatal Attraction
- The Other Woman
- Overboard
- I Want You Back
- The Legend of Jack and Diane
- Cruel Intentions
- Revenge
- The Last of the Mohicans
- This Is Where I Leave You
- Gone Girl

Books:

- Hooked by Emily McIntire
- Twisted Love by Ana Huang
- Tis the Season for Revenge by Morgan Elizabeth
- The Sacrifice by Shantel Tessier
- Good Girl Complex by Elle Kennedy
- Savage Hearts by J.T. Geissinger

- Stolen Heir by Sophie Lark
- The Risk by S.T. Abby
- Painted Scars by Neva Altaj
- King of Wrath by Ana Huang
- The Words by Ashley Jade
- Love at First Spite by Anna E. Collins
- From Blood & Ash by Jennifer L. Armentrout

27

RUINED/SCANDALOUS HERO/HEROINE

DEFINITION

While most people tend to associate being scandalous or having a ruined reputation with historical romance, the reality is this has been and continues to be a huge problem in every time period. Entire companies today are devoted to the business of restoring people's online reputations, in fact. Hence, this remains a relevant story type and qualifies as a universal trope of romance.

The only difference between a scandalous character and a ruined character for the purposes of this trope is timing. The scandalous character has just done something that will ruin his or her reputation, whereas the ruined character has done it far enough in the past that the ruin of his or her reputation is a fait accompli.

In both cases, however, the main character has done or is doing something that breaks the rules of the society in which he or she lives, which flouts conventions or goes against the norms of family, friends, or coworkers.

In this trope, the main character has done something or has been accused of doing something that has or will ruin his or her reputation. Right or wrong, this scandal and ruin of reputation may also ruin the main character's entire life.

This trope typically follows this character's journey to redemption or to a new life. The main character may find a way to restore his or her reputation, or the main character may simply move away from the scandal and ruin to build a new and better life somewhere else. This new "place" may be geographical, or it may be societal. The main character may choose to move into a different workplace, a different friend group, or a different stratum of society.

A great deal of social pressure is usually applied to this character to slink away from his or her scandal/ruination and exile himself or herself. Although the societal expectation is that this person should disappear or go into hiding, this is yet another norm of behavior your main character may choose to ignore or flout outright.

In the world you build, you'll need to decide what its social and behavioral norms are, what constitutes a behavior that would be scandalous, and what ruin would look like when a person violates these rules of polite behavior.

The action that ruins the main character may be one of intentional rebellion against the rules of the society he or she lives in. Or it may be unintentional—a mistake, an accident, something he or she was forced into doing, or an action he or she didn't realize violated the norms or rules of society.

And, of course, it's entirely possible your scandalous or ruined main character did nothing wrong at all. Rather, he or she is rumored to have violated the norms or has only been accused of breaking the rules, and that is enough to create scandal and destroy his or her reputation.

In the case where the main character did break the rules, you'll need to decide what his or her intentions were and whether the main character knew what would happen if he or she was caught breaking the rules. Your main character may not care that he or she flouted conventions...or your main character may have expected to get away with his or her behavior. In either case, your story will undoubtedly address the fallout from scandal and a ruined reputation, how the main character feels about it, and how he or she responds to it.

In this trope, the love interest also has some big decisions to make. Is he or she so in love with the scandalous/ruined character that he or she is willing to accept the ostracism and scorn from polite society that the main character is already experiencing? Is the love interest willing to destroy his or her own reputation—willingly and intentionally—by becoming involved with a societal pariah?

Indeed, the love interest's dilemma may prove more interesting and captivating to your audience than the main character's. The love interest faces a choice—preserve his or her reputation and stay away from the scandalous/ruined main character or join the main character in scandal and ruination in return for true love.

For the main character, this story may or may not be one of rebellion. But for the love interest, this story is absolutely a rebellion against the norms and rules of the society he or she lives in.

ADJACENT TROPES

- Redemption
- Rebellious Hero/Heroine
- Bad Boy/Girl Reformed
- Forbidden Love
- Straight Arrow Seduced

WHY READERS/VIEWERS LOVE THIS TROPE

- who doesn't love a good bad boy or girl
- getting to break the rules and thumb your nose at authority figures
- flinging off caring about what anyone else thinks of you
- breaking out of your boring life and doing something exciting, forbidden, or taboo

- not being outcast or blamed anymore for a past mistake
- not feeling other-ed, no longer being an outsider, and finding a tribe that accepts you exactly as you are

OBLIGATORY SCENES
THE BEGINNING:

The main character and love interest meet. This is often a meet cute in which the main character does something scandalous and the love interest is completely scandalized.

You may choose not to reveal to the love interest immediately that the person he or she has just met and is wildly attracted to is scandalous or ruined. That may come as a nasty shock to the love interest only after he or she is fascinated by and already half in love with the main character.

The main character may warn off the love interest early in the story, telling the (naïve) love interest to stay away and avoid becoming embroiled in scandal and ruin. Or the main character may want or need the companionship of someone who doesn't automatically spurn him or her ad delay revealing his or her scandal or ruined reputation.

This main character typically starts the story an embittered and angry soul. But it's fully possible to create a main character who blithely doesn't care about being scandalous/ruined or who is oblivious to his or her terrible social status.

It's also possible to start out with a main character who has already withdrawn from society or who is in the process of withdrawing from society. This character isn't necessarily a recluse but is or is becoming isolated and alone.

The external story problem can revolve around something the main character needs to do that his or her scandalous/ruined status prevents or makes very difficult. Or the story may revolve around something the love interest needs, either from the main character or that the main character could help with if only he or she wasn't so scandalous or ruined already.

In either case, your external plot problem should usually be made immeasurably more difficult to deal with because of the scandal in your main character's life or because of his or her ruined reputation.

The beginning typically ends with a mini-crisis of some kind—either a complication to the external plot problem or some sort of confrontation between the main character and the guardian(s) of polite society in your story.

THE MIDDLE:

This is where you'll really put the screws to your love interest. The main character's fate is sealed—he or she is expelled from polite society—but the love interest still has a choice. Does the love interest follow his or her heart and dive into true love with the scandalous/ruined main character or does the love interest step back from love and retain his or her position, status, acceptance within polite society?

Your main character may have big opinions about the love interest's decision of whether to join him or her in scandal and ruin or stay close to family and friends and retain status within society. This may be a major source of conflict between your lovers, in fact.

The secondary characters are especially important to this story. They represent and enact the main character's expulsion from society, judgment of the main character's scandalous behavior, and are the gatekeepers who will prevent the main character from returning to polite society until he or she has suffered enough punishment or made enough amends—assuming there even is a path back to acceptance within the society you've created.

Usually, some or all of the development of this relationship takes place in secret, away from the judgment and disapproval of the people who have ostracized the main character.

The conflict between the main character and love interest intensifies toward a crisis. The main character may try to push away the love interest to save the person he or she is falling in love with from the same scandal and ruin the main character is experiencing. Meanwhile, the love interest is wrestling with the dilemma of giving up his or her position in polite society for the sake of love.

While the love interest's choice may seem, at a glance, to be a rather shallow one, it's up to you to set up a close-knit family, a job the love interest really needs, or a societal status that's very important to maintain for some compelling reason. The stakes for the love interest abandoning the norms of polite society need to be high enough to make the choice between love and social acceptance a terrible one.

Pressure from the secondary characters builds throughout the middle of the story—pressure on the main character to disappear and pressure on the love interest to disengage from the main character.

The external story problem also builds toward a crisis that will force these two people to make impossible choices.

BLACK MOMENT:

Interestingly, this black moment can revolve around either of the lovers. The main character can be forced to choose between his or her feelings for the love interest and accepting exile from polite society. Or the love interest can be forced to choose between his or her love for the main character and his or her position within polite society. Or of course, they can both be forced to choose.

Regardless of which option you select, the character(s) being forced into a choice ultimately choose badly. Rather than choose love, each character may choose self-sacrifice in the name of protecting the person they love from any more harm. These two characters may choose to solve the plot problem instead of making the problem worse by choosing love.

After their bad choices, the relationship between the lovers implodes.

Worse, the love interest is probably embroiled in a scandal of his or her own regardless of the main character's and the love interest's best efforts to keep the love interest clear of the scandal/ruin blast zone.

The outside characters who've been trying to break up the lovers all along have finally succeeded, and they relish their victory.

THE END:

Devastated by their separation, one or both of the lovers regrets choosing norms over love and decides to give it one last try to put the relationship back together. This may include confronting the external plot problem. Or resolving the external plot problem may be the catalyst to draw the lovers back together one last time.

Once they're back together, apologies can be made and forgiveness granted. The couple can move forward together, confronting society as a united couple. Together, they can make amends for the scandal(s) they've caused, or they can shame society into accepting them back, or they can declare their defiance of society's norms.

Happily ever after for this couple may include the pair resuming their rightful place in society, or it may be that the couple leaves this place and this society altogether to go somewhere new and make a fresh start.

It's possible the couple chooses to stay and continue to be social outcasts...at least from the society that exiled them both. Instead, the couple may find a new tribe, a new family, a new society to live in, one that accepts them as they are and doesn't judge them for the scandal or ruin.

KEY SCENES

- the moment the love interest finds out about the scandal surrounding the main character

- someone important or in a position of authority over the love interest tells him or her to steer clear of the main character
- a secret meeting between the main character and love interest in which they nearly get caught and nearly ruin the love interest's reputation
- a confrontation between the main character and a gatekeeper of polite society
- the main character tells the love interest not to have anything to do with him or her lest the scandal and ruin rub off on the love interest
- the main character and love interest are caught together
- the love interest is publicly attacked or humiliated as his or her own scandal becomes public
- the love interest is given an ultimatum by a family member, friend, or authority figure to choose between love and scandal/ruination and social exile of their own

THINGS TO THINK ABOUT WHEN WRITING THIS TROPE

What is the world your story will take place in and what are the rules and norms of good behavior within it? How will you make these rules and norms relatable to your audience or at least believable?

What has the main character allegedly done that breaks the rules and norms of polite behavior? Did the main character actually do it or not?

How does the main character feel about what he or she is accused of having done? Does he or she care about reputation or social ruin?

What are the consequences to the main character of this scandal and ruin? Can you make those worse for him or her? Can you make those consequences MUCH worse?

What was the main character's previous position in society? How far has he or she fallen from it?

Who is the love interest? What is his or her position in society prior to your story beginning?

How do the main character and love interest meet? What tone does their meeting set for the rest of your story?

Does the main character reveal his or her scandal/ruin to the love interest right away or not? Does the love interest know who the main character is right away or not?

Who tells the love interest about the main character's scandal and ruin? How does the love interest react? How does the main character react to the love interest's reaction?

Who are the people around the couple that enforce the rules of polite behavior? Who are the gatekeepers of acceptance or rejection from the "society" of your story?

What is this society? Is it a town? A place of employment? A social stratus? A group of friends?

Why does the main character care or not care about being part of this societal group? What does he or she lose by being ostracized from it?

What is the love interest's position within this societal grouping? What does he or she stand to lose by being ostracized from it? How can you make that loss worse? How can you make it much, MUCH worse for the love interest?

How does the love interest feel about the dilemma he or she is being put into?

Will the relationship between your lovers develop in secret or in plain sight of the people ostracizing the main character?

What about these two people irresistibly attracts them to each other? What about each other irritates or angers each of them?

What are the points of friction in their relationship where they vehemently disagree with each other?

How will you contrive to get your lovers together frequently to be together? What's the device in your story that throws them into repeated proximity or at least gives them chances to choose to be in close proximity?

Will any secondary characters aid and abet the lovers having trysts? If so, who? How? Why?

What is the external story problem? How does the main character's scandal or ruin relate to that problem? How does the love interest's potential scandal and ruin relate to that problem?

How can you make the consequences of failing to resolve the plot problem absolutely devastating to one or both of your lovers?

How will the external story problem cause a crisis for the lovers regarding the scandal and ruination they're both facing?

What constitutes choosing wrong for each of your lovers that provokes the breakup and black moment?

What event or moment of epiphany will show each of the devastated lovers that they've made a terrible choice they'll regret forever?

How will your lovers resolve the external story problem? Will they work together toward a solution? Will each of them try to solve it on their own? Will they work at cross-purposes to each other in the process of trying to fix the problem (a là The Gift Of the Magi?)

Who owes whom an apology by the end of this story? Will any secondary characters ever apologize to one or both of the lovers? Does one of the lovers owe the other one an apology?

Will one of your lovers make some sort of grand gesture of love to the other? If so, who? What will the big gesture be?

How will your lovers, now a couple, rejoin polite society? Will they go to a new geographic place? Find a new friend group? Enter a new stratum of society? Or will they blow of polite society for good and go their own way in life entirely?

What does happily ever after look like for this couple? This is an especially important question in this particular trope.

TROPE TRAPS

Creating a scandal that (while it may be historically or setting accurate) is too lame for your audience to buy as the cause of so much scandal and ruin for your main character.

Creating a love interest who's so popular and beloved in the societal grouping that he or she can freely interact with the ruined main character without negative blowback, and your audience doesn't buy it for a second.

Creating a love interest who's so naïve the audience doesn't like him or her.

Creating a main character who's so dark, brooding, and antisocial that your audience doesn't believe he or she would ever bother going to the trouble of rejoining polite society.

Failing to create big enough consequences for the love interest getting involved with the main character.

Failing to create an external story problem that has anything at all to do with the scandal and ruin of one or both of your lovers, rendering the whole scandal and ruin little more than a side show to annoy your characters (and probably your audience).

Creating secondary characters so hateful and judgmental that they become caricatures and don't seem plausible to your audience.

Creating such a rigid system of behavioral rules and judgment that no sane character wouldn't know the rules or would dream of breaking the rules.

That said, failing to create bad enough consequences for breaking the rules and norms of polite behavior.

Failing to create bad enough potential consequences for the love interest choosing to be with the scandalous/ruined main character.

Making the love interest's choice between his or her own reputation and true love so straightforward that your audience doesn't believe that the love interest faces any dilemma at all. Your audience dislikes your love interest for waffling in the face of a simple and obvious decision.

Creating a main character who breaks the rules without caring in the least about having done it, then having him or her meet the love interest and ALL OF A SUDDEN, the main character is totally invested in getting back into society's good graces.

Making one of your lovers do all the compromising and suffering to have the other one. BOTH of your lovers should have to make hard choices and sacrifices.

One of your lovers completely overshadows the other one in your story because he or she is the only one facing any terrible choices.

Your audience thinks your couple is lame or dumb for giving a darn about the rules of the society they live in.

You create a society and set of norms that your audience doesn't relate to and doesn't care about.

You set up a story where your audience is rooting for the lovers to do one thing and you have the couple do the opposite. For example, your audience wants the lovers to thumb their noses at society, but instead the lovers kowtow to the keepers of the norms and rules. Or vice versa, your audience wants the lovers to apologize and resume their rightful places in society, but instead you have them walk away.

RUINED/SCANDALOUS HERO/HEROINE TROPE IN ACTION
Movies:

- A Walk to Remember
- Keith
- Grease
- Mean Girls
- Easy A
- Eat Pray Love
- Never Been Kissed

Books:

- Glow by Raven Kennedy

- Tempt Me At Midnight by Lauren Royal
- The Traitor Queen by Danielle L. Jensen
- Pride, Prejudice, and Other Flavors by Sonali Debv
- Delilah Green Doesn't Care by Ashley Herring Blake
- Priest by Sierra Simone
- Suddenly You by Lisa Kleypas
- Unlawful Contact by Pamela Clare
- Addicted to You by Krista and Becca Ritchie
- The Crown of Gilded Bones by Jennifer L. Armentrout
- Bringing Down the Duke by Evie Dunmore

28

RUNAWAY BRIDE/GROOM

DEFINITION

In this trope, a bride or groom who is on the verge of getting married flees at the very last second and doesn't go through with the wedding.

In the traditional and deeply clichéd version of this story, bride or groom runs away from the church or wedding venue minutes before the wedding is scheduled to begin. The guests are in their seats, the music is playing, and the bride or groom chickens out...or finally listens to his or her heart...and decides at the very last second not to go through with the wedding. Also in the clichéd version, the person who first meets the fleeing bride or groom—often by picking up the runaway at the side of a road in a ruined wedding gown or ruined tuxedo—ends up being the love interest.

In its most cliché form, it's still a delightful romantic romp and wildly popular with readers and viewers. This is one of those tropes where delivering exactly the story your audience expects isn't necessarily a bad thing.

That said, multiple variations on this trope are possible. For example, the bride or groom can choose to break off the engagement before the wedding is about to start, days or weeks before the wedding. What distinguishes the runaway bride or groom from one who just ends the engagement and calls off the wedding is the act of running.

The runaway bride or groom calls off the wedding without offering an explanation to his or her intended spouse, possibly without an explanation to his or her family and friends, and probably without any explanation to the jilted near-spouse's family and friends.

Another factor specific to the runaway bride/groom is the act of leaving. Not only does this person call off the wedding abruptly and likely without explanation, but this bride or groom also tends to physically leave the proximity of their intended, and often the proximity of all the family and friends associated with the canceled wedding.

While running away from a wedding at the last minute is the inciting incident of this trope, the story arc to follow involves unwinding the reason(s) why the bride or groom ran away, resolving the relationship with the jilted fiancé(e), and possibly building a whole new relationship with the True Love who shows up on the heels of the bride or groom's run from marriage to the wrong person.

The jilted intended may or may not try to reconcile with the runaway bride/groom. This will depend on the underlying reason(s) why the bride/groom ran away, how humiliated the intended is by being left at the altar, and whether or not the intended perceives the relationship as repairable.

It is possible for this trope to start with a bride or grooming running away from a wedding, and then the remainder of the story revolving around a journey back to the altar for the same two people. First, they must resolve whatever problem caused the bride/groom to flee in the first place, and only then will their path be clear to marriage and happily ever after.

If your plan is to cast the jilted intended as the wrong person for your runaway bride/groom and you plan to introduce the "right" person as a love interest to the runaway, the entire relationship with Mr./Ms.

Right must develop at the same time the runaway is unwinding and ending the relationship with Mr./Ms. Wrong. It's the juxtaposition of these two relationships against each other that provides much of the movement and conflict of the Runaway Bride/Groom trope.

At its core, this story is almost always a love triangle. However, one of the pairings of the love triangle has already fractured by the time your story begins. Often, at its core, this story is also a rescue by a knight in shining armor, which I personally believe explains the enduring popularity of this trope.

ADJACENT TROPES

- Commitment Phobia
- Stop the Wedding
- Only One Not Married
- In Love With the Wrong Person
- Fear of Intimacy
- Reconciliation/Second Chance

WHY READERS/VIEWERS LOVE THIS TROPE

- for anyone who has ever had a fight with their spouse and in a moment of frustration asked themselves, "why did I think it was a good idea to marry this person?", this trope is the answer
- being rescued by a knight in shining armor and taken away to a new and better life
- recognizing soon enough that someone isn't Mr./Ms. Right for us...before the damage is done

- running away from everything and everyone in our life and starting over from scratch in a completely new life created solely by me, for me
- hosing over the jerk who has treated us badly or done us wrong. Revenge is sweet
- what would my life have been like if I'd made a different decision at a critical moment
- is there someone more perfect for me out there not settling for the okay partner, and furthermore, finding the perfect partner for me

OBLIGATORY SCENES
THE BEGINNING:

No surprise, this story almost always begins with a bride or groom in the final moments before walking down the aisle. We see his or her moment of panic, decision, epiphany, or a last second revelation of shocking information, and we see him or her run away from the wedding.

Someone usually helps the bride or groom run away. This can be a friend or family member, or this person can be a kind stranger.

Often this rescuer is the future love interest...who is magically in the exact right place at the exact right moment and is the exactly perfect true love for our runaway. What are the *odds*?

In all seriousness, your audience will suspend its disbelief to go along with this stunning coincidence. This trope is so beloved that audience members are entirely willing to put up with the improbability of the rescuer being Mr. or Ms. Right...likely because this is such an alluring fantasy.

Who doesn't want a knight in shining armor to come along and sweep you away from the awful thing or person you're fleeing?

Who doesn't want to be whisked off to the knight's enchanted castle where you're safe and protected from harm, cherished and loved the way you deserve to be loved, and all your problems go away?

The beginning typically ends with the first intrusion of the jilted ex-fiancé(e) or someone close to him or her showing up to demand an explanation or showing up to intensify the problem that caused the runaway to flee.

The external plot of this trope typically revolves around the reason the bride or groom decided not to go through with the wedding.

While the true reason may be personal and emotional in nature— a fundamental flaw in the intended's personality or a fundamental mismatch between the runaway and intended—there may be an external, plot-based reason your runaway fled.

For example:

- the intended cheated on the runaway
- the intended is involved in some nefarious activity the runaway finds out about just before the wedding
- the intended has an ulterior reason for marrying the runaway that doesn't involve true love.

Whatever this external reason is, it's usually introduced in Act One. Indeed, this may be the source of the mini-crisis that leads your story into Act Two.

THE MIDDLE:

The complications get really messy in the middle of this story. Not only is the runaway falling in love with his or her rescuer, but the jilted ex is probably demanding answers or attempting to reconcile with the runaway. If there's going to be a love triangle, it's fully established and the runaway is being pulled in warring directions.

If your intent is ultimately to reconcile the runaway and the intended, the problems that broke up the first wedding come roaring to the fore and have to be wrestled with in the middle of your story.

The external plot of your story puts all kinds of pressure on the runaway, who must lean on the new love interest for help and support.

Family and friends catch up with the runaway and are outraged at the runaway's decision to flee the wedding at the last minute. The fallout from your main character's impulsive decision lands squarely upon his or her head in the middle of this story.

Some friends and family may support the decision to run, and these people probably enter into drama and conflict with the friends and family who hate the decision and want to reverse it.

Any drama that swirled around the wedding and its planning process probably only escalates after the bride or groom decamps.

While the love interest acts as a bulwark against the drama, criticism, and efforts to change the runaway's mind, the love interest may find himself or herself fighting romantic feelings toward the recently rescued runaway. The runaway already has a lot on his or her emotional plate, and the love interest may find himself or herself in the unenviable position of having to sit back, suppress his or her growing feelings, and support the distraught runaway without expressing his or her true feelings.

Because the love interest is usually a knight in shining armor, he or she is typically going to be self-sacrificing and will set aside his or her own happiness to help the runaway find happiness, even if it means going back to the intended or moving on from the love interest.

As the middle ends, a confrontation with the jilted ex looms. The runaway has to make a decision once and for all about who he or she wants to be with (intended or new love interest). The external plot problem that complicates this decision is becoming a crisis that may make the decision even harder for the runaway.

The love interest may decide to remove himself or herself from the equation in the name of doing what's right. He or she will step aside so the pre-existing relationship can recover. Even though the love interest may be completely in love with the runaway by the end of the middle, the love interest may not think it's honorable to interfere with the previous relationship.

BLACK MOMENT:

Faced with a choice between the original intended and the new love interest, the runaway chooses wrong. He or she may choose to go back to the old fiancé(e), or the runaway may choose neither potential partner.

The external plot problem that is forcing the runaway back into the arms of the jilted ex explodes and exerts maximum pressure on the runaway to go back to the intended. Any consequences of not going back to the former fiancé(e) happen, and the runaway has no choice at all anymore. He or she must go back.

The love interest is devastated. He or she has lost the perfect partner, the love of his or her life. The love interest knows for sure that the runaway is the right person for him or her and vice versa that he or she is the right person for the runaway.

In the story where the runaway and jilted intended are struggling to reconcile, the black moment is when their attempt at reconciliation and fixing the problem looming between them fails utterly. They've failed to get together for a second time—which is somehow even more devastating that failing the first time around.

THE END:

The runaway, faced with reuniting with the former intended recalls why he or she fled the first time. Furthermore, the runaway now has the comparison between the perfect love interest and the flawed fiancé(e) to make his or her decision to flee before even more justified.

The runaway decides once and for all to leave behind the former intended and be with the love interest forever. This may require one last run, away from the intended and back into the arms of the love interest.

The love interest, devastated by having lost the love of his or her life may finally decide to take action to win back the runaway and may help the runaway get away from the intended for a second time.

The external plot problem is solved. Sometimes, the runaway resolves it, sometimes the love interest may step in and solve it. Because this external plot problem is generally not that vital to the runaway's ultimate decision to choose the love interest over the jilted ex, the external plot problem is occasionally solved by other secondary characters or the problem takes care of itself.

For example, the runaway found out about some criminal activity the intended or intended's family was involved in. By the end of the story, law enforcement catches up with the intended and his or her family and they're taken out of the picture, leaving the runaway and love interest free to get back together.

For the runaway and fiancé(e) who ultimately get back together, the big problem keeping them apart must be solved in the ending of the story. The conflicts between them that have flawed their relationship until now must be resolved as well. Apologies must be made, forgiveness granted, and then this couple can reconcile.

The end of this story almost always includes the final ending of the original relationship between runaway and jilted ex, and the commitment to forever between the runaway and love interest.

This commitment can take the form of a wedding the runaway doesn't run from, an engagement, or an agreement never to marry each other but a declaration of true love forever.

For what it's worth, this trope is ripe for a sequel. The gun-shy runaway may prefer not to commit to marriage by the end of this story, which leaves plenty of room for a second story where he or she must overcome commitment phobia once and for all and the long-suffering love interest must wait a little bit longer for his or her happily ever after.

. . .

KEY SCENES

- the jilted fiancé(e) and guests discover the bride/groom has fled the wedding
- the distraught runaway is rescued after fleeing
- the runaway finally reveals to the love interest why he or she fled the wedding
- the love interest and jilted ex meet for the first time
- the runaway and his or her ex meet for the first time
- the love interest pulls back from a romantic moment in the name of respecting the previous relationship to which the runaway is committed

THINGS TO THINK ABOUT WHEN WRITING THIS TROPE

What's the backstory of the bride/groom and fiancé(e) before your story starts? Which parts of it are necessary to include in your story so your audience eventually understands why the bride or groom ran away from the wedding?

When does your bride or groom run away? Does he or she run from the wedding ceremony itself? Just before heading to the wedding? Days or weeks before the wedding?

Why does your bride or groom run away from getting married?

Why does the bride or groom actually run instead of sticking around and breaking up in person?

Does anyone who knows the runner help the bride or groom flee? If so, who and how?

Who is the love interest in your story? Does he or she rescue the bride/groom or help the bride/groom flee the wedding?

Does the bride or groom know the love interest before the story begins? If so, how and for how long? Are they friends? Enemies? Frenemies? Something else?

If the bride/groom does not know the love interest, how do they meet (if it's not the love interest rescuing the bride or groom)?

Who is the love interest? What's his or her story? Why is he or she in the right place at the right time to meet and/or rescue the runaway bride or groom?

What about the runaway and love interest attracts them to each other? Is it immediate, or does the attraction grow over time?

How will you keep the runaway and love interest in close proximity throughout your story?

What is the external plot problem besides the runaway having to sort out the end of his or her relationship with the jilted ex-fiancé(e)?

Does the external plot problem have some bearing on why the bride or groom ran instead of going through with the wedding? If so, what?

How do the friends and family of the runaway react to his or her running?

How do the family and friends of the fiancé(e) left at the altar react to the bride or groom's running?

Do the friends and family of both the runaway and the jilted ex try to get the couple back together or to sabotage them reuniting? Why?

What does the love interest think of the bride/groom having run from his or her own wedding?

At what point does the jilted fiancé(e) show up in your story again? What does he or she want? Is he or she trying to reconcile with the runaway, get something from the runaway, or finish the breakup?

What does the love interest think of the jilted ex when the two of them meet? Is there a confrontation between them?

What conflict besides the existence of a prior fiancé(e) develops between the runaway and love interest?

Is your love interest a traditional knight in shining armor type or not? Does he or she nobly resist falling in love with the runaway or resist getting into a romantic relationship with the runaway before the runaway has completely broken up with the jilted fiancé(e)?

What does the runaway think of the love interest's noble forbearance in love?

When does the love interest almost but not quite give in to his or her attraction to the runaway but then not act on it at the last second? How does the runaway react to this moment?

When the love interest finally does give in and indulge in a romantic moment with the runaway (at a heat level commensurate with your story's overall heat level), how does he or she react afterward? Is the love interest appalled to have been so weak? Relieved to have finally expressed his or her feelings? Worried that he or she has put the runaway in a terrible dilemma? All of the above? Some other reaction?

How does the runaway feel about the jilted fiancé(e) in general? In love? Friendly? Betrayed? Furious? NOTE: Hate is not the opposite of love. Apathy is. If the runaway still feels rage, anger, or betrayal toward the ex, your runaway is not fully done with that person, yet.

When and how do the love interest and jilted fiancé(e) finally confront each other? How does that go? What's said and felt by both of them?

How does the external plot problem put pressure on the runaway to go back and follow through with marrying the jilted fiancé(e)? How can you really up that pressure? How can you make it nearly impossible for the runaway NOT to go back and marry the fiancé(e)?

What are the consequences of the runaway NOT going back and marrying the fiancé(e)?

What are the consequences of the runaway not staying with the love interest and ultimately being with him or her? How can you make those consequences worse...and much worse...for the runaway?

In the black moment between the runaway and love interest, who breaks it off and walks away? Why? How?

Does the runaway return to the jilted fiancé(e) after he or she breaks up with the love interest?

What does the runaway learn about himself or herself that makes him or her ready to commit to a long-term relationship with the love interest now?

How will you resolve the external plot problem? Will the runaway, the love interest, the jilted ex, and/or some other outside force actually fix the problem?

How will you get the runaway and the love interest back together in physical proximity? Who will follow or go back to whom? How will they resolve their personal conflicts?

Who has to apologize to whom? Does the runaway owe the jilted ex an apology or not?

Who makes a grand gesture of love to whom? What's the gesture?

How will you resolve any conflict between the jilted ex and the love interest?

How will you resolve any conflict between the runaway and his or her family and friends?

Do you need to resolve friction, anger, or resentment between the runaway and the family and friends of the jilted ex, or can you leave things between them alone at the end of your story with the understanding that they'll all go their separate ways?

Will the runaway move into a new life in a new place with the love interest?

Do the love interest and runaway make their life in close proximity to the jilted ex or will their lives never intersect again?

What does happily ever after look like for this couple?

Is the runaway willing to marry the love interest having now found the right person? Or is the runaway leery of marriage and, while happy with the love interest, prefers to wait for a while to jump into another wedding situation?

TROPE TRAPS

Creating a runaway who runs for a bratty reason and is unlikable.

Creating a runaway who leaves in a bratty or bitchy way and is unlikable. (It was recently in the news that a bride, when it was time to read the vows she'd written for her groom in the middle of her wedding, instead read aloud a series of texts from his phone where he cheated on her with another woman. Ouch.)

The bride or groom sneaks out of the wedding in a way that surely would get him or her seen and caught, and your audience doesn't buy that he or she slipped out successfully. Let's face it. Wedding dresses and tuxedos are not inconspicuous.

Nobody tries to stop the runaway and your audience doesn't buy it.

The reason the bride or groom flees his or her own wedding is simple enough that he or she should have stuck around and explained it to the jilted fiancée(e).

The runaway is immature and selfish to just run from the wedding and not offer an explanation or apology to the fiancé(e) and to the assembled wedding party and guests.

The plot problem you choose has nothing to do with why the bride or groom fled and ends up not feeling connected to the core trope of a runaway bride or groom.

The reason the bride or groom ran should have been dealt with and confronted WELL before getting all the way to the wedding or very close to the wedding. Which is to say, the bride or groom knew about the problem long enough before the wedding to deal with it in some more mature and reasonable way but chose not to.

The love interest moves in on the upset, grieving, or angry runaway and takes advantage of his or her vulnerable emotional state...thereby coming across as selfish or a crass opportunist.

The love interest doesn't fight hard enough or soon enough for the love of the runaway.

The love interest is so self-sacrificing that he or she never thinks of his or her own happiness and irritates your audience with his or her determination to be personally unhappy.

The love interest isn't different enough from the jilted ex to make the runaway's choice to fall in love with the new person but run from the ex make sense.

The jilted ex is decent enough that the audience sympathizes with him or her and thinks he or she is too good for the runaway and doesn't deserve the runaway or deserve to have been jilted.

The audience disagrees with the runaway's decision to run away.

The runaway is too eager and willing to jump into marriage with the love interest after having just run from another such commitment and without having learned some big, important lesson first.

The same reason the runaway left the first wedding applies to a second potential wedding with the love interest, and your audience doesn't buy that he or she would go through with this wedding after not going through with the last one.

You fail to assure your audience that the runaway won't ever run away from the love interest. Once a flight risk, always a flight risk.

RUNAWAY BRIDE/GROOM TROPE IN ACTION
Movies:

- Runaway Bride (Duh)
- It Happened One Night
- Dirty Grandpa
- Till Death Do Us Part
- Made of Honor
- Different Flowers
- It had To Be You

Books:

- Runaway Love by Melanie Harlow
- Things We Never Got Over by Lucy Score
- Powerless by Elsie Silver
- Dirty by Kylie Scott

- Neon Gods by Katee Robert
- A Court of Mist and Fury by Sarah J. Maas
- The Kiss of Deception by Mary E. Pearson
- Runaway Groom by Lauren Layne
- Matched With Her Runaway Groom by Britney M. Mills

29

SPINSTER/BLUESTOCKING/ON THE SHELF

DEFINITION

Traditionally, this trope is about a woman who has never married and is considered past the appropriate age in which women are supposed to marry.

I'm a big fan of turning tropes on their heads, so I hereby declare that this trope can also be about a man who has never married and is considered past the usual or appropriate age for men to marry!

The term bluestocking traditionally refers to educated, intellectual women. It comes from the 18th-century Blue Stockings Society in England led by the hostess and critic Elizabeth Montagu, the "Queen of the Blues."

The reference to blue stockings may arise from the time when woolen stockings were informal dress, in contrast to formal, fashionable black silk stockings. The term later developed negative implications and is now often used in a derogatory manner.

The phrase "on the shelf" or "left on the shelf" appears to have originated in the 19th century to refer to a single woman who is past the usual age of marrying and has no prospects or possibilities of getting married.

SIDE NOTE: In the 19th century, that would have been around the age of 30.

The arc of this trope, then, is for the main character to be single, never married, and older than what's considered the usual marriageable age in your story setting. Over the course of your story, this person will (improbably) meet someone who finds him or her attractive, they fall in love, and against society's expectations, they eventually marry.

Because the very premise of this trope is that the main character is not marriageable, this trope almost without exception ends with a wedding (or whatever the equivalent is in the world you've built). That said, it's possible for this character to find true love and a permanent relationship that doesn't end in a traditional marriage but that does end in a happily ever after for your lovers.

This main character may have had a close call with romance or marriage in the past. He or she might have been involved in a scandal that ruined the relationship, might have been left at the altar, or perhaps engages in unrequited love.

This main character might also be embarrassed about his or her single state and bring a fake boyfriend, girlfriend, or fiancé(e) to some family event or perhaps engage in a pretend marriage.

This main character may be unloved or unlovable, may be a Plain Jane, have a fear of intimacy, have commitment phobia, or have been burned by love in the past.

This main character may be looking for a makeover, a fresh start, or be an ugly duckling who blossoms in your story. He or she may also be willing to enter into an online or pen pal relationship, a pretend marriage, or an unconsummated marriage.

Which is to say, this is one of the tropes most likely to be layered with any number of other tropes. At its core this is a classic love story of a person not in love or not looking for love who finds love when or where they least expect it and ends up married and living happily ever after.

. . .

ADJACENT TROPES

- Only One Not Married
- Socially Awkward Hero/Heroine
- Shy Hero/Heroine
- Nerdy/Geek/Genius
- Ruined/Scandalous Hero/Heroine

WHY READERS/VIEWERS LOVE THIS TROPE

- for every person who has not yet found true love, there is still hope
- it's NEVER too late to find love
- embracing one's own insecurities or quirks, being true to oneself, and still finding true love eventually
- there's a perfect someone out there for each and every one of us...we just have to be patient and keep looking and hoping until Mr. or Ms. Right comes along

OBLIGATORY SCENES
THE BEGINNING:

The main character and love interest meet. This trope often relies on a meet cute to set the tone for the story. The main character is typically awkward, shy, socially clueless, or skeptical of the love interest. The main character has usually accepted his or her perpetually single state. If he or she hasn't made peace with it, he or she has at least accepted being romantically alone as his or her fate in life.

Hence, when the love interest first shows up on the scene, the main character isn't going to immediately hope that this is the One. The main character isn't going to throw himself or herself into romantic speculation and instantly swoon over the dreamy love interest.

The main character is potentially scarred, hardened, or resigned to his or her inability to find love and it is this emotional baggage that will provide much of the conflict in the story as the main character works through it with or in spite of the love interest.

As for the love interest, the act of becoming romantically interested in and involved with the spinster/bluestocking/on the shelf character is an act of rebellion against the norms of the society they live in. Obviously, something about the main character fascinates the love interest enough for him or her to stick around and get to know the main character better.

The more the love interest learns about the main character, the more interesting and alluring that person becomes...and the more of a dilemma the attraction between them poses for the love interest who is not supposed to be falling in love with this older, unacceptable potential partner.

The budding romance may start in secret to avoid the judgment and condemnation of others, or it may start as a platonic friendship that's socially acceptable at first.

The beginning often ends with the exposure of the relationship to others as becoming too romantic. Or it may end with the couple realizing their friendship has become something more—something that could ruin the reputation of the love interest and possible what good reputation the main character still retains.

THE MIDDLE:

This is where the relationship develops into full-blown love...and where being in love causes all kinds of complications. Whatever emotional baggage the main character has developed through the years of not being chosen as someone's mate has to be dealt with before he or she is ready to embrace being truly loved.

This could involve old humiliations, self-esteem or self-image problems, perhaps anger at the structures of society, or a rebellious streak that drove the main character to pursue a passion that was not socially acceptable.

Whatever emotional scars have formed, these must be faced, addressed, and healed before the main character is ready to believe the love interest truly loves him or her.

Meanwhile, pressure grows on the love interest not to continue down the romantic path with this flawed main character who is too old, too different, too...whatever...to be considered marriageable within the society they exist in.

Friends and family of both characters may interfere in the romance.

If there's an external plot, it usually revolves around why the love interest shouldn't marry the main character, or why the main character hasn't married before now.

Traditionally, the external plots in this trope are very secondary to the main storyline, which is overcoming society's objections to this couple falling in love and getting married. That said, in my quest to turn tropes on their heads, I'm a fan of external plot problems that pose a real and serious obstacle to this couple ending up happily married.

This can be a fiancé(e) or arranged future partner of the love interest, some will or estate that dictates who the love interest or main character can or cannot marry, a secret the main character is keeping about his or her identity, past, or family—have fun with this and feel free to be creative!

At any rate, whatever plot problem you choose will grow toward a crisis in the middle of your story and explodes at the end of the middle, threatening the romance between your lovers.

BLACK MOMENT:

In the black moment, the external plot problem explodes, helping to tear apart your lovers. Additionally, whatever conflicts they've had growing between them also explode, and one or both of them breaks up the relationship.

The main character who has dared to hope that he or she has finally found love at last is devastated, perhaps more so because he or she has lived without love for so long already and now knows just how lonely and incomplete his or her life was before.

The love interest, pressured into breaking up, pushed away by the main character, or supremely frustrated with some aspect of the relationship has finally "done the right thing" according to society. He or she has verified everyone else's perception of the main character not being marriageable and may finally return to the good graces of the society he or she has been flouting up until now. While this should be satisfying for the love interest, the loss of the person they love overwhelms any feelings of relief or return to society.

These two people are completely devastated.

THE END:

In their devastation, the lessons are learned and epiphanies had for both lovers. They both realize the thing(s) they need to realize to understand exactly what they've lost and how miserable they are without the other person. They regret the choices that led to their breakup, and they resolve to find a way to fix their mistakes.

Either individually or together, the main character and love interest do the thing they were unwilling or unable to do before to be with their true love. They may make a grand sacrifice, may make a grand (possibly public) gesture, they may have to apologize to each other, forgive each other, or in some other way repair the relationship. But whatever it takes, no matter how hard, they're both willing to do it to be together.

Their love is more important than anything else in the world to both of them. And, having learned this, they find the strength, resources, or wherewithal to move heaven and earth to be together.

Their grand romance and great love wins out in the end, and they can finally get married and be happy together forever.

KEY SCENES

- the main character's spinster/bluestocking/on the shelf status is revealed to the love interest
- the main character tells the love interest outright that he or she is unmarriageable
- the love interest declares his or her romantic interest in spite of the main character's unmarriageable status
- the love interest wants to advance the relationship and the main character puts on the brakes
- they're nearly caught in a romantic situation by a gatekeeper of society's opinion of the main character
- they *are* caught in a romantic situation by a gatekeeper of society's opinion of the main character
- the main character is publicly humiliated for daring to seek love for himself or herself
- the love interest is publicly humiliated for becoming romantically involved with the main character

THINGS TO THINK ABOUT WHEN WRITING THIS TROPE

What is the main character's backstory? Who is he or she? Why did he or she miss getting chosen for marriage in the normal time-frame? What about the main character made him or her unmarriageable?

How did/does the main character continue not to fit into the society you've built into your story?

Who is the love interest? What is his or her position within society? Is he or she happy to go along with society's values when the story begins? Is he or she a rebel when the story begins and happy to buck society's rules and norms? (Bonus question: how can both of these things be true at the same time?)

How do the main character and love interest meet? What's the tone of this meeting? How does it set the tone for the rest of your story?

Are they friends initially? Platonic initially? Do sparks fly right away—romantic, friction, or infuriated sparks? Are they instant enemies? Frenemies initially?

Does someone put the love interest up to approaching the main character? If so, who and how? When will the main character find out about this in your story and how will he or she feel about it? How will the love interest feel about it later?

Why does the love interest want to interact with the main character a second time? How does he or she make this happen? (Or does the main character engineer a second meeting?)

How will they continue to meet up and get to know each other over the course of your story? What plot device will you use?

What's the external plot problem one or both of them is dealing with over the course of the story? How does this problem work to force them together or pull them apart...or does it do both?

What obstacle(s) to being romantically involved must they overcome? Who represents those obstacles? How will your lovers overcome them?

How does this gauntlet of obstacles become ever more difficult to navigate? How does each obstacle get more difficult than the last one to overcome?

Do your lovers form a romantic relationship in secret or in plain sight of society?

If they fall in love in secret, how will they meet secretly? Will anyone help them? If so, who and how? How will they nearly get caught...possibly more than once? How will they ultimately get discovered and exposed?

If they fall in love very publicly, what kind of pushback will they face? From whom?

How does society react when the couple's relationship does become public knowledge? How do friends and family react?

Will the main character resist falling in love with the love interest initially? If so, why?

Will the love interest resist falling in love with the main character initially? If so, why?

To the previous two questions, how can you make it a much more difficult dilemma? How can you make it even more difficult than that?

What are the negative consequences if these two do get married? How can you make those worse? How can you make those much worse? How can you make them impossible to overcome or ignore?

What emotional baggage and emotional scars does the main character begin the story with? How will he or she confront those and heal them? Will the love interest help in this process? If so, how?

What sacrifice will the love interest have to make or be forced to make if he or she goes ahead and marries the main character? How can you make that much bigger?

What conflicts will the lovers struggle to overcome between them? Do they have some sort of disconnect in values, beliefs, opinions, norms of behavior or something else?

What external plot problem ultimately breaks them up?

What internal, personal conflict ultimately breaks them up?

How do they each react and feel about breaking up?

How do the people around them react and feel about the breakup?

What lesson does each character learn or what epiphany does each character have that makes them each willing to make one last try to put the relationship back together?

When in your story will the couple actually get married? Will you wait till the very end of the story after everything else is resolved and use the wedding as their happily ever after moment?

OR

Will you have them marry earlier? You can use their wedding to precipitate the black moment, you can have the wedding be how they solve the external plot problem, or they can marry to defy society one last time, or the grand gesture can be the wedding ceremony itself.

How will they solve the external plot problem? Who will do what needs to be done?

Is there some consequence to their getting married that actually happens to them and that they cannot avoid? If so, what is it and how do they feel about it?

Who makes a grand gesture, grand apology, grand sacrifice or grants grand forgiveness so these two can reconcile?

How does society react to this grand reconciliation event? (Is society present for it or hears about it secondhand?)

Does the couple gain the forgiveness of polite society for bucking the norms and ending up together? How does your couple feel about that?

What does happily ever after look like for this couple? Do they re-enter polite society as a married couple or not? Where do they go to start a life together?

TROPE TRAPS

The main character is entirely marriageable in the eyes of your audience from page one...which leads your audience not to buy the premise of your story or to find the rules of society your story is set in to be stupid or implausible.

The main character and love interest hate each other so instantly and completely that your audience doesn't buy the two of them spending enough time together to ever fall in love.

The main character and love interest are so different from each other that your audience doesn't believe they would ever fall in love.

The couple's fundamental values, beliefs, and morals are so

disparate that they would never fall in love. Furthermore, even if they fall in love, at some point these fundamental differences will cause them irreconcilable differences.

The love interest approaches the main character on a bet or dare and comes across as a giant jerk the audience hates.

The love interest lacks any or enough redeeming qualities to be forgiven by your audience for initially disliking or disrespecting the main character or buying into society's reasons for why the main character is unmarriageable.

The love interest is a chauvinist or man-hater who treats the main character badly, possibly only in the beginning, but enough to tick off your audience on the main character's behalf.

The main character is a chauvinist or man-hater who wouldn't ever plausibly change his or her mind and agree to get married.

The strictures of society in which these two people exist would never bend enough to allow them to marry...and live. (Or without being exiled, at any rate.)

The audience doesn't buy that this couple will be happy together forever, probably because they are so different or live such wildly different lives from each other.

One character has to change, a lot, for the couple to end up together...and the audience either doesn't buy the change or doesn't buy that the change is permanent.

One or both characters fails to learn a significant enough lesson or have a significant enough epiphany to explain whatever big change(s) of heart is/are necessary for them to reconcile.

There are no consequences for ignoring the rules of society.

Society forgives them way too easily for ignoring the rules of society.

They have to make no amends or apologies to anyone for rebelling against their assigned positions in society and rebelling against the rules of polite or proper behavior the way they have.

The external plot problem doesn't add anything to the story...it's just a placeholder for why the couple is in proximity and is boring or uninteresting to your audience.

The couple doesn't have to sacrifice anything to be together.

Your audience is bored by all the angst and hesitation between these two people about following their hearts...which is to say, you fail to create any real or serious potential consequences for these two following their hearts and getting married.

SPINSTER/BLUESTOCKING/ON THE SHELF TROPE IN ACTION
Movies:

- Persuasion
- Phantom Thread
- A Room With A View
- Something's Gotta Give
- Great Expectations
- While You Were Sleeping
- Hush...Hush, Sweet Charlotte
- The Mirror Has Two Faces
- The Witches of Eastwick
- The African Queen

Books:

- The Viscount Who Loved Me by Julia Quinn
- Devil in Winter by Lisa Kleypas
- To Seduce a Sinner by Elizabeth Hoyt
- Lord of Scoundrels by Loretta Chase
- Persuasion by Jane Austen
- Flowers From the Storm by Laura Kinsale

- The Ugly Duchess by Eloisa James
- Frederica by Georgette Heyer
- And Then He Kissed Her by Laura Lee Guhrke
- Ravished by Amanda Quick
- Soulless by Gail Carriger

30

STEPSIBLING/STEPPARENT ROMANCE

DEFINITION

This trope is actually two separate tropes, but their arcs are so similar, I've combined their descriptions into a single entry. In this story, the main character falls in love with their stepsibling or stepparent. The couple overcomes the obstacles before them and ends up together, happily ever after.

Both of these tropes rely for conflict on the taboo of incest with a close family member. Yes, the stepsibling or stepparent is not technically a blood relative, so the main character is not technically engaging in incest.

But psychologically and emotionally, getting into a romantic relationship with a perceived family member, DNA-match or not, is going to *feel* like incest.

Its prevalence is difficult to generalize, but research has estimated 10-15% of the general population as having had at least an incestuous sexual contact, with less than 2% involving intercourse or attempted intercourse. Among women, research has yielded estimates as high as 20%.

I would like to point out, though, that when you include the number of people within families who are aware of these wildly inappropriate contacts, the percentage of people affected indirectly by incest is probably much higher.

This crime touches a much higher proportion of the general public—and your audience—than you might expect and has a high likelihood of being a trigger or hot button for many of them.

Also worth noting, incest is illegal in every state in the U.S. ***even if the contact is consensual by both parties***. It's often combined with statutory rape in the case of a minor and is frequently charged as a felony.

It's also one of a very few crimes that is illegal in every single country on Earth (with some international variations in how close a family member one may legally engage in a sexual relationship with).

> **Assuming it's not your actual intent to write an incest romance, which is a valid—if ethically fraught—choice, the easiest and most obvious way to avoid crossing over the line into taboo is to make sure the main character and love interest have not had time, proximity, or inclination to form any significant familial-style relationship before they fall in love.**

For example, the main character and stepsibling become romantically involved almost immediately after meeting. They never get to know each other as siblings and are strangers until they meet, are attracted, and move straight into a romantic relationship.

The stepparent relationship is trickier to navigate since the stepparent has necessarily married or been the legal partner of one of the main character's (usually biological) parents prior to becoming romantically involved with the main character.

The odds of the main character and stepparent having known each other for a while before they become romantically involved are fairly high. In the case of a main character whose parent married the love interest while the main character was a minor or young adult, the odds of the main character having attached "parent figure" to how he or she identifies the stepparent are also very high.

In the main character-stepparent relationship, you must account for two things:

1. Why the love interest has never stepped into a parental role with the main character in the past (or has stepped out of it now).
2. How and why the relationship between the main character's parent and the love interest-stepparent has ended.

In both the stepsibling and stepparent romance, the main decision you must make is how close to incest you plan to go with your story. The closer to an incestuous relationship you move, the more conflict and resistance your lovers will encounter from the people around them, some of whom may have (possibly legal) authority to intervene to break up the relationship.

Also, the more backlash you're likely to face from reviewers, readers/viewers, and the general public who may or may not have consumed your story.

Generally, these two tropes revolve around resistance, both internal and external, to the very existence of this relationship.

Why did I put this in a volume of backstory tropes instead of external tropes? Because a prior relationship between the main character and stepsibling and stepparent necessarily exists. One of the main character's parents married or partnered with someone in the past and introduced a stepsibling or stepparent into the main character's life.

The newer this "step" relationship is, the less incestuous it's likely to feel in your story. Vice versa, the longer this relationship has been in existence, the likelier your story is to skirt close to incest in feel.

You will have to make certain ethical choices as you approach this trope. Stepsibling and stepparent romances sell, so obviously it's a fantasy some people have. And where there's a market and money to be made, writers are going to step into that space.

Is incest a real and devastating problem that real people face? Absolutely. Is it not only illegal but wrong and immoral, especially when forced upon minors or when minors are groomed or coerced into cooperating? Absolutely.

And yes, it's a titillating taboo for some people; therefore, it is going to get written about, ethics notwithstanding.

If you choose to write about this as a fantasy or wish fulfillment type of story, by all means, please do your research and be sensitive to the criminal implications and the intense physical, psychological, and emotional damage that can and do result from exactly these types of interactions between close family members.

Yes, but they're only "steps" I hear some writers shouting at me.

If a person perceives another person as a sibling figure or parental figure, the DNA involved doesn't matter psychologically or emotionally when that brother-figure, sister-figure, or parent-figure crosses a boundary with him or her that should never, ever be crossed within a family.

Incest—and perceived incest—are supreme violations of trust and exploit the most intimate of family bonds in a devastating betrayal of trust.

Be careful with this trope.

ADJACENT TROPES

- Guardian/Caretaker Romance
- Forbidden Love
- Right Under Your Nose
- May-December Romance

WHY READERS/VIEWERS LOVE THIS TROPE

- fantasy of engaging in a totally taboo relationship
- sneaking around and getting away with doing something really bad
- a giant Eff You to society and its rules or to a family member(s) who are judgmental, straitlaced, stuffy, or overbearing
- Warning, serious answer here: because your reader/viewer has an unhealthy, twisted, or broken view of what constitutes love that this trope accurately reflects

OBLIGATORY SCENES
THE BEGINNING:

The main character and stepsibling or stepparent come into physical proximity. They may be meeting for the first time or have never been around each other much or at all in the past.

Romantic or sexual sparks fly.

Houston, we have a problem.

The main character and love interest know without a shadow of a doubt their relationship is wrong, and they fight the attraction they each feel for the other. They may or may not discuss their attraction and its wrongness and weirdness.

This is almost always a secret relationship, engaged in furtively. One or both participants knows it to be wrong and possibly knows it skirts the line of being illegal. Depending on ages and prior relationship type, it might actually be criminal.

The external story problem is something that throws these two people into repeated physical proximity. While most story problems pull lovers apart, this trope turns that on its head and the story problem does its level best to thrust this couple—who should not be together—into each other's arms.

The beginning often ends with someone finding out they may be flirting with the idea of entering into a relationship and freaking out— or forbidding the relationship. The beginning may also end with the couple almost getting caught together and being forced to acknowledge to each other that they shouldn't do this.

THE MIDDLE:

The middle is often a series of approaches and retreats as the couple fights their attraction, the wrongness of what they're doing, and can't resist being together one more time.

Friends and family around this pair become suspicious, start watching the couple, warn off the couple, threaten the couple, and eventually expose the couple's illicit relationship to other friends and family. The social pressure to break up probably becomes nigh unbearable as everyone piles on the pair.

The couple knows what they're doing is technically wrong but they spend much of the middle trying to justify it to themselves and others. But it feels so right. But nobody else is being hurt. But we were never sibling-like or parent-child-like before. We were just two strangers who met and fell in love...

The external story problem grows in intensity, forcing the couple together more and more, closer and closer, until an inevitable explosion is bound to occur.

BLACK MOMENT:

The couple breaks up. The pressure has become too much to bear, or perhaps the guilt, or the threat of legal action, or some other reason. Whatever internal conflicts have been happening within the lovers and between the lovers may have been too much to stand.

To be clear, this is a black moment for the lovers themselves. Most of the people around them may see this moment in the story as a triumph or a relief rather than a tragedy. Indeed, when this couple finds a way to be together in the end, those around them probably are disappointed.

Your challenge then, is to make your audience empathize with the lovers strongly enough that the moment of their being torn apart is, indeed, a black one...and not cause for celebration by your audience.

THE END:

The couple is so miserable apart that they can't stay away from each other. They both realize this or have some other similar epiphany that gives them the strength to push back against society and all the forces pulling them apart and to try one last time to find a way to be together.

The external plot problem is resolved and moved out of the way as an obstacle to love. The lovers either reconcile with family and friends and find a way to make these people understand why they're so in love and how it's right for them to be in love.

Once these external obstacles are taken care of, the last piece left is for the lovers to overcome their personal, internal conflicts so they can be together. This may involve apologies, forgiveness, resolving past emotional baggage, learning to ignore what others think, or whatever other conflicts you've brewed between these lovers over the course of your story.

Somewhere in the story, and definitely by the end, the legality of what your lovers are doing must be established so your audience won't wonder forever if the pair was ever caught and prosecuted.

KEY SCENES

--the first time they acknowledge their mutual attraction for each other

--the moment they acknowledge to each other that the relationship is wrong

--when they're almost caught together by someone who would be disastrous to be

caught by

--the couple's first big fight

--the lovers are caught together in a romantically compromising situation

--one or both of the lovers is confronted by someone who declares such a

relationship to be wrong, immoral, toxic, or illegal

--the lovers try to stay away from each other but fail

--individually, and then together, your lovers are confronted by friends, family,

colleagues, or social/cultural/legal authority figures about the wrongness of what

they're doing

--one or both lovers pay(s) a heavy price for the illicit relationship

--individually or together, the lovers question what they're doing and if they should

walk away from this relationship

THINGS TO THINK ABOUT WHEN WRITING THIS TROPE

When, where, and how did the main character and stepsibling or stepparent first meet? How old were they both?

Did a brotherly/sisterly or parental relationship develop in the past between the main character and the step-love interest? If so, what was that relationship like? If not, why not and what kept them from developing this familial relationship?

Have the lovers ever spent time in physical proximity or together in any way in the past? If so, how, when, and where?

What has changed in one or both characters' lives that throws these two people together now? Why now?

In the case of a stepparent, why did that marriage end?

What happened to the main character's parent? Is he or she alive? Present in the story? Divorced or separated from the stepparent?

If the main character's parent is alive, what role does he or she play in the story? Does he or she freak out at the stepparent romance? Does he or she try to break it up? Or does the parent see how these two people he or she loves could work as a couple and help them get together? (Side note: the potential squick factor of a parent setting up their child with their ex is extremely high. Tread very carefully if you go there.)

Alive or dead, will the main character's parent play a major role in your story? If so, what? What does he or she think of this new relationship? What will he or she do? Will the parent support or sabotage the new relationship? If so, how and why?

What story device throws your main character and love interest into close and repeated physical proximity in your story?

What do the lovers find fascinating and irresistibly attractive about each other? What about each other bothers or irritates them to no end?

What problems will this couple encounter in their relationship that's not related to the illicitness of their relationship?

Will the relationship be secret, at least at first? Who do the main character and love interest feel a need to hide their relationship from? Why?

Who nearly catches them in a romantically compromising position the first time? Who in your story would be the worst possible person to catch them together? Can you make this person almost catch them at some point in your story?

How do the lovers initially feel about getting involved with this forbidden person? What do they think about it? What do they do about these thoughts and feelings?

Do the lovers individually or as a couple try not to get romantically involved with each other? Do they ever talk about it? If so, what do they say? If not, why not?

Do they both know their relationship is wrong according to the society they live in? If so, why do they proceed? If not, why not?

What's the external plot that you'll hang this romance story upon? How does this external plot and its problem push the lovers together? How does it pull them apart? Is the external story problem a source or the source of the potential consequences if these two people go ahead and insist on becoming romantically involved?

How can you make the consequences of following through on this relationship worse? Much worse? Terrible? Unbearable?

Who around the lovers knows or finds out about their relationship?

How do the people around the lovers react to the existence of this relationship? Do they try to break it up or help the couple along?

At what point in the story do your lovers decide to ignore what everybody else thinks and go for it with each other? What does that moment or event look like?

How will your lovers individually and as a couple deal with guilt, doubt, or regrets regarding being in this relationship?

Who in your story will bring the backlash to your lovers if and when they get caught?

What consequences will actually happen to your lovers as a result of their relationship?

What breaks them up? Who walks away? Why?

How do the people around them react to the breakup?

How do the lovers react to the breakup?

What makes one or both of them decide to try to repair what's broken in their relationship or what's in the way of it, and get back together?

How will they overcome each and every obstacle standing in their way to being together?

Who owes apologies to whom? What do those apologies look like? Are they accepted when given?

Does the couple reconcile with the people who thought they shouldn't be together, or will the couple leave the place where they've met and fallen in love and start a new life elsewhere with less emotional baggage and judgment?

How will you convince your audience that this couple has what it takes to be happy forever? Will you successfully convince the character in the story around this couple of that? If so, how?

Is this couple ever forgiven by society and the people around them?

Do they forgive themselves? If so, how? When? Where? Why?

TROPE TRAPS

Creating a relationship that feels too incestuous to your audience and they don't like it.

Treating the pseudo-incestuous elements of the romance cavalierly and triggering or upsetting a big chunk of your audience

Writing (implausibly) that nobody around this pair has any idea they're falling in love and building a romantic relationship—it's very hard to hide this kind of activity from people who know you well and certainly from family members. Which is to say, creating TSTL (too stupid to live) secondary characters whom your audience doesn't buy or like.

Failing to create enough physical separation in the main character and love interest's back story to keep them from plausibly having formed a familial relationship before your story starts.

Creating a hokey reason your audience doesn't buy for why the stepsibling or stepparent never got involved in the main character's life before now.

Failing to plausibly account for where the parent/spouse of the main character and love interest has disappeared to and failing to explain why that marriage has ended.

Going for the cliché where the only living birth parent of the main character dies, which throws the step-spouse and main character together to handle the dead parent's final affairs and final effects while they grieve together...and oh, fall in love. When you're grieving the recent loss of a parent or spouse, odds are outstanding you're in no fit emotional condition to fall madly in love with anyone.

You fail to factor in an age difference between your lovers and the sorts of problems that can and should cause.

Your main character is a spoiled brat, narcissist, or focused only on what feels good in the moment. He or she won't listen to reason and does whatever he or she wants, regardless of who it hurts...and your audience hates this person.

Your love interest knows full well that a romantic relationship with the main character is off limits, but does it anyway, knowing it's wrong, and alienates your audience.

If one of your lovers is so naïve that he or she doesn't realize this relationship is ethically and morally wrong, then he or she is too naïve to be in a serious relationship...and the love interest is taking gross advantage of this incredibly naïve character by seducing him or her.

Failing to consider how your story might trigger or upset a good chunk of your audience. Failing to handle the flirtation with incest with any sensitivity, honesty, or care.

Failing to include some sort of overt or covert trigger warning to your audience in your packaging and marketing materials.

Being a jerk when a reader or viewer approaches you and is upset over the subject matter of your story and failing to realize he or she may be horribly triggered by

past, real-life trauma along the lines of this trope.

STEPSIBLING/STEPPARENT TROPE IN ACTION
Movies:

- Butterfly
- Beau-père
- Welcome the Stranger
- Daddy's Girl
- Angel Eyes

- Mini's First Time
- Sweet Temptation

Books:

- Love Unexpected by Q. B. Tyler
- Stepbrother Dearest by Penelope Ward
- Brutal Intentions by Lilith Vincent
- Power by Cassandra Robbins
- Eyes on Me by Sara Cate
- The Devil by Ashley Jade
- Lords of Pain by Angel Lawson
- Prick by Sabrina Paige
- Fallen Too Far by Abbi Glines
- Culpa Mia by Mercedes Ron

31

STOCKHOLM SYNDROME/SLAVERY ROMANCE

Don't. Do. It.

But if you must...

DEFINITION

Having now gotten your attention, we need to have a serious conversation about the ethics of this trope.

But first, let's define Stockholm Syndrome. It's when a victim experiences such intense psychological distress that it causes him or her to identify with and empathize with his or her kidnapper or abuser and said kidnapper/abuser's goals...or in the case of this as a romance trope, to fall in love with his or her kidnapper/abuser.

It was first observed in 1973 when Jan-Erik Olsson, a convict on parole, and an associate took four employees (three women and one man) hostage during a failed robbery of Kreditbanken, a large bank in Stockholm, Sweden. He and an associate held the hostages captive for six days in one of the bank's vaults. When the hostages were released, none of them would testify against their captors in court. Instead, they began raising money for the robbers' defense.

Four key elements comprise Stockholm Syndrome:

1. A hostage's development of positive feelings towards the captor
2. No previous relationship between hostage and captor
3. A refusal by hostages to cooperate with police and other government authorities
4. A hostage's belief in the humanity of the captor, ceasing to perceive them as a threat, when the victim holds the same values as the aggressor.

Stockholm Syndrome is thought to arise from the extreme power imbalances of hostage-taking, kidnapping, and abusive relationships.

Also worth noting, psychologists believe that many enslaved people experience(d) Stockholm Syndrome with regard to their enslavers.

Here's where this becomes problematic in crafting a romantic relationship:

- The kidnapper/abuser is doing direct harm to the victim/love interest.
- The abuser never changes his or her behavior to "protect" the victim. He or she continues to inflict harm on the victim throughout the relationship.
- The victim is non-consensually forced to participate in this relationship.
- Any feelings the victim perceives himself or herself having are a result of intense psychological distress. We're talking desperate, visceral fear for one's life, here. **The victim is trying to find a way to survive… not legitimately falling in love with anyone**.

The act of "falling in love" in this situation is, in fact, an unconscious psychological response to the stress, trauma, and threat of the situation. It is not a conscious choice the victim makes.

The frantic, frightened victim will try everything and anything to convince the captor/abuser/enslaver not to harm or kill them. It's a human survival response akin to a wolf chewing off its own leg when caught in a hunter's trap.

Convincing yourself and your captor/abuser/enslaver that you're in love with him or her is a similar act of desperation.

This is where Stockholm Syndrome and Slavery Romance differ from BDSM/Power Exchange Romance tropes. The former two are entirely non-consensual on the part of the hostage/victim/enslaved person and the act of "falling in love" is entirely nonconsensual in nature. Whereas in a BDSM or power exchange relationship—done ethically—absolutely every single bit of the relationship is consensual by both parties and can voluntarily be exited at any time.

It's important to note that romances between enslaved persons and their enslavers contain most of the same elements of a Stockholm relationship:

- They're entirely non-consensual on the part of the enslaved person.
- They include an extreme power dynamic of utter control by the enslaver.
- They almost always include emotional or physical abuse.
- The enslaved person experiences feelings of complete helplessness and fear for his or her life.
- Any feelings an enslaved person develops for his or her enslaver are purely the result of trying to survive rather than any legitimate romantic feelings the enslaved person has for their enslaver.

Let's look at another trope that can tread close to the Stockholm Syndrome/Slavery Romance trope—the Mafia Romance.

In a mafia romance, the main character may, indeed, do something bad, even criminal, to the love interest at the beginning of the story. But the mafioso, who is romantically attracted to the love interest, quickly has an epiphany and repents of his or her bad actions toward the love interest.

The mafioso spends the rest of the story protecting the love interest and/or making up for his or her terrible opening mistake.

While the main character may remain a criminal throughout a mafia romance, and the love interest may end up accepting that criminality and empathizing with the criminal, the main character uses his or her criminal skills or criminal connections to protect and care for the love interest. He or she never harms the love interest after the inciting event, or quickly STOPS harming the love interest, and actively works to earn the trust and love of the love interest.

The key differences between Stockholm Syndrome/Slavery Romance and Mafia Romance are:

- In the Stockholm/Slavery story, ***the main character never stops harming the love interest***.
- In the Stockholm/Slavery story, ***the hostage/victim/enslaved person never has any agency, freedom, power, or choice to participate or not participate in the relationship***.

These two tropes may only be an inch apart, but that inch makes all the difference. Which brings us to the ethical crux of the matter:

Is it okay or not to write stories based on non-consensual relationships based in abuse, psychological distress, fear, threat to life and limb, and desperation to survive with no real, romantic love being possible between the kidnapper/abuser/enslaver and the hostage/victim/enslaved person?

It's only fair to point out that these stories are being written, and they're selling enough copies and generating enough views to convince writers to write more of the same.

It's also fair to point out that writers often work out their own traumas and pain through writing about experiences that imitate or approximate their lived experience.

Is the fantasy of being kidnapped or held hostage and ravished part and parcel of the fantasy of being allowed to do something very bad but still retaining one's good girl/boy status after the fact, that is, staying pure after doing something impure in the eyes of others? Possible. In some cases, probable.

But I would like to point out that this trope revolves around **falling in love** with one's abuser...not simply being helpless and ravished. And personally, I do believe that makes a huge difference in where the ethical line lies with this trope.

In the same vein, readers and viewers sometimes work out their traumas and pain by reading or watching characters who've experienced a similar situation to their own, particularly if those fictional characters end up finding a positive outcome.

The reality is many people do experience abuse at the hands of others who have rendered them powerless. As part of the human experience, it's certainly fair game for writers to write about.

But romanticizing abuse, normalizing it as courtship, suggesting that one should love one's abuser and embrace physical and psychological trauma as demonstration of love—this is tantamount to telling a victim of the worst sort of abuse to shut up and take it...and while they're at it, learn to love the person doing it to them.

Likewise, portraying an enslaved person happily falling in love with his or her enslaver is tantamount to suggesting to your audience that they should relax and accept slavery. It's breathtakingly unethical at best and monstrous at worst, not to mention unspeakably racist.

I would *never* tell anyone not to write at all about having been the victim of a kidnapping, abuse, or enslavement. Nor would I dream of telling a reader or viewer not to consume stories about it, particularly if it's a trauma they've experienced directly or indirectly.

There's tremendous value in fiction that exposes and sheds light on mankind's worst excesses and acts as a cautionary tale of why *not* to act in certain ways. And there's enormous value in depicting people of courage, strength, and resilience surviving and transcending terrible trauma to be able to love and trust other people after recovering from their terrible experience.

But I am suggesting that writing about Stockholm Syndrome and enslavement without the most extreme sensitivity to them, without awareness of the potential to normalize horrific abuse or the potential to reinforce tolerating intense psychological suffering is deeply unethical.

Abuse is not love. Period.

I debated long and hard whether or not to include this trope at all in a book of romance tropes. I even consulted with publishing industry experts and DEI professionals over my decision. It would've been much easier to skip this whole discussion or pretend stories of this type don't exist, and to avoid the potential blowback of declaring love stories based on this trope to be generally unethical.

But my purpose stands to dissect and analyze all the romance tropes being written in the romance industry today, even the unethical ones.

Indeed, if the purpose of storytelling is for readers or viewers to vicariously live through fictional people, to learn lessons about themselves and how to survive, to play out possible scenarios in their imaginations and learn from them without having to experience them, then it's reasonable to expect some writers to write about kidnappings, abuse, or enslavement, all of which do, in fact, happen.

What I'm objecting to is suggesting to your audience the notion that, out of these tragic and horrendous traumas, true love with your kidnapper, abuser, or enslaver is a possible outcome. I'll repeat what I said before:

Abuse is not love. Abuse is never love. Real love never grows from abuse.

ADJACENT TROPES

- Mafia Romance

. . .

STOCKHOLM SYNDROME/SLAVERY ROMANCE TROPE IN ACTION
Books:

- Wench by Dolen Perkins-Valdez (the one and only book I've found that handles an enslaver/slave relationship well)
- The Way Forward by Eliana West

AUTHOR'S NOTE: I'm happy to include more movies and books that handle this difficult trope through an ethical lens and with sensitivity. If you know of any, please feel free to contact me, and I'll update this list in a future edition.

32

SURVIVIOR'S GUILT/PTSD

DEFINITION

In this trope something terrible has happened to the main character or very close to the main character in the past. He or she has survived this terrible thing but not without significant scars and emotional baggage.

PTSD (Post-Traumatic Stress Disorder) is the norm to expect as an aftereffect when someone has experienced a major trauma. As its name suggests, it's a psychiatric disorder that results from exposure to some sort of traumatic, life threatening event or harmful trauma.

People with PTSD have intense, disturbing thoughts and feelings related to their experience that last long after the traumatic event has ended. They may relive the event through flashbacks or nightmares. They may feel sadness, fear or anger. They may feel detached or estranged from other people.

People with PTSD may avoid situations or people that remind them of the traumatic event, and they may have strong negative reactions to something as ordinary as a loud noise or an accidental touch.

I'm not going to belabor this trope description with a lengthy discussion of the causes, treatments and remedies for PTSD. There's a ton of information available on the subject, and there are a bunch of different ways it can be caused, ways in which it can manifest, and ways it can be treated.

You'd be wise to do your research before diving into a portrayal of it in your story. Many of your audience members will be intimately familiar with it, and they'll know immediately if you do or don't know what you're talking about.

The possible traumas that can result in PTSD are endless Because of this, you'll need to research the type of PTSD specific to the past trauma you've chosen to subject your main character to.

Please realize that not only does PTSD affect the person who has it, but it also affects everyone who loves or cares about him or her.

PTSD greatly raises the risk of mortality in all its victims and is the leading cause of suicide in those who suffer from it. This is a very serious condition that good people die from every single day.

You owe it to your audience to portray accurate information about the symptoms, causes, treatments, consequences, and outcomes of PTSD or to be crystal clear in both a trigger warning and disclaimer that you're a) portraying it, and b) doing so fictionally and not factually.

One last note: although survivor's guilt and PTSD have been lumped into one trope description, they're not the same thing. While they are both trauma responses, which is why I've combined them, don't conflate one with the other.

Having survivor's guilt doesn't mean you necessarily have PTSD. Vice versa, the presence of PTSD in a character does not necessitate that he or she also experience survivor's guilt.

Okay. Public Service Announcement over. Where were we with the trope?

Right.

The main character suffering from survivor's guilt or PTSD is moving on with his or her life—or at least is trying to—when the main character meets someone new to whom he or she is attracted. Can the main character overcome the pain and emotional damage of the past to find a way forward and find true love?

At its core, this is a trope of healing. The main character must come to terms with past trauma lest it interfere with present events and prevent a possibly wonderful future.

The love interest may have nothing to do with the past tragedy. Or the love interest may trigger thoughts or memories of the past tragedy without having been part of the tragedy directly. Or, the love interest may have been intimately involved in the past tragedy, having also experienced it, having survived it as well, or perhaps as a witness.

The love interest may have healing of his or her own to do, or the love interest may serve as someone who loves the main character enough to stick by him or her while the main character launches a journey of self-healing.

The external plot problem of this sort of story often dredges up the past and forces the main character to confront his or her guilt over having survived or to confront his or her PTSD.

At the same time the possibility of falling in love and being able to have a forever relationship with someone the main character loves may act as the catalyst that finally pushes the main character to confront his or her past and guilt.

ADJACENT TROPES

- Recovery/Rehabilitation
- Dangerous Secret
- Forgiveness
- Redemption

WHY READERS/VIEWERS LOVE THIS TROPE

- getting to release guilt held over past events would be such a relief
- it's possible to come back from a terrible mistake and find happiness
- it's possible to heal from anything given enough time and love (and good therapy)
- loves heals all wounds
- someone comes along and lifts the unbearable burden off my back
- the person I love who's lost in survivor's guilt or PTSD can recover someday and return to being the person I once knew and loved

OBLIGATORY SCENES
THE BEGINNING:

The main character and love interest meet. Commonly a meet-cute of some kind, cuteness is not necessarily required. The main character may not initially expose his or her guilt or PTSD to this person he or she has just met. Survivor's guilt and PTSD are pretty personal things and the main character may not choose to share it with just anyone.

If, however, the love interest is somehow tied to the event(s) that caused the main character's survivor's guilt or PTSD, it's entirely possible the love interest knows already or immediately who the main character is and can surmise what the main character might be feeling. In this case the relationship may jump past superficial to intensely personal very quickly.

This jump may put off the main character and may make one or both of your lovers quite uncomfortable.

Something about the love interest is fascinating enough to the main character that he or she contemplates the notion of confronting his or her demons once and for all to clear the path to true love.

The main character is intriguing and wonderful enough that the love interest is willing to wait through the main character's recovery and healing process to be with him or her. The love interest may even be willing to go through the healing process with the main character.

The beginning typically ends with something triggering an emotional crisis for the main character. It may be the first time in the story that he or she has directly confronted his or her unresolved feelings. It may be the moment when the main character realizes he or she has survivor's guilt or PTSD. Or there may simply be some event that's too painful for the main character to handle in his or her current emotional and psychological state.

THE MIDDLE:

The main character consciously decides to get better so he or she can be with the love interest. The love interest may issue an ultimatum first that the main character must get his or her head and heart right before the love interest will enter into a serious relationship with him or her.

The romantic relationship is typically punctuated by advances and retreats as the main character takes two steps forward and one step back in his or her healing process. The love interest may become frustrated and have to fight to be patient as he or she waits for the main character to deal with his or her issues.

The love interest may be recruited to help the main character work through his or her baggage and feelings. The love interest's job may be to stand aside and merely lend support and cheerleading to the main character.

The external plot of the story often has something to do with the event(s) that caused the main character's survivor's guilt or PTSD in the first place. The current events may trigger even more guilt or PTSD or amplify the guilt and PTSD that's already present.

It's not uncommon to have some sort of mystery or unknown information about the past tragedy that is uncovered over the course of your story. The revelation may change the main character's perception of the event, might let the main character off the guilt hook, or might change everything the main character thinks he or she knows about the past tragic event.

As the main character pushes himself or herself harder and harder, closer and closer to the heart of his or her trauma, he or she may resist going any further in his or her recovery at some point. This can trigger the black moment as the main character puts the brakes on the healing process.

The external plot problem gets worse before it gets better. As the middle ends and the black moment unfolds, the external problem becomes a full-blown crisis.

The pressures from inside the romantic relationship reach a boil and bubble over as well, adding more steam to an already fraught situation.

One or both lovers walk(s) away from the romance. The main character may be unwilling to face the core of his or her wound. Or the love interest may lose patience for how long the main character's journey to healing is taking.

BLACK MOMENT:

Now that they're apart, the lovers realize how miserable they are without the other one in their life. The main character's recovery from guilt/PTSD stalls or heads in the opposite direction. He or she may spiral emotionally.

The main character has failed to conquer his or her demons and remains or returns to being consumed by guilt or lost in PTSD. No matter how hard the love interest has loved the main character, the main character was unwilling or unable to change for the love interest. This realization is devastating to both characters.

They've both taken a chance on love and have lost. Love wasn't enough to overcome the guilt or PTSD that one or both of them is struggling through.

THE END:

It's into this soup of pain and loss that one or both lovers realizes some lesson of import or experiences some sort of epiphany. While this ah-hah moment may not fix everything, it does succeed in putting the past, the past tragedy, and the current feelings of guilt/PTSD into a new and more manageable perspective.

This epiphany does succeed, however, at convincing the lovers that they belong together. No matter how hard it is nor how long it takes, they'll find a way to be together. To that end, the main character takes one last shot at confronting his or her demons.

This moment may coincide with the big climax of the plot problem. The main character must face his or her fears/guilt/PTSD to be able to fix the problem once and for all. It's a moment of supreme courage, self-sacrifice, and blind belief for the main character to take this leap of faith. But, at the other end of the jump awaits the love of his or her life.

As the lovers reunite, there may be confessions, admissions of past mistakes, and forgiveness is granted for past bad behavior. The love interest typically acknowledges the monumental scale of the journey the main character has taken to be with him or her.

The couple can finally come together healthy, healed, and capable of the full measure of love. This is typically an angst-filled story, and your audience is going to want a swoon-worthy moment of romantic connection between the lovers before you end your story.

KEY SCENES

- the love interest connects the main character to the past tragic event. The main character may make the

connection, or someone else might do it, or the love interest might discover it for himself or herself
- the main character talks about his or her feelings for the first time with the love interest
- the main character pulls back in a romantic moment from the love interest and it's upsetting to one or both of them
- someone close to one of the lovers warns the couple against getting too close
- the main character lashes out in his or her pain and hurts the love interest's feelings
- the first major romantic encounter either goes well and then takes a terrible turn for the worse in the aftermath, or the romantic encounter itself goes terribly as the guilt and PTSD intrude and sabotage the main character's happiness
- the love interest absolves the main character from responsibility for the past tragedy
- the main character (finally) absolves himself or herself for having survived or for having PTSD

THINGS TO THINK ABOUT WHEN WRITING THIS TROPE

What past event or events has the main character experienced? How has it traumatized him or her?

What form has the trauma taken? Survivor's guilt? PTSD? Both?

How has this guilt/PTSD caused the main character's regular, healthy behavior to change? How does the guilt/PTSD manifest itself in the main character's actions and decisions?

How do the main character and love interest meet?

Does the love interest have any connection to the past event(s) that traumatized the main character? If so, how, and how has the love interest been affected by the same set of events? Has the love interest reacted the same way as the main character or in some different way? Why?

When does the love interest find out about the past trauma and from whom? Does the love interest ask about it or does someone volunteer the information?

How does the main character's guilt/PTSD impact his or her relationship with the love interest early in the relationship?

Does the main character self-sabotage in some way? If so, how? Why?

What does the love interest think of the main character's trauma and response to it?

How will the love interest try to help the main character confront his or her demons? Does it work? Why or why not?

What problems beside the main character's guilt/PTSD do the lovers have to deal with?

How do the people around this pair treat them? Does anyone else blame the main character for what happened?

Is the love interest protective of the main character? Why?

Does the love interest ever grow impatient with the main character's manifestation of guilt/PTSD? What does that impatience look like?

How does the external plot problem provoke the main character's guilt/PTSD? Does the problem force him or her to confront his or her feelings or not? How and why?

What causes the main character to pull back from the romantic relationship? What triggers the retreat? What does it look like? How does the love interest react?

What about the setting of your story triggers the main character's guilt/PTSD?

What about the secondary characters triggers the main character's guilt/PTSD?

What about the love interest triggers the main character's guilt/PTSD?

What breaks up the lovers? Who walks away from whom? Why? How?

How will your main character ultimately face and deal with his or her trauma and pain? Will he or she get professional help? Help from the love interest? Go it alone?

What event in your story will demonstrate in deeds and actions the main character's ultimate confrontation with his or her guilt/PTSD?

Does the love interest have an epiphany of some kind after the breakup? If so, what? How does it change him or her? What does he or she learn? How does it affect his or her decision to give the relationship one last try?

What besides losing the love interest will be the consequence(s) of the main character NOT confronting and overcoming his or her survivor's guilt/PTSD? How can you make that worse? Much worse?

Will the lovers work together to solve the external plot problem or will one of them handle it alone? If so, who? How?

How will the lovers reconcile? Will it take an honest discussion or something more? If so, what? What does that look like in your story?

Are there any amends to be made? If so, by whom to whom? Will we see these on the page, stage, or screen?

What does happily ever after look like for this couple?

TROPE TRAPS

Failing to portray PTSD in a believable or sensitive way.

Giving out misinformation that could potentially be damaging to a real person who reads or watches your story, particularly without including any disclaimers.

Creating a main character so damaged that they can't possibly build or sustain a romantic relationship in their current emotional state.

Creating a past event so traumatic that the main character will never plausibly recover, particularly without intervention from mental health professionals.

Creating a past tragedy that your audience thinks the main character SHOULD feel guilty over...and that your audience thinks they should continue to carry their guilt over.

Creating a love interest who's as damaged as your main character and together they should go to therapy, not to bed...which is to say your audience thinks a relationship between them is a terrible idea.

The love interest has the patience of a saint and puts up with behaviors that no sane person would stand for. (Side note: for couples who've married or made a long-term commitment before the trauma that caused the guilt/PTSD, the love interest may be willing to hang in there for much longer than the new boyfriend/girlfriend would.)

Creating a lame past or past tragedy that wouldn't trigger the amount of guilt or PTSD your main character is experiencing.

Failing to do your homework on how survivor's guilt and PTSD actually manifest in people experiencing them. Getting the behaviors, responses, and triggers wrong. Much of your audience has experienced survivor's guilt or PTSD themselves or have watched someone they love deal with it. They'll KNOW what it looks like, up close and personal.

Getting so bogged down in the tragic past or trauma that your story has no lightness, no humor, nothing to spark enjoyment or hope in your audience.

Getting too preachy about guilt or forgiveness and turning off your audience.

The main character forgives himself or herself too easily...or too reluctantly.

The main character never forgives himself or herself and yet manages to achieve true love in the end without completing the healing arc of this trope.

SURVIVIOR'S GUILT/PTSD TROPE IN ACTION
Movies:

- Guardians of the Galaxy, Vol. 3
- Avengers: Endgame
- Ordinary People
- The Normal Heart
- Snow Cake

NOTE: I was unable to find any credible movies that portray a love story where a main character is wrestling with PTSD. There are any number of spectacular portrayals of PTSD on TV/film/stage...but not romantic stories. Here are a few of the best movies featuring PTSD, though:

- Born On The Fourth of July
- The Deer Hunter
- American Sniper
- The Hurt Locker
- The Hunger Games
- Taxi Driver
- The Fisher King
- Mystic River

Books:

- Collision Course by S.C. Stephens
- Loving Vin by Sloane Kennedy
- A Life of Shadows by Kristen Banet
- After the Crash by Emma Alcott

- Unlikely Date by Samantha Christy
- The Alpha Awakens by Anna Fury
- That Second Chance by Meghan Quinn
- To Desire a Devil by Elizabeth Hoyt
- Psycho Shifters by Jasmine Mas

33

TEEN CRUSH

DEFINITION

In this trope, the main character and love interest knew each other as teens (or even as children), and the main character—as the name implies—had a crush back then on the love interest. The love interest may or may not have been aware of the crush back then, but in either case, didn't respond to it or act upon it. Time has passed, life has moved on for both people, and now they've come back together for some reason.

The renewed acquaintance may revive the teen crush, or the main character may wonder what he or she ever saw in the love interest. Regardless, as these two people spend time together, an adult romance is kindled, and the main character finally gets to be with the person they had a crush on in the past.

Given that a teen's (unrealistic or at least inexperienced) expectations of how a romance might go, the adult main character may be surprised when he or she actually gets to know the person he or she once had a crush on. The crux of this trope is nostalgia versus reality, imagined perfection versus the reality of imperfection, the imaginary lover versus the real one.

· · ·

ADJACENT TROPES

- Reconciliation/Second Chance Romance
- Oblivious to Love
- Childhood Sweethearts/Friends
- Girl/Boy Next Door
- Right Under Your Nose
- First Love
- Unrequited Love

WHY READERS/VIEWERS LOVE THIS TROPE

- what would've happened if I got together with my teen crush?
- my life would be so different now
- getting swept out of the difficult, mundane life I have now and carried away to a better life
- I wasn't invisible then, after all, and I'm not invisible now
- a do-over of our teen years and teen mistakes
- setting right the mistakes of the past

OBLIGATORY SCENES
THE BEGINNING:

The main character and love interest meet again. This is often a meet-cute. The love interest may or may not recognize the main character, but it's likely the main character knows instantly who the love interest is. After all, the main character probably obsessed about the love interest day and night at some point in the past.

The main character may or may not admit to having had a teen crush to the love interest early in your story. Likewise, the love

interest may or may not admit to having been aware of the main character's crush back in the day.

There's usually some sort of external storyline or plot problem
that brings these two people into proximity with each other and
keeps them in proximity long enough for their relationship to
develop.

The couple may enjoy reminiscing about their shared past, or one
or both may wince about it. This pair may also have wildly differing
memories of their common past. After all, the main character's crush
never panned out back then and the love interest never took advantage of the crush to have a teen romance with the main character.

As a relationship begins to develop between these two people,
conflict or obstacles must arise. The beginning usually ends with
some sort of problem cropping up that threatens to derail the budding
romance.

THE MIDDLE:

This is where the lovers must get to know each other again. They
compare recollections of their shared past and conflict may arise over
how they each remember past events.

They have both changed and grown and lived a lot of life since
they last saw each other, and those not-shared experiences may be a
source of conflict for the pair.

In the past, there was potentially some sort of power dynamic or
status difference between this pair. But, given that the main character
and love interest never acted upon the main character's crush back
then, it's probable that they did not share similar social statuses in
high school. And, given that a popular kid always has the option to
reach out to a less popular kid (but not vice versa), it's likely the main
character with the crush had lower social status than the person he or
she had a crush on.

However, in the present, the tables may have turned. The main
character may have equal or higher social standing, power, success,

wealth, or other attributes than the love interest. As that changed social dynamic makes itself felt in the middle of your story, this may be a major source of conflict for your lovers.

Secondary characters may have a strong opinion about a possible romance between these two people and may hinder or help along the relationship.

The conflicts between nostalgia and imagined love slam up against the reality of the now and the imperfections of a real relationship, and disillusionment is an unpleasant consequence.

The external storyline that has brought them together now threatens to tear them apart and races toward a crisis.

BLACK MOMENT:

All of the old conflicts, insecurities, failures to communicate, and teen drama have come back and done their worst. The new adult conflicts between the lovers have failed to be resolved, and the obstacles caused by passage of time and having lived separate lives for a long time have proved to be unsolvable. The disconnect of expectations from reality may throw the biggest wrench of all into the romance.

On top of all that, the external plot problem has gone terribly wrong and is doing its part to tear the lovers apart.

One or both lovers walks away from this flawed and disappointing relationship, but both of them are devastated when their hopes and dreams failed to pan out.

THE END:

Often in this trope, it's the external storyline or plot problem that forces the estranged lovers back into proximity. Having failed to make a relationship work, it's likely these two people want nothing to do with each other initially after their breakup. Failing to get it right once is bad enough. But failing to get it right when another chance presents itself to try is exponentially worse.

This devastating breakup provokes reflection and self-examination. The lovers may individually or together accept that they had unrealistic expectations, or that they're miserable apart, or that they can't rely on the social norms and behaviors of their teen years to sustain an adult relationship, or they may both have to learn some other lesson about themselves, about their expectations, or about life before they're ready to give the relationship one last chance.

The lovers confront their unsolved problems individually or together. They solve the external plot problem, they resolve to change the things that broke them up, and they move forward hopefully into a future together.

KEY SCENES

- obviously, the scene where the main character confesses his or her teen crush to the love interest
- the scene where the love interest admits that he or she was or wasn't aware of the main character's teen crush
- the couple returns to their teen stomping grounds or reminisces about their teen days, and they recall the past VERY differently
- the power dynamic in the relationship equalizes or flips for the first time
- the first big romantic scene—a fantasy fulfilled...or disappointed...for the main character
- the imagined romance and reality of this actual romance collides, hard
- something or someone from one of the lover's life since they last saw each other intervenes to cause a big problem between the lovers

. . .

THINGS TO THINK ABOUT WHEN WRITING THIS TROPE

What's the shared past between these two characters? How did they know each other as teens, in what context, and where? What were they each doing during that time?

What was the social status of each of them during their teen years? For example, was one of them a science nerd and the other one a jock?

Was one of them more popular than the other? If so, which one?

Was the love interest aware back then of the main character's crush? What did the love interest do or not do about it?

Did the main character ever reveal his or her teen crush back then? If so, how? If not, why not? Did the main character try to reveal his or her crush to the love interest and fail? If so, how and why?

How do the main character and love interest meet again in your story? In what context? Who has the higher social status now? Has it equalized or flipped? If so, how? Why? When? How do they each feel about this?

Did their respective friends back then know about the main character's crush on the love interest? What did the friends do or not do about it? Did they tell the love interest? Run interference to keep the main character away from the love interest?

Are those friends from back then still friends with main character and love interest now? If so, what will their role in your story be? Will they be supportive or skeptical? Will they interfere? Try to help along the romance? Sabotage it? Be jealous? Be nostalgic?

How do the main character and love interest's recollections of their teen years differ? How is this a source of conflict for them?

What has happened in each of their lives in the intervening years they've been apart?

What aspects of their intervening lives will pose obstacles to their being together now?

What has changed for the better in each of them since they last knew each other? What has changed for the worse?

How have they grown together? How have they grown apart?

What issues from their teen years will you pull forward to cause conflict, disagreements, or obstacles to love now?

What new conflicts will you introduce between them now that are adult differences as opposed to teen issues?

Why are they both willing to get into a relationship with each other now? What about now makes romance possible when it wasn't back in their teen years?

What is the external storyline or plot problem that brings these two together now? How will it push them together? How will it pull them apart?

What crises, those internal to them individually, those pertaining to problems in the relationship, and external plot problems will explode and tear the lovers apart?

What realization or lessons will each person learn after they fail at this relationship that makes them ready to get it right next time?

What will bring these two back together again to talk out or fight out their problems?

How will the couple resolve the external plot problem? Do they have to work together to fix it, or can one of them take care of it alone?

What elements from their intervening, separate lives, will they carry forward into their current romance? (Jobs? Kids? Homes? Friends? Health problems?)

What about their nostalgic memories or imagined love story turns out to be real and exist today? What recollections or fantasies do they have to let go of so they can be happy together now?

Who makes a grand gesture, apologizes, or grants forgiveness to whom? For what? How do they do it?

How will you convince your audience that this couple has what it takes to stay together and be happy forever, particularly in light of not one, but two, major missteps in getting together?

What does their new life together going to look like going forward?

TROPE TRAPS

Creating a love interest who was such a jerk back in their teen years that the main character wouldn't plausibly give him or her a chance to redeem himself or herself now.

Creating a main character who was so shy, so insecure, so socially awkward back in his or her teen years that he or she wouldn't plausibly be as confident, secure, or outgoing as he or she is now.

Writing adult characters who still act like the teenagers they once were and failing to let them grow up.

Creating adults who still engage in teen-like drama and bad behavior that's unlikable to your audience.

Failing to create plausible intervening lives that have happened to each character. Failing to create successes, failures, changes, new family, new friends, and real obstacles to the couple getting together now.

Not equalizing the power dynamic from then to now. For example, if the love interest was the quarterback of the football team and the main character was a nobody back then, and the love interest is an NFL quarterback today and the main character is still a shy, insecure, mouse, why would the love interest give the main character any notice now?

Both characters remember the past accurately and identically—no audience member will buy that. It's not how life works and everyone knows it.

The lovers are so caught up in the nostalgia of the past they fall in love with that past and their past selves and fail to bring themselves or the relationship forward into the present.

One or both characters only wants to relive their "glory days" and is unlikable to your audience.

One or both characters is so set in his or her ways, so inflexible, that this relationship will never survive in the long-term.

The conflict that breaks up the couple now is sophomoric and immature. Which is to say, your characters have failed to grow up.

You fail to convince your audience that this couple has learned the lessons or made the changes necessary to build a mature, long-term relationship. Or you fail to convince the audience that the lessons learned or changes made will stick for the long-term.

Happily ever after means living in the past for this couple. Nope. At some point, they have to move into the future, and will they be happy then?

TEEN CRUSH TROPE IN ACTION
Movies:

- Crazy, Stupid, Love
- Grease
- Class Reunion
- Peggy Sue Got Married
- Beautiful Girls
- Romy and Michele's High School Reunion
- Grosse Point Blank
- Zak and Miri Make a Porno

Books:

- Best Friends Forever by Jennifer Weiner
- Love, Comment, Subscribe by Cathy Yardley
- Tease by Melanie Harlow
- The Four Leaf by Lee Jacquot
- Prom King by Penny Wylder

- Licked by Brooke Blaine
- Santa Cruise by Fern Michaels
- Doing It Over by Catherine Bybee
- Something In The Way by Jessica Hawkins
- Powerless by Elsie Silver
- Edge of Dusk by Colleen Coble

34

APPENDIX A – UNIVERSAL ROMANCE TROPES LISTED BY VOLUME

Volume 1, THE TROPOHOLIC'S GUIDE TO INTERNAL ROMANCE TROPES

Accidental Pregnancy

Amnesia

Anti-Hero

Bad Boy/Girl Reformed

Beauty-and-the-Beast

Burdened by Beauty/Talent

Celibate Hero

Clumsy/Thoughtless/Bumbling Hero/Heroine

Cold/Serious/Uptight Hero/Heroine

Commitment Phobia

Damaged Hero/Heroine

Dangerous Secret

Disabled Hero/Heroine

Fear of Intimacy

Fresh Start/Do-Over

Goody Two Shoes

Hero/Heroine in Disguise

Makeover
Nerdy/Geek/Genius
Newcomer/Outsider/Stranger
Oblivious to Love/Last to Know
Only One Not Married
Plain Jane/John
Plus Size Love
Rebellious Hero/Heroine
Reclusive Hero/Heroine
Shy Hero/Heroine
Single Parent
Socially Awkward Hero/Heroine
Transformation/Fixer Upper
Ugly Duckling
Virgin Hero/Heroine
Widowed Hero/Heroine

Volume 2, THE TROPOHOLIC'S GUIDE TO EXTERNAL ROMANCE TROPES

Across the Tracks/Wrong Side of the Tracks
Best Friend's Sibling/Sibling's Best Friend
Best Friend's Widow/Widower
Childhood Sweethearts/Friends
Couples Therapy
Cross-Cultural/Interethnic/Interracial
Divided Loyalties
Everyone Else Can See It
Evil/Dysfunctional Family
Feuding Families
Fish Out of Water/Cowboy in the City
Following Your Heart
Forbidden Love
Friends to Lovers

Girl/Boy Next Door
Hero/Heroine in Hiding
Hidden/Secret Wealth
Home for the Holiday/Vacation Fling
Long Distance Romance
Love Triangle
Marriage Pact/Bargain Comes Due
Marriage of Convenience/Fake Marriage
No One Thinks It Will Work
Nursing Back to Health
On the Run/Chase
Quest/ Search for MacGuffin
Rags to Riches/Cinderella
Rescue Romance/Damsel or Dude in distress
Riches to Rags
Rivals/Work Enemies
Secret Baby
Secret Identity
Secret Organization/Secret World
Twins Switch Places/Lookalikes

Volume 3, THE TROPOHOLIC'S GUIDE TO BACKSTORY ROMANCE TROPES

Back From the Dead
Billionaire
Bully Turned Nice
Burned By Love
Dangerous Past
Enemies to Lovers
Engaged to/Marrying Someone Else
Estranged Spouses/On the Rocks
Ex-Convict Hero/Heroine
Finding a Home

First Love
Forgiveness
Guardian/Caretaker
Instant Family
In Love With the Wrong Person
Is the Baby Mine
Left At the Altar/Jilted
Lone Wolf Tamed
Mafia Romance
Not Good Enough for Him/Her
Rebound Romance
Reconciliation/Second Chance
Recovery/Rehabilitation
Redemption
Reunion
Revenge
Ruined/Scandalous Reputation
Runaway Bride/Groom
Spinster/Bluestocking/On the Shelf
Stepsibling/Stepparent Romance
Survivor's Guilt/PTSD
Teenage Crush

Volume 4, THE TROPOHOLIC'S GUIDE TO HOOK ROMANCE TROPES

Arranged Marriage
Baby On the Doorstep
Boss-Employee
Bodyguard
Coming Home
Deathbed Confession
Disguised as a Male
Drunk/Vegas Wedding

Fake Fiancé(e)/Boyfriend/Girlfriend
False Identity
Fated Mates/Soul Mates
Fling/One Night Stand
Grumpy/Sunshine
Hate/Snark to Love
Innocent Cohabitation
Love At First Sight
Love-Hate Relationship
Matchmaker/Matchmaker Gone Wrong
May-December Romance
Mistaken Identity
Nanny/Teacher & Single Parent
Online Love/Pen Pals
Opposites Attract
Pretend/Celibate Marriages
Raising a Child Together
Right Under Your Nose
Road Trip/Adventure
Running Away From Home
Secret Crush/Secret Admirer
Stop the Wedding
Straight Arrow Seduced
Stranded/Marooned/ Forced Proximity
Terms of the Will
Treasure Hunt
Tricked into Marriage
Unconsummated Marriage
Unrequited Love

ALSO BY CINDY DEES

THE TROPOHOLIC'S GUIDES:

UNIVERSAL ROMANCE TROPES

Volume 1, The Tropoholic's Guide to Internal Romance Tropes

Volume 2, The Tropoholic's Guide to External Romance Tropes

Volume 3, The Tropoholic's Guide to Backstory Romance Tropes

Volume 4, The Tropoholic's Guide to Hook Romance Tropes

NOTE: I've chosen not to make future volumes in this series available as pre-orders because I'm committed to getting each book right instead of hurrying to meet a deadline.

If you'd like to be notified when the next volume goes on sale, please visit www.cindydees.com/tropes and sign up for my (rather infrequent) tropes newsletter.

FICTION

Second Shot, A Helen Warwick Thriller

Double Tap, A Helen Warwick Thriller

The Medusa Project

The Medusa Game

The Medusa Prophecy

The Medusa Affair

The Medusa Seduction

Medusa's Master

The Medusa Proposition

I've received and heard your requests (with great delight, I might add) for more books covering the tropes of specific genres of fiction.

I'm currently developing lists of tropes for what I expect will amount to something like a dozen more genre fiction books covering genres including but not limited to:

- The Tropes of Sexual Tension
- Historical and Paranormal Romance Tropes
- Sweet, Clean & Wholesome, and Inspirational Romance Tropes
- Cozy Mystery Tropes
- Noir Mystery Tropes
- Crime Fiction Tropes
- Thriller Tropes
- Horror Tropes
- Science Fiction Tropes
- Fantasy Tropes
- Paranormal Tropes
- Action/Adventure Tropes

If I've missed any genres you'd like to see books on, please feel free to contact me at www.cindydees.com and let me know!

ABOUT THE AUTHOR

New York Times and USA Today bestselling author of over a hundred books, Cindy Dees has sold over two million books worldwide. She writes in a variety of genres, including thrillers, military adventure, romantic suspense, fantasy, and alternate history.

Cindy is the creator and executive producer of an upcoming Netflix television series based on her Helen Warwick thriller novel series about a woman assassin, and Cindy has multiple additional television and film projects in development.

A two-time RITA winner and five-time RITA finalist, she is also a two-time Holt Medallion winner, two-time winner of Romantic Times' Romantic Suspense of the Year Award and a Career Lifetime Achievement Award nominee from Romantic Times.

Cindy taught novel writing courses for seven years at a major university and has taught dozens of workshops on every aspect of writing, screenwriting, and the publishing and TV/film industries.

A former U.S. Air Force pilot and part-time spy, she draws upon real-life experience to fuel her stories of life (and sometimes love) on the edge of danger. Her social media links are at www.cindydees.com and www.cynthiadees.com.

For more information on:

- Cindy's upcoming books on genre tropes (including cozy mystery, noir mystery, thrillers, sci fi, fantasy, horror, action-adventure, and various sub-genres of romance, and more)
- deep dives into individual tropes
- analysis of popular movie, book, and TV show tropes
- and much, much more

visit www.cindydees.com/tropes to sign up for her Tropoholic's newsletter.

Made in United States
Troutdale, OR
11/06/2024